# Privacy, Security and Accountability

# Privacy, Security and Accountability

## Ethics, Law and Policy

Edited by Adam D. Moore

ROWMAN &
LITTLEFIELD
———————— INTERNATIONAL

London • New York

Published by Rowman & Littlefield International, Ltd.
Unit A, Whitacre Mews, 26-34 Stannary Street, London SE11 4AB
www.rowmaninternational.com

Rowman & Littlefield International, Ltd. is an affiliate of Rowman & Littlefield
4501 Forbes Boulevard, Suite 200, Lanham, Maryland 20706, USA
With additional offices in Boulder, New York, Toronto (Canada), and London (UK)
www.rowman.com

**British Library Cataloguing in Publication Information Available**
A catalogue record for this book is available from the British Library

ISBN: HB 978-1-78348-475-1
ISBN: PB 978-1-78348-476-8

**Library of Congress Cataloging-in-Publication Data**

Privacy, security and accountability : ethics, law and policy / edited by Adam D. Moore.
p. cm.
Includes bibliographical references and index.
ISBN 978-1-78348-475-1 (cloth : alk. paper) — ISBN 978-1-78348-476-8 (pbk. : alk. paper) —
ISBN 978-1-78348-477-5 (electronic)
1. Privacy, Right of. 2. National security. 3. Liability (Law) I. Moore, Adam D., 1965– editor.
JC596.P759 2016
172'.1—dc23
2015031883

♾™ The paper used in this publication meets the minimum requirements of American
National Standard for Information Sciences Permanence of Paper for Printed Library
Materials, ANSI/NISO Z39.48-1992.

Printed in the United States of America

# Contents

# Acknowledgements

I want to thank Katie Mayer for editing the chapters, as well as the Information School at the University of Washington for providing research assistant support. Katie's hard work and perseverance have been invaluable. I also want to thank Sarah Campbell, Sinead Murphy and the other editors at Rowman & Littlefield International for all their help in preparing and editing the manuscript. Acknowledgements and thanks go to Michael Katell for reading and commenting on all of the articles.

Several of the chapters published in this volume were originally presented at the Information Ethics Roundtable: "Information Ethics and Policy: Intellectual Property, Privacy, and Freedom of Speech," University of Washington, April 24–26, 2013. This conference was supported by the Walter Chapin Simpson Center for Humanities, the Department of Philosophy, the Information School and the Program on Values in Society.

Special thanks goes to my family and loved ones—Kimberly Moore, Alan Moore and Amy Moore—for putting up with all of the time I have spent staring at computer screens during this project.

# Introduction

## *The Value of Privacy, Security and Accountability*

## Michael Katell and Adam D. Moore

Within democratic societies, privacy, security and accountability are often seen as important values that must be balanced appropriately. If we accept or permit too much privacy, the result may be too little accountability and security. Conversely, when privacy is minimized, individuals may be constrained and denied the space to grow, experiment, and engage in practices not generally accepted by the majority. In our increasingly networked and algorithmically analyzed society, new technical capabilities are forcing a continuing reevaluation of previously accepted norms governing privacy and its tension with other values, including accountability and security.

Predictive analytics will soon be able to determine with a high degree of probability where you will be next week and what you might be doing. Facial-recognition technology, heat-sensing cameras, license-plate readers, and data mining will soon enable police to engage in what has been called "virtual frisking." Moreover, the reidentification of anonymized data sets is promising to make public the most private areas of our lives by exposing information we believed to be protected and unavailable for use by marketers, hiring managers, or government actors.

Against the ever-growing apparatus of technology-based surveillance are those who champion privacy and direct technical talent and resources towards its enablement. Data encryption, anonymization systems like Tor, the so-called dark web, and virtual currencies such as bitcoin may provide technologically based privacy protections. Aside from technical approaches, a diverse collection of authors and scholars is ushering in a cogent articulation and defense of privacy. Moreover, there is a growing interdisciplinary movement within the European Union, the United States and Canada to legislatively protect privacy, while at the same time insisting on accountability for those in power. However, there is a multitude of dynamic technical, ideological, and legal issues that makes the preservation or reacquisition of informational privacy complex and politically fraught.

In bringing together leading scholars to address the tensions between privacy, security, and accountability, this anthology is intended to address the thorny value propositions of an increasingly interconnected and monitored society. Our hope is that by clarifying the moral, legal, and social foundations of privacy, security, and accountability, we can move towards determining the appropriate balance between these contested values. Advances in information technology development have introduced concerns and considerations that simply weren't on the minds of most people as little as twenty years ago. The capabilities, opportunities, and anxieties being articulated by the authors in this collection are novel, ethically complex, and badly in need of sustained inquiry. We begin by providing an overview of the values under study.

## PRIVACY: ITS MEANING AND VALUE

Privacy has been defined in many ways over the last century.[1] Samuel Warren and Louis Brandeis, following Judge Thomas Cooley, called it "the right to be let alone."[2] Roscoe Pound and Paul Freund have defined privacy in terms of an extension of personality or personhood.[3] Alan Westin and others have described privacy in terms of information control.[4] Julie Inness defined privacy as "the state of possessing control over a realm of intimate decisions, which include decisions about intimate access, intimate information, and intimate actions."[5] Others have characterized privacy as a socially constructed realm that emerges from relationships and interactions.[6] According to Julie Cohen, privacy is "an interest in breathing room to engage in socially situated processes of boundary management.[7] Judith Wagner DeCew has proposed the "realm of the private to be whatever is not, according to a reasonable person in normal circumstances, the legitimate concern of others."[8] Anita Allen describes privacy as an act of "self care" and a moral obligation of individuals to society.[9] This brief summary indicates the variety and breadth of the definitions that have been offered.

In addition to the different conceptions already noted, there are two distinctions that have been widely discussed related to defining privacy. The first is the distinction between descriptive and normative conceptions of privacy. A descriptive or nonnormative account describes a state or condition where privacy obtains. An example would be W. A. Parent's definition: "Privacy is the *condition* of not having undocumented personal knowledge about one possessed by others."[10] A normative account, on the other hand, makes references to moral obligations or claims. For example, when DeCew talks about what is of "legitimate concern of others," she includes ethical considerations. Similarly, Allen's conception of privacy as an obligation to others is based in a normative moral theory.

Reductionist and nonreductionist accounts of privacy have also been offered.[11] Reductionists argue that privacy is derived from other rights, such as life, liberty, and property rights—there is no overarching concept of privacy but rather several distinct core notions that have been lumped together. Viewing privacy in this fashion might mean jettisoning the idea altogether and focusing on more fundamental concepts. For example, Frederick Davis has argued, "If truly fundamental interests are accorded the protection they deserve, no need to champion a right to privacy arises. Invasion of privacy is, in reality, a complex of more fundamental wrongs. Similarly, the individual's interest in privacy itself, however real, is derivative and a state better vouchsafed by protecting more immediate rights."[12] Unlike Davis, the nonreductionist views privacy as related to, but distinct from, other rights or concepts.

It is our view that these distinctions are not as important as some have thought. First, while it is important not to confuse normative and descriptive accounts of privacy, it is possible and proper to define privacy along both dimensions. Intellectual property is also defined descriptively and normatively. We may, for example, define intellectual property without making any essential references to normative claims. We can even give a description of the conditions that surround an intellectual property right. Moreover, we can define intellectual property in normative terms by indicating the moral claims that surround persons and their property. The same is true of privacy.

Second, without considering the justification of the rights involved, it is unclear whether privacy is reducible to other rights or the other way around.[13] And even if the reductionist is correct, it does not follow that we should do away with the category of privacy rights. The cluster of rights that comprise privacy may find their roots in property or liberty yet still mark out a distinct kind. Finally, if all rights are nothing more than complex sets of obligations, powers, duties, and immunities, it would not automatically follow that we should dispense with talk of rights and frame our moral discourse in these more basic terms.

We favour what has been called a "control" based definition of privacy.[14] A right to privacy is a right to control access to, and uses of, places, bodies, and personal information. For example, suppose that Smith wears a glove because he is ashamed of a scar on his hand. If you were to snatch the glove away, you would be violating not only Smith's right to property (the glove is his to control) but also his right to privacy—a right to restrict access to information about the scar on his hand. Similarly, if you were to focus your X-ray camera on Smith's hand, take a picture of the scar through the glove, and then publish the photograph widely, you would violate a right to privacy.

While your X-ray camera may diminish Smith's ability to control the information in question, it does not undermine his right to control access.

Privacy also includes a right to choose, within limits, the scope of control over information. Sharing information with others does not necessarily render it public and no longer subject to any privacy rights. As noted by Daniel Solove, information disclosures should not be assumed to be limitless or universal.[15] Smith may choose to show the scar on his hand to the members of his motorcycle club. He may choose to tell a colorful story about its origin at a club meeting. Sharing that information with the club does not then permit Jones, who is unaffiliated with the club and not present when Smith shared the information, to view Smith's scar, either by snatching off the glove or by using an X-ray device after Smith's limited disclosure. A disclosure to some is not a license of access to all.

Privacy also includes a right over the use of bodies, locations, and personal information. If access is granted accidentally or otherwise, it does not follow that any subsequent use, manipulation, or sale of the good in question is justified.[16] In this way, privacy is both a shield that affords control over access or inaccessibility and a kind of use and control right that yields justified authority over specific items—like a room or personal information.[17]

A strict definition of "personal information" is elusive, but the European Union Data Directive defines it as "any information relating to an identified or identifiable natural person . . . one who can be identified, directly or indirectly, in particular by reference to an identification number or to one or more factors specific to his physical, physiological, mental, economic, cultural or social identity."[18] For example, information about a specific individual's sexual orientation, medical condition, height, weight, income, home address, phone number, occupation, and voting history would be considered personal information on this account.

To get a sense of the importance of privacy and separation, it is helpful to consider similar interests shared by many nonhuman animals. While privacy rights may entail obligations and claims against others—obligations and claims that are beyond the capacities of most nonhuman animals—a case can still be offered in support of the claim that separation is valuable for animals. Alan Westin, in *Privacy and Freedom*, notes,

> One basic finding of animal studies is that virtually all animals seek periods of individual seclusion or small-group intimacy. This is usually described as the tendency toward territoriality, in which an organism lays private claim to an area of land, water, or air and defends it against intrusion by members of its own species.[19]

More important for our purposes are the ecological studies demonstrating that a lack of private space, due to overpopulation and the like, will threaten survival. In such conditions, animals may kill each other or engage in suicidal reductions of the population.

Given that humans evolved from nonhuman animals, it is plausible to think that we retain many of the same traits. Bruce Schneier, citing comments by the biologist Peter Watts, suggests that there is an instinctual inclination to seek privacy and feel discomfited by its absence because "animals in the natural world are surveilled by predators. Surveillance makes us feel like prey."[20] Empirical data supports this. Lewis Mumford notes similarities between rat overcrowding and human overcrowding. "No small part of this ugly urban barbarization has been due to sheer physical congestion: a diagnosis now partly confirmed by scientific experiments with rats—for when they are placed in equally congested quarters, they exhibit the same symptoms of stress, alienation, hostility, sexual perversion, parental incompetence, and rabid violence that we now find in [large cities]."[21] These results are supported by numerous more recent studies.[22] Household overcrowding and overcrowding in prisons has been linked to violence,[23] depression,[24] suicide,[25] psychological disorders,[26] and recidivism.[27]

Cultural universals have been found in every society that has been systematically studied.[28] Based on the Human Relations Area Files at Yale University, Alan Westin has argued that there are aspects of privacy found in every society—privacy *is* a cultural universal.[29] Barry Schwartz, in an important article dealing with the social psychology of privacy, provides interesting clues as to why privacy is universal.[30] According to Schwartz, privacy is group preserving, maintains status divisions, allows for deviation, and sustains social establishments. As such, privacy may be woven into the fabric of human evolution.

While privacy may be a cultural universal necessary for the proper functioning of human beings, its form—the actual rules of association and disengagement—is culturally dependent.[31] The kinds of privacy rules found in different cultures will be dependent on a host of variables including climate, religion, technological advancement, and political arrangements. Nevertheless, we think it is important to note that relativism about the forms of privacy—the rules of coming together and leave-taking—does not undermine our claim regarding the objective need for these rules. We have strong evidence that the ability to control access to our bodies, capacities, and powers, and to sensitive personal information, is an essential part of human flourishing or well-being.

## THE VALUE OF SECURITY

At the most basic level, security affords individuals control over their lives, projects, and property. To be secure at this level is to have sovereignty over a private domain—it is to be free from unjustified interference from other individuals, corporations, and governments. At this level, it would seem privacy and security come bundled together.

At a second level, security protects groups, businesses, and corporations from unjustified interference. Corporations need to be secure from industrial espionage, theft, and the like. Without this kind of control, businesses and corporations could not operate in a free market—not for long, anyway. In any case, if we ask the question, "Why do we care about corporations and free markets?" we are quickly led back to security at the individual level. We value security at the level of groups, businesses, and corporations because these entities are intertwined with security at the personal level. It is through these groups that many of us pursue lifelong plans and projects and order our lives as we see fit. Few would maintain that these groups are valuable independent of their impact on individual lives. Privacy and security come bundled together at this level, as well, although in a different way. Through the use of walls, guards, and fences, groups are able to secure a private domain that may be necessary for the continued existence of groups and group activities.

There is also national security to consider. Here we are worried about the continued existence of a political union. Our institutions and markets need to be protected from foreign invasion, plagues, and terrorism. But again, it seems that we value national security not because some specific political union is valuable in itself, but because it is a necessary part of ensuring the safety of individuals. As Kenneth Himma argues in chapter 8, classical social contract theory implies that the main reason citizens submit to state authority is to attain security, and that "security is the ultimate value that the state is morally obligated to protect."[32] Armed services, intelligence agencies, police departments, public health institutions, and legal systems provide security for groups, businesses, and, at the most fundamental level, individuals. Group security, whether small or large, is valuable only in relation to the lives, projects, and sovereignty of individuals.

When considered in the form of individual safety, security is a powerful value that speaks to some of our deepest fears. While this value has likely been with us for millennia, it has taken on new meaning in recent years and sparked a great deal of technological drama. In the current climate of fear stemming from legitimate and hyperbolic threats posed by international terrorists, governments have felt compelled to employ every tool available to protect citizens and business interests from potential harm. This response has often been controversial. Cutting-edge electronic surveillance technologies and sophisticated analysis techniques have been embraced by myriad military and law-enforcement organizations, and their rapid adoption has bewildered the civilian politicians whom we entrust to regulate them. Many agencies and organizations are engaged in "policy by procurement," allowing the affordances of surveillance and analysis technologies to dictate the terms by which they are used—sidestepping meaningful deliberation and frequently pitting the value of security against that of privacy for individuals and accountability for government officials. In this technologically enabled, fear-inspired environment, balancing the legitimate needs of law enforcement with cherished rights and competing values is an ongoing struggle for a deliberative democracy and society in general. Several of the authors in this collection have specifically responded to this tension.

## THE VALUE AND MEANING OF ACCOUNTABILITY

There are at least three different forms of accountability, and each of these forms can be defined normatively or nonnormatively. While admittedly imprecise, we find the categories of legal, social, and moral accountability to be useful. In each case, a person or institution is subject to some form of sanction, punishment, praise, or benefit. As with normative and nonnormative conceptions of privacy, we need to be careful not to confuse or mix normative and nonnormative definitions of accountability. A normative conception of accountability begins with moral "oughts," "shoulds," or "permissions." To hold someone accountable on this view is to be morally justified in sanctioning, punishing, praising, or benefiting someone. In a nonnormative state of accountability, we may hold someone accountable without moral legitimacy. This sort of mistake is nicely illustrated in a case offered by Anita Allen. When discussing the divorce of Leonard and Alice Rhinelander, Allen writes,

> Alice Rhinelander was the eventual victor in the case. . . . Bizarrely, Al Jolson, the famous blackface entertainer, was dragged into court to deny an affair with Mrs. Rhinelander, solely because she once mentioned in a letter that someone she met at work called "Al Jolson" was a flirt. That a perfect stranger to the litigants was held accountable for his sex life, too, is evidence of the sweeping character of private life accountability at the time. [33]

We agree that Al Jolson was held legally accountable by being forced to testify, but this does not justify this instance of accountability now, or at the time of this case. As philosophers love to note, mere descriptive claims do not automatically entail value claims or "ought" claims. Social accountability and moral accountability have a similar structure. Just because someone *is* held socially or morally accountable does not automatically entail that these practices are *justified*.

A normative conception of accountability begins with moral "oughts," "shoulds," or "permissions." To hold someone accountable on this view is to be morally justified in sanctioning, punishing, praising or benefitting someone. Consider this example: Smith has a moral obligation with respect to Jones, Smith fails to deliver, and thus Jones may justifiably compel or sanction Smith. In this case, Jones may hold Smith to account. In order for Jones to know whether Smith has delivered on his obligation, Jones must have the ability to monitor Smith. In this view, when someone is accountable, they are justifiably subject to being monitored or watched. They may be compelled to give evidence or it would be permitted to seek such evidence, and they may be punished or rewarded depending on what is revealed. This is not true for those who are not accountable.

How we are normatively accountable to others depends on a substantial account of what we owe each other. John Stuart Mill, noted by Anita Allen as "one of the fathers of Libertarianism," famously argued that "the individual is not accountable to society for his actions, insofar as these concern the interests of no person but himself."[34] Short of harming others in terms of violating basic rights or violating a contract, Mill argued that individuals are not accountable to society or other citizens. The public/private, society/individual distinction is one way to mark the boundary of what we owe each other as citizens. In this reading of Mill, the moral landscape is rather impoverished. Individuals simply don't morally owe each other that much. If so, the domain of normative accountability would be small as well.

Imagine a different, more socialist, extreme. Consider that we are "our brother's keeper" and owe a great deal to others in our society. Aside from the basic rights of life, liberty, and property, we add rights to health care, jobs, food, education, income, retirement, respect, and so on. In this possibility, the moral landscape would be thick with obligations and duties. As a result, the domain of normative accountability would be correspondingly large. Obligation, it would seem, begets accountability.

In Mill's world, where we owe each other relatively little, demanding that a doctor be held accountable for failing to provide routine medical care would be unjustified, as would any associated monitoring of his or her practice. Obtaining an administrative subpoena and searching this doctor's files, office, and home would be understood as a privacy violation. In the more socialist world, such normative accountability practices would be justified. If doctors owe citizens routine medical care, then they could also be subject to monitoring to determine whether they are fulfilling the obligation to provide it. In that case, then, it may be perfectly appropriate to search files, offices, and homes.

All of this becomes rather complex as soon as we recognize that privacy rights, or other moral norms, can trump the demands of accountability in some cases. Perhaps the only way to hold the doctor accountable in our socialist world is to read her mind. Unless there was some way to filter and capture only thoughts relevant to the case—why did this doctor fail to provide routine medical care—most would agree that privacy should outweigh accountability. But also note, to the extent that the doctor violates a right and the violation leads to a bad outcome for the patient, we may well conclude that mental privacy should yield to accountability.

While there are numerous explanations for why accountability is valuable, we draw on evolutionary theory. Imagine that in certain conditions nature selected for a specific trait in humans—say, a predisposition to be moved by ethical principles like promise keeping and accountability practices.[35] In these conditions, groups of humans who keep promises, uphold contracts, and recognize duties to cooperate for mutual benefit do better than groups who do not act on such principles. G. E. M. Anscombe calls these "Aristotelian necessities," writing, "[G]etting one another to do things without the application of physical force is a necessity for human life, and that far beyond what could be secured by . . . other means."[36]

Given the mutation, the selection for, and the enhancement of the life prospects of groups who act on moral principle rather than force or fear, we find that acting morally and holding each other accountable becomes a part of human flourishing. Ethical and moral principles are common to every culture and are necessary for the continued functioning of societal groups. Robert Nozick puts the point the following way: "Perhaps ethical capacity of some sort was biologically instilled . . . perhaps ethics is so important a cultural tool that every society (or at least every society that has survived for some time) has found its way to culturally instill it."[37] Binding ourselves with promises, restricting certain sorts of behaviour, and establishing accountability practices would not only provide for stability in one's social group but also allow for coordination to mutual benefit across groups.

By contrast, failing to maintain accountability is likely to reduce group cohesion and interfere with cooperation across groups. In the United States, it has been argued, the lack of accountability to the public of certain federal law-enforcement agencies engaged in domestic and international spying is a challenge to the foundations of our system of government. For both Alan Rubel and Bryce Clayton Newell (in this collection), the issue is not just a question of the legality of actions made by state agents but also one of the inability of citizens to assert their rights because they lack the ability to hold those who may be violating them accountable. Being unable to exercise our rights threatens that they will simply wither away, taking our conceptions of democracy and liberty with them.

If the analysis so far is more or less correct, we have good reason to conclude that privacy, security, and accountability are all morally valuable. Moreover, we are now in a position to consider the central questions addressed in this anthology. What is the appropriate balance between privacy, security, and accountability? What do we owe each other in terms of information sharing and access? Why is privacy more or less important than other values, such as security or free speech? Are whistleblowers like Edward

Snowden or Julian Assange heroes or villains? This book was put together so that many of the leading scholars of privacy, security, and accountability could address these challenging questions.

## OVERVIEW OF ANTHOLOGY CHAPTERS

Anita L. Allen begins this anthology with our first chapter by arguing that individuals have an ethical duty to protect their own privacy. Stating that "the culture of disclosure and self-disclosure that recognizes no meaningful limit . . . is ethically flawed, whatever its practical rewards," Allen shows us that privacy can be understood as both a duty to oneself and a duty to others since what is private to ourselves is often also private to others. Disclosing the details of my divorce reveals the details of my ex-spouse's failed marriage. Sharing my genome also shares genomic data about my relatives. However, our privacy is not merely a matter of concern to others. Invoking Kant, Allen demonstrates privacy's deontological foundations as an act of self-care. Morality can be "self-regarding." Utilitarian arguments also can be construed as a duty to protect one's privacy since one's own happiness is contributive to the calculus of utility for the greatest number. Preventing harm to others flows from being responsible for oneself. If we have an obligation to protect our own privacy for the good of others, it logically follows that we can demand a code of conduct from the institutions and businesses we interact with who have the power to invade and exploit our privacy. Meaningful and effective privacy policies and regulations would emerge to serve consumers and citizens striving to meet their moral obligations.

In chapter 2, Helen Nissenbaum focuses optimistically on the future of privacy law by examining the Obama administration's proposed Consumer Privacy Bill of Rights, evaluating its potential to provide some modicum of improvement to the current state of online privacy. A key section in the proposal is the "Respect for Context" provision that requires the holders of private data to use that data only within the constraints dictated by the context in which it was gathered. As Nissenbaum points out, the problem is one of interpretation. Without clarification, each reader is likely to believe this provision benefits their interests, which puts its legitimacy and effectiveness at risk. Nissenbaum argues that her work in "contextual integrity" offers a useful framework for clarifying the proper interpretation of "context."

In a turn to conceptual investigations, in chapter 3 James Stacey Taylor considers the moral question of privacy and the dead. This question may hinge on considerations as to whether or not the dead can be harmed and to what extent aspects of the living persist into death. It appears that a dead person retains some moral agency because the actions taken by someone while living can impact others after her death. Similarly, one's identity may continue to evolve after death, as with the case of dying, yet still being recognized as a newborn's grandmother. As to the ability to be harmed after death, the question may be one of a person's "interests," which can survive him or her and can therefore be thwarted by the living. Taylor rejects the idea that any of these characterizations neatly imply that privacy violations after death are truly harmful by comparing the risk of harming dead people to the risk of harming others who "do not exist." If it is not morally wrong to do harm to people who do not exist, it may not be wrong to harm the dead. Ultimately, it is the interests and well-being of the living that must be considered, and through considerations of those interests, Taylor reaches his conclusion about the extent of our moral responsibilities to the dead.

In chapter 4, Judith Wagner DeCew outlines the many conceptions of privacy and the three areas of law that have arisen in the United States to define its scope. DeCew argues that privacy is not a new or novel concept, finding evidence of privacy in the writings of Aristotle and John Locke. Countering arguments that detract from privacy's legal and moral claims, DeCew demonstrates that the protection of individual privacy is fundamental to liberty and personhood, and that it distinguishes a free and civil society from one characterized by tyranny and oppression. One of the important legacies of Warren and Brandeis is the idea that privacy rights don't need to be explicitly stated in the Constitution to be rights. They can be (and have been) persuasively extended from other rights over person and property, in much the same way a right against assault is an extension (and presumption) of original intent despite any specific reference to assault in the Constitution. While there are cases where privacy must be carefully balanced with other rights and should be strategically restrained to prevent harm to others, we should not allow fear or intolerance to diminish a value that is "at the heart of one's right to define one's own existence."

In chapter 5, Dorota Mokrosinska extends the problem space for privacy laid out by DeCew, arguing that privacy has been improperly upheld in the legal realm as an individual interest rather than a democratic value. This has resulted in an unwarranted overvaluing of free speech when it comes into conflict with privacy because speech is always assumed to be a democratic value. Reframing privacy in a political dimension strengthens claims for privacy to compete compellingly with other political interests—free speech in particular. Mokrosinska's argument extends the traditions of political liberalism and its concept of "public justification," which provides a framework for determining how people who deeply disagree can reasonably engage in political discourse by choosing mutually acceptable terms of argument. Privacy's critical role here is to enable the setting aside of deep disagreements in order for political engagement to proceed. By applying the ideals of political liberalism and public justification, Mokrosinska offers a strategy for mediating between privacy and speech where they come into conflict.

In chapter 6, Annabelle Lever prompts us to consider the critical role privacy plays in achieving and maintaining a democratic society, while also showing how democracy, thoughtfully implemented, is a potent response to global terrorism. Like Mokrosinska, Lever argues that privacy and democracy are intertwined. To a large extent, privacy is what makes civil society possible. Adding nuance to arguments about the nature of privacy in public, Lever argues that impersonal surveillance in the name of security is an arbitrary application of power that contravenes democratic principles and may, in fact, diminish security for people on the margins of society. Taking care to differentiate acts of terror from the social and political aims its proponents seek to achieve, Lever argues that an accessible and participatory *deliberative* democracy offers alternative models that can empower alienated political actors to achieve their goals without resorting to violence and destruction.

In chapter 7, Kay Mathiesen examines the importance of citizen access to open government data (OGD) as a means of ensuring government accountability and a functioning democracy. Starting with a descriptive deconstruction of "accountability" that requires both transparency and consequences to be complete, Mathiesen builds a normative case for the value of OGD generally, and for the importance of making OGD truly accessible so people can actually use it. As is clear from Mathiesen's characterization, the simple availability of information doesn't lead to a democratic and accountable government. Comprehension of government data is best achieved through thoughtful interpretation and dissemination by intermediaries. A free press, interest groups, and scholars, working both with and without explicit government support, are crucial agents in the effort to create an informed society that is capable of choosing and guiding its government.

Turning to the value of security, in chapter 8 Kenneth Einar Himma argues that security is a more important right that always "trumps" privacy, which is not an absolute or fundamental right, but merely "instrumental" to other rights. Privacy's claims are significantly weaker when in conflict with security because survival is far more valuable than the preservation of privacy, which is not a duty or obligation of the state. Reviewing the philosophical arguments that legitimize state authority, including those argued by social contract theorists from Hobbes and Locke to Rawls and Nozick, Himma suggests that privacy is not a right that is explicitly included in the social contract binding a citizen to her state. Despite the losses or harms we might incur from invasions of privacy, Himma argues that risks of bodily injury and death are far more impactful and grave, thereby negating privacy considerations except as "instrumental" to other rights. Privacy is, therefore, not an absolute right and is easily trumped by our desire for security.

In chapter 9, Adam D. Moore responds to the tension between individual privacy and security by conceptualizing the four main arguments employed to demonstrate how privacy must bow before the value of security. Moore characterizes arguments that elevate security over privacy as "just trust us," "nothing to hide," "security trumps privacy," and "consent." In each case, Moore demonstrates the weaknesses and deterministic paradoxes that undermine the argument. Specifically countering arguments—including those of Himma—that the prevention of bodily harm requires us to prefer security over privacy, Moore demonstrates the importance of privacy as a bulwark against the tyrannical excesses of an unchecked security state. We may have reason to fear a secret and powerful security apparatus in much the same fashion as we fear external threats. Because of its importance in preserving personal autonomy and security, privacy should not be construed merely as an "instrumental" value or right, but rather as a crucial tool for holding state power accountable, ensuring that the state cannot unduly violate individual rights and personal autonomy.

In chapter 10, Alan Rubel identifies problems of legality, privacy, and transparency in the data collection practices of the National Security Agency (NSA). By deconstructing the flawed interpretation of the laws that supposedly grant the NSA authority to conduct bulk surveillance, and by illustrating the apparent ineffectiveness of that surveillance, Rubel suggests we have endured violations of our constitutional rights without even accomplishing the stated goals of these surveillance programs. A significant problem with the practice of bulk surveillance is its secrecy, which is a powerful obstacle to accountability. Rubel argues that state secrecy concerning surveillance devalues people's rights. Citizens are prevented from asserting their rights because they can't know whether or how those rights are being violated. As Rubel states, "What matters here is the *objective* value of the right, or the ability of the right-holder to make use of the right or to benefit from the right should the right-holder need to." Rubel argues that the government's actions deny right-holders the opportunity to meaningfully make use of their rights, and the government's actions thereby rebuke democratic standards and the rule of law.

Bryce Clayton Newell echoes Rubel's concerns in chapter 11 by comparing recent court cases which attempted to hold state actors accountable for surveillance practices. Notably, in *Klass and Others vs. the Federal Republic of Germany*, the European Union Court of Human Rights found that lawyers representing likely surveillance subjects could contest state surveillance that may have included them, even though they lacked evidence that the surveillance had occurred. Meanwhile, in *Clapper v. Amnesty International*, the U.S. Supreme Court found that the plaintiffs could *not* challenge state surveillance practices because they could not show that they themselves had been subjects of the surveillance. Newell examines these contrasting cases using neorepublican political theory, which holds that a state of domination exists when the state has the capacity to interfere with *impunity* and in an *arbitrary fashion* with the choices that the dominated agent otherwise has the capacity to make. Newell argues that this accurately describes a legal land-scape in which subjects under surveillance are unable to challenge their surveillance within the law.

In chapter 12, Nadine Strossen closely examines the federal government's interpretation of the PATRIOT Act and, similarly to Rubel, concludes that many law enforcement actions based on this interpretation are both illegal and ineffective. Citing national security experts, courts, lawmakers, and the federal agencies themselves, Strossen shows us that the NSA's "suspicion-less surveillance" practices have vastly exceeded the intents of the drafters of the PATRIOT Act and have frequently abused even the limited oversight of the courts and legislative committees meant to supervise them. Strossen iden-tifies a long-standing culture of secrecy as the enemy of accountability, one that has actually put the American population at greater risk of harm. She argues that greater accountability and adherence to the spirit and precedent of the Fourth Amendment are crucial for restoring the balance of protections guaranteed by the US Constitution.

In this collection, we have gathered together some of the most eminent authors working today in the legal, philosophical and conceptual areas of information technology to provide the reader with a rich overview of the current debates over privacy, security, and accountability. We are specifical-ly concerned with the interplay between these values in a networked world that presents fresh challenges to the work of philosophy, technology, and law in a rapidly changing and disrupted cultural moment. We find ourselves in new terrain featured with astonishing threats, exciting opportunities, and con-fusing moral and social obligations. The authors in this collection have availed themselves of the challenge to make sense of this evolving reality, seeking intellectual clarity to guide us through uncertain and exciting times.

## NOTES

1. Parts of this section draw from Adam D. Moore, "Privacy: Its Meaning and Value," *American Philosophical Quarterly* 40, no. 3 (2003): 215–27. For a rigorous analysis of the major accounts of privacy that have been offered, see Judith Wagner DeCew's *In Pursuit of Privacy: Law, Ethics, and the Rise of Technology* (Ithaca, NY: Cornell University Press, 1997), chaps. 1–4; Adam D. Moore, "Defining Privacy," *Journal of Social Philosophy* 39, no. 3 (Fall 2008): 411–28, and *Privacy Rights: Moral and Legal Foundations* (University Park: Pennsyl-vania State University Press, 2010), chap. 2–3; and Daniel Solove, "A Taxonomy of Privacy," *University of Pennsylvania Law Review* 154, no. 3 (2006): 477.

2. See Thomas M. Cooley, *Cooley on Torts*, 2nd ed. (1888); Samuel D. Warren and Louis D. Brandeis, "The Right to Privacy," *Harvard Law Review* 4, no. 5 (1890): 193–220.

3. Roscoe Pound, "Interests in Personality," *Harvard Law Review* 28 (1915): 343; Paul A. Freund, "Privacy: One Concept or Many?," in *Privacy: Nomos XIII*, ed. J. Roland Pennock and John W. Chapman (New York: Atherton, 1971), 182.

4. Alan Westin, *Privacy and Freedom* (New York: Atheneum, 1968); Adam D. Moore, *Intellectual Property and Information Control* (New Brunswick, NJ: Transaction, 2001, 2004); Anita L. Allen, *Why Privacy Isn't Everything: Feminist Reflections on Personal Accountability*

(Lanham, MD: Rowman & Littlefield, 2003); Ruth Gavison, "Information Control: Availability and Control," in *Public and Private in Social Life*, ed. Stanley I. Benn and Gerald F. Gaus (New York: St. Martin's Press, 1983), 113–34.

5. *Eisenstadt v. Baird*, 405 U.S. 438, 453 (1972). See also Joel Feinberg, "Autonomy, Sovereignty, and Privacy: Moral Ideas in the Constitution?," *Notre Dame Law Review* 58, no. 3 (1983): 445; H. Tristram Engelhardt Jr., "Privacy and Limited Democracy," *Social Philosophy and Policy* 17, no. 2 (Summer 2000): 120–40; Julie Inness, *Privacy, Intimacy, and Isolation* (New York: Oxford University Press, 1992), 140.

6. 7. Daniel Solove, *Understanding Privacy* (Cambridge, MA: Harvard University Press, 2008), 28.

7. Julie Cohen, *Configuring the Networked Self: Law, Code, and the Play of Everyday Practice* (New Haven, CT: Yale University Press, 2012), 149.

8. Judith Wagner DeCew, *In Pursuit of Privacy: Law, Ethics, and the Rise of Technology* (Ithaca, NY: Cornell University Press, 1997), 62.

9. See chapter 1 in this volume.

10. W. A. Parent, "Privacy, Morality, and the Law," *Philosophy and Public Affairs* 12, no. 4 (1983): 269.

11. For an analysis of the reductive versus non-reductive debate, see Amy Peikoff, "No Corn on this Cobb: Why Reductionists Should Be All Ears for Pavesich," *Brandeis Law Journal* 42, no. 4 (2004): 751. See also Judith Jarvis Thomson, "The Right to Privacy," *Philosophy and Public Affairs* 4, no. 4 (1975): 304n1. For a critique of Thomson's view of privacy, see Thomas Scanlon, "Thomson on Privacy," *Philosophy and Public Affairs* 4, no. 4 (1975): 315–22.

12. Frederick Davis, "What Do We Mean by 'Right to Privacy'?," *South Dakota Law Review* 4 (1959): 20.

13. See DeCew, *In Pursuit of Privacy*, 29, citing Scanlon, "Thomson on Privacy," and Jeffrey Reiman, "Privacy, Intimacy, and Personhood," *Philosophy and Public Affairs* 6, no. 1 (1976): 26–44.

14. See also Allen, *Why Privacy Isn't Everything*; Gavison, "Information Control"; Charles Fried, *An Anatomy of Values* (Cambridge, MA: Harvard University Press, 1970), chap. 9; Richard Wasserstrom, "Privacy: Some Assumptions and Arguments," in *Philosophical Law*, ed. Richard N. Bronaugh (Westport, CT: Greenwood Press, 1979), 148; Ernest Van Den Haag, "On Privacy," and Hyman Gross, "Privacy and Autonomy," in Pennock and Chapman, *Privacy*, 147, 170; and Richard Parker, "A Definition of Privacy," *Rutgers Law Review* 27, no. 2 (1974): 280.

15. Solove, *Understanding Privacy*, 23. Solove outlines this concept while describing the failings of the "privacy-as-secrecy" theory, citing the views of Edward Shils and Kenneth Karst. More generally, see also Solove, "Taxonomy of Privacy."

16. We reject the so-called third party doctrine established by Supreme Court decisions in *Miller* and *Smith*. The doctrine was largely invalidated by the *Jones* decision in 2012. See *United States v. Miller*, 425 U.S. 435 (1976), *Smith v. Maryland*, 442 U.S. 735 (1979), and *United States v. Jones*, 132. U.S. 565 (2012). For a concise summary of those cases and their impact on the privacy/surveillance debate, see John Villasenor, "What You Need to Know about the Third-Party Doctrine," *Atlantic*, December 30, 2013, http://www.theatlantic.com/technology/archive/2013/12/what-you-need-to-know-about-the-third-party-doctrine/282721.

17. This way of defining privacy is not without difficulties. For a defense of this account see Moore, *Privacy Rights*, chap. 2; Moore, "Privacy: Its Meaning and Value"; and Moore, "Defining Privacy."

18. Directive 95/46/EC of the European Parliament and of the Council (1995) OJ L 281 0031-0050. As with "privacy," defining the term "information" is difficult. See, for example, Michael K. Buckland, "Information as Thing," *Journal of the American Society for Information Science* 42, no. 5 (1991): 351–60; Andrzej Chmielecki, "What Is Information?," in Proceedings of the Twentieth World Congress of Philosophy, 1998, http://www.bu.edu/wcp/Papers/Cogn/CognChmi.htm; and C. E. Shannon, "A Mathematical Theory of Communication," *Bell System Technical Journal* 27 (1948).

19. Westin, *Privacy and Freedom*, 8.

20. Bruce Schneier, *Data and Goliath: The Hidden Battles to Capture Your Data and Control Your World* (New York: W. W. Norton, 2015), 127.

21. Lewis Mumford, *The City in History* (New York: Harcourt Brace, 1961), 210, cited in Theodore D. Fuller et al., "Chronic Stress and Psychological Well-Being: Evidence from Thailand on Household Crowding," *Social Science Medicine*, 42, no. 2 (1996): 267. This view is echoed by Desmond Morris, who writes, "Each kind of animal has evolved to exist in a certain amount of living space. In both the animal zoo and the human zoo [when] this space is severely curtailed . . . the consequences can be serious." Desmond Morris, *The Human Zoo* (New York: McGraw-Hill, 1969), 39.

22. See, for example, Andrew Baum and Stuart Koman, "Differential Response to Antici- pated Crowding: Psychological Effects of Social and Spatial Density," *Journal of Personality and Social Psychology* 34, no. 3 (1976): 526–36; Jes Clauson-Kaas et al., "Urban Health: Human Settlement Indicators of Crowding," *Third World Planning Review* 18, no. 3 (1996): 349–63; John N. Edwards and Alan Booth, "Crowding and Human Sexual Behavior," *Social Forces* 55, no. 3 (1977): 791–808; Fuller et al., "Chronic Stress"; Griscom Morgan, "Mental and Social Health and Population Density," *Journal of Human Relations* 20, nos. 1–2 (1972): 196–204; David P. Farrington and Christopher P. Nuttall, "Prison Size, Overcrowding, Prison Violence and Recidivism," *Journal of Criminal Justice* 8, no. 4 (1980): 221–31; Paul Paulus, Garvin McCain, and Verne Cox, "Death Rates, Psychiatric Commitments, Blood Pressure and Perceived Crowding as a Function of Institutional Crowding," *Environmental Psychology and Nonverbal Behavior* 3, no. 2 (1978): 107–16; R. Barry Ruback and Timothy S. Carr, "Crowd- ing in a Woman's Prison," *Journal of Applied Social Psychology* 14, no. 1 (1984): 57–68.

23. Edwin I. Megargee, "The Association of Population Density Reduced Space and Un- comfortable Temperatures with Misconduct in a Prison Community," *American Journal of Community Psychology* 5, no. 3 (1977): 289–98 and Frank J. Porporino and Kimberly Dudley, *An Analysis of the Effects of Overcrowding in Canadian Penitentiaries* (Ottawa, ON: Research Division, Programs Branch, Solicitor General of Canada, 1984).

24. Verne C. Cox, Paul B. Paulus, and Garvin McCain, "Prison Crowding Research: The Relevance for Prison Housing Standards and a General Approach Regarding Crowding Phe- nomena," *American Psychologist* 39, no. 10 (1984): 1148–60.

25. Garvin McCain, Verne C. Cox, and Paul B. Paulus, *The Effect of Prison Crowding on Inmate Behavior* (Washington, DC: US Department of Justice, 1981).

26. Paul Paulus, Garvin McCain, and Verne Cox, "Death Rates, Psychiatric Commitments, Blood Pressure and Perceived Crowding as a Function of Institutional Crowding," *Environ- mental Psychology and Nonverbal Behavior* 3, no. 2 (1978): 107–16.

27. David P. Farrington and Christopher P. Nuttall, "Prison Size, Overcrowding, Prison Violence and Recidivism," *Journal of Criminal Justice* 8, no. 4 (1980): 221–31.

28. Cultural universals have been found in every society that has been systematically stud- ied. See George Murdock, "The Universals of Culture," in *Readings in World Anthropology*, ed. E. Adamson Hoebel, Jesse D. Jennings, and Elmer R. Smith (New York: McGraw-Hill, 1955).

29. This view is supported by John Roberts and Thomas Gregor. See Roberts and Gregor, "Privacy: A Cultural View," in Pennock and Chapman, *Privacy*, 225.

30. Barry Schwartz, "The Social Psychology of Privacy," *American Journal of Sociology* 73, no. 6 (May 1968): 741–52.

31. See Herbert Spiro, "Privacy in Comparative Perspective," in Pennock and Chapman, *Privacy*, 121–48.

32. See chapter 8 in this volume.

33. Anita L. Allen, "Privacy Isn't Everything: Accountability as a Personal and Social Good," *Alabama Law Review* 54, no. 4 (2003): 1381.

34. John Stuart Mill, *On Liberty* (1859), chap. 5, cited in Allen, "Privacy Isn't Everything," 1377.

35. For a more detailed exposition of this view, see Robert Nozick, *Invariances: The Struc- ture of the Objective World* (Cambridge, MA: Belknap Press of Harvard University Press, 2001), 236–301. "Ethics and our normative capacities arise because they extend the domain of

coordination to mutual benefit beyond that which is accessible through evolutionarily instilled behavior patterns plus operant conditioning," 278.

36. G. E. M. Anscombe, *Collected Philosophical Papers of G. E. M. Anscombe* (Minneapolis: University of Minnesota Press, 1981), 18, cited in Philippa Foot, *Natural Goodness* (Oxford: Oxford University Press, 2001), 15.

37. Nozick, *Invariances*, 239.

## Chapter One

# The Duty to Protect Your Own Privacy

## Anita L. Allen

What good might privacy do or represent for us? Philosophers, lawyers, political theorists, and policy makers are hard at work seeking to understand the value of privacy. They are asking, for example, "Whether and, if so, why privacy is valuable in a democratic society, and what implications privacy has for the ways we see and treat each other."[1] As summed up by Annabelle Lever, "Proponents of privacy believe that it promotes people's freedom, equality, and happiness. . . . [P]rivacy can help to protect people from unjustified scorn, humiliation and recrimination, as well as from bribery and coercion."[2] Privacy is indeed valuable for democratic societies like ours, in which people need the capacity to think and act independently.[3] Privacy has value for individuals, and in the words of Julie Cohen, "generate[s] large positive spillovers for society."[4]

The question I take up in this chapter is not, however, the familiar one of whether privacy has value—intrinsic or instrumental, personal or collective. Instead, it is a broad question about the ascription of ethical responsibility: in addition to any moral obligation to protect others' information privacy,[5] do individuals also have a moral obligation to protect their own information privacy? Moreover, could protecting one's own information privacy be called for by important moral virtues, as well as obligations or duties?[6] I broached the issue of protecting one's own privacy as a requirement of ethics in a recent book about physical and information privacies.[7] But limited space and a broad, ambitious agenda prevented me from fully examining the case for and against the ascription of ethical duties to protect one's own privacy to individuals. So, I return to it here.

Safeguarding others' privacy is widely understood to be a responsibility of government, business, and individuals. The "virtue" of fairness and the "duty" or "obligation" of respect for persons arguably ground other-regard-

ing responsibilities of confidentiality and data security. But is anyone ethically required—not just prudentially advised—to protect his or her own privacy? If so, how might a requirement to protect one's own privacy and related
ethical virtues properly influence everyday choices, public policy, or the
law?[8] I want to test the idea of an ethical mandate to protect one's own
privacy, while identifying the practical and philosophical problems that bear
adversely on the case.

## THE GREAT INFORMATION PRIVACY GIVE-AWAY

With respect to information privacy, the question of a duty to protect one's
own privacy is an especially timely and important one. I focus on information privacy—as opposed to decisional or physical privacy—for that reason.[9]
We are in the midst of an Era of Revelation.[10] Our time is characterized by
what I term the "Great Privacy Give-Away."[11] People are giving away more
and more personal data to intimates and strangers for a variety of self-interested, altruistic, or civic-minded reasons.

Some scholars and other commentators have expressed admiration and
support for individuals who choose freely to share personal information, and
some have concluded that it is good for society that individuals are choosing
to share personal data.[12] Indeed, there can be good reasons to share, even
what is deemed highly sensitive personal data, as a recent report of the
Presidential Commission for the Study of Bioethical Issues found with respect to individuals' sensitive whole genome sequencing data sought by
biomedical researchers.[13]

In the United States and most other parts of the world, contemporary
modes of communication feature extensive, high-technology-aided personal-
information sharing that is enjoyable, rewarding, often practically necessary,
and publicly beneficial. The benefits of information disclosure are sufficiently numerous, in fact, that it may strike some as facially implausible that there
could be any such thing as an ethical obligation not to disclose. How could
we be duty-bound to withhold information about ourselves?

Of course, we all recognize special professional duties of confidentiality
and secrecy, which are specific modes of legally and ethically mandated
information privacy. Thus, in the usual case, a federal government employee
cannot ethically reveal classified information without authorization.[14] A lawyer cannot ethically share many of the secrets she discusses with her clients
in the course of representation.[15] But in the Era of Revelation, I surmise
many would argue that there is no moral or ethical basis for disapproving if a
government employee, a lawyer, or anyone else freely chooses to share intimacies about her *own* life. According to this perspective, without any moral
or ethical shadow, a person can always reveal that she practices celibacy, has

breast cancer, is burdened by a pile of unpaid debts, or dislikes foreigners. Only norms of tact, manners, and taste apply. (A philosopher might argue, building on Helen Nissenbaum's powerful descriptive account of information privacy, that there are ethical norms of appropriateness, not mere guidelines of taste and tact at stake here. [16])

A new, technophilic generation appears to have made disclosure the default rule of everyday life, and cannot imagine things any other way. Commentators excitedly claim that a new generation has rejected or redefined informational privacy. [17] Some older people welcome the change. "Let us celebrate the insouciance of youthful privacy indifference!" one of my grey-haired legal colleagues asserts, ironically repeating market-economy efficiency arguments for transparency articulated more than fifty years ago, pre-Internet. [18] The young and young at heart may indeed look back and snicker at the high-toned insistence of Judge Richard Posner in *Haynes v. Alfred A. Knopf, Inc.* [19] that the mysteries of privacy universally extend to graphic details of the intimacies of the bedroom and toilet. [20] "Big Brother"—not the Orwell character but the European and American reality TV show that places young adults on public display nearly 24/7— is already vintage. [21]

Yet, if we are to take normative ethics seriously—and I recognize that not everyone wants to or can—we have to be open to the possibility that some of what we do and enjoy doing may not be ethically good or best. We may have ethical reasons and obligations to do things differently. The fact that a new generation has rewritten the rules of privacy or abandoned privacy as a value altogether would not prove that privacy was or is mostly worthless. Admittedly, values do erode; values can outlive their times. [22] In my lifetime, it was widely considered immoral—and illegal—for unmarried people and people of different races to cohabitate. [23]

It is not especially problematic to say, with ethics in mind, that someone has an obligation to protect other people's privacy. That we can understand and agree with. We have no problem saying that people have a moral obligation not to make gratuitous, cruel, unconsented-to information disclosures about others. In 2010, Rutgers University student Dharun Ravi violated that ethical duty with horrendous consequences. He surreptitiously webcast his roommate Tyler Clementi being intimate with another man, which prompted a mortified Clementi to commit suicide. More than an excusable prank, it is plain wrong to secretly broadcast someone's date with a consenting adult in his own home.

Now, as to duties to protect your own privacy, can we sensibly ascribe these? With prudence in mind, it is fairly common to ascribe obligations of self-care relating to informational privacy and data protection. To protect my reputation and feelings, there are certain practical precautions I should take. Prudent self-interest demands that I password-protect electronic access to my banking accounts at Wells Fargo. If I download my medical records from www.myuniversitymedicine.com, I should use the password-protect option. I should periodically change my university.edu email password. I should think hard about what I put into Dropbox,[24] about what I reveal about my location via Foursquare,[25] and about the content of my Tumblr[26] postings. But are self-regarding moral duties, as well as self-interested practical strategies, implicated in online life?

Sometimes people are so inattentive to their privacy that moral and ethical values do appear to come into play. Recall former congressman Anthony Weiner, a Democratic member of the U.S. House of Representatives from New York.[27] Congressman Weiner sent sexually suggestive images of his pelvic region clad in tight-fitting underwear that revealed the outlines of his penis. He sent the images in Twitter messages to young women, ages twenty-one and seventeen, whom he did not know.[28] As a consequence of this reckless behaviour, Weiner was forced to resign from office in 2011. Weiner disrespected himself, displaying little regard for the privacy of his body and sexual urges.[29] The Weiner case shines a light on the specific question I want to explore in this chapter: whether anyone has a moral obligation to protect his or her own information privacy, and, if so, whether such an obligation ought to influence choice, policy, or the law.

If people have an ethical obligation to protect their own privacy, there are more than merely prudential grounds for privacy vigilance. If a person has a moral obligation to protect her own privacy, then, assuming moral obligations creates *prima facie* reasons for acting, she would have a reason over and above prudent self-interest to adopt measures to safeguard important privacies. To protect informational privacy, ethical goodness might require that she, for example, not aim sexy pictures at minors or the general public. Ethics might require that she secure financial information when transacting business online. Ethics might require that she keep secret whole-genome-sequencing data generated from clinical care or research. She might even have an obligation to moderate free speech and the use of social media that widely reveal her location, plans, activities, feelings, and beliefs.

Of major significance, if people have an obligation to protect their own privacy, there could be special "corporate responsibility" grounds for implementing meaningful and effective consumer privacy policies.[30] We could praise firms who embrace strong privacy-protection policies and adhere to codes of "fair information practices,"[31] "generally accepted privacy principles,"[32] or "privacy by design"[33]—these measures facilitate morally prescribed data management practices by individuals. (The analogy here is praising manufacturing firms for installing safety devices on dangerous products like guns, automobiles, and circular saws to help consumers meet their obligation to use products safely.)

The fact that Facebook offers ways for its globally popular social networking site to be used for restricted communications within intimate circles takes on ethical weight.[34] Facebook makes it easier for users to comply with ethical duties by hosting less accessible secret pages than it would if it did not. While Facebook has greatly contributed to the culture of extreme self-revelation, I am suggesting that Facebook and other social media firms understand themselves as partners in our ethical goodness. The fact that computer rental companies extracted sensitive data from machines used by their customers[35] has a two-fold unethical dimension. Not only did such firms malevolently engage in spying,[36] but they also undermined their unsuspecting customers' abilities responsibly to protect personal data from falling into the hands of unwanted third parties.

If people have an obligation to protect their own privacy, we might applaud public laws and government entities which confer rights of anonymity, restrict wiretapping, and limit access to stored communications.[37] Indeed, public law, rules, and judicial choices have implications for the ease with which persons can satisfy the moral duty I am probing. In 2012, a court in Minnesota found that a Facebook user had a reasonable expectation of privacy under the Fourth Amendment in her password-protected Facebook wall postings.[38] The federal district court that made this finding honoured the choice many make, whether for moral or prudential reasons, to protect their own informational privacy. The court, like Facebook, functioned in the case as a partner in empowering Facebook users' moral compliance.

## THE CHALLENGE OF MORAL THEORY

The complex question of whether and why privacy is an important ethical value is related to but distinct from the question of whether persons have a moral (or ethical) duty (or obligation) to protect their own privacy. Privacy could be a preeminent ethical good with widespread political and legal implications, and yet it still may be highly problematic to ascribe to individuals the ethical responsibility to protect their own privacy.

First, the ascription may be problematic because the very concept of duties or obligations of self-regard is analytically incoherent. Second, there could be normative problems. For instance, there might be a plenitude of practical reasons for a person to try as hard as he or she can to protect his or her own informational privacy without it making good normative sense to ascribe to him or her an ethical duty to do the same thing. For example, we should all try hard to eat vegetables to promote our health, but surely there is no moral duty as such to eat vegetables!

Let me suggest the schematic of an argument in favour of self-regarding information privacy duties. It goes like this. There are moral duties obliging moral agents to act in some ways rather than others. Moral duties include duties to others and duties to oneself. Among duties to self is a duty to protect one's own informational privacy. One ought to limit disclosures of information about oneself for utility reasons, pertaining to one's reputation and future opportunity; and/or virtue reasons, pertaining to modesty, reserve and temperance; and/or Kantian reasons, pertaining to dignity, self-respect, autonomy, and freedom. In addition to "first-order" duties to protect one's own privacy, there may also be "second-order," derivative duties to protect one's own privacy for the sake of specific others or the community. My genome is also my siblings' genome, so I have an obligation to protect the privacy of my genome. My checking account number is also my husband's checking account number, so I have an obligation to protect the privacy of my checking account number. Among duties to others (family, friends, community) is a second-order duty to protect one's own informational privacy.

The outlined argument starts with a distinction between duties to oneself and duties to others, and therefore immediately faces a challenge. The distinction embraces a controversial perspective whereby moral agents' moral obligations extend not only to the world but also to the moral agents themselves.[39] Morality is in this sense both other-regarding and self-regarding. Though I am not a pure Kantian deontologist—I do not rule out that the moral grounds for obligations can be consequentialist as well as nonconsequentialist—I share with Kantians the controversial belief that moralists can ascribe coherently duties to—or at least duties regarding[40]—the self.

Kant derived both duties to oneself and duties to others from the categorical imperative to "[s]o act that you use humanity, whether in your own person or in the person of any other, always at the same time as an end, never merely as a means,"[41] or alternatively—Kant advanced several formulations—to "act only in accordance with that maxim through which you can at the same time will that it become a universal law."[42] For Kant a moral duty is "the necessity of an action from respect for [moral] law,"[43] the categorical imperative. Only actions performed from a good will, from the motive of duty, have true "moral worth" in Kant's special sense. Duties Kant recognized included the duty of honesty, the duty to preserve one's life, and the duty of beneficence.

Kant himself further divided duties to others and duties to self into "perfect" and "imperfect" duties.[44] (He also distinguished between positive and negative duties.[45]) Kant described "perfect" duties that are strict, narrow, and unremitting,[46] such as the duty to tell the truth. He labeled "imperfect" the wide and meritorious duties, such as the duty of beneficence and the duty to develop one's talents.[47]

My views about moral duty are Kantian in flavour but are not views Immanuel Kant himself precisely held. According to my understanding, duties to others are duties of care and respect. They are imperatives to act and omit in particular ways. Duties to others require that we not gratuitously cause bodily harm, that we keep our promises, and that we not degrade and deceive. Duties to oneself are duties of self-care and self-respect. Among such duties are, first, duties to act so as to promote one's rational interests in safety, security, freedom, and opportunity and, second, duties to strive to be the kind of person who acts with self-regard, dignity, and integrity. It would potentially violate duties to the self of the first sort to, for example, make oneself ill through easily avoidable medical neglect and would violate duties of the second sort to waste the bulk of one's time on trivial or demeaning pursuits.

The Kantian-flavored perspective I embrace with respect to duties to oneself is far from universal among moralist theorists. Indeed, many prominent philosophers flatly reject the notion that anyone has a duty to himself or to herself. The philosopher Marcus G. Singer rejected the idea as logically untenable.[48] Kurt Baier called it "absurd," as Lara Denis has pointed out, while at the same time pointing out that several other major philosophers—Aristotle, F. H. Bradley, and Bernard Williams—did not mention the idea of duties to oneself at all.[49]

I take solace, however, in the fact that many philosophers do subscribe to the concept of duties to oneself and have mounted defenses.[50] But because there is disagreement and because I want to apply the concept to a new area of moral life and public policy, it seems appropriate that I should engage the philosophic debates to the extent it makes sense for a lawyer to do so, articulating reasons for embracing the notion of duties to oneself in the face of detractors.

## Is Morality Only Other-Regarding?

The Kantian tradition notwithstanding, the idea that there are only or primarily duties to others has been described as an "axiom" of Anglo-American philosophy.[51] On this idea, the ethics we embrace are presumed social and other-regarding.[52] It is wrong to injure other people, but when it comes to yourself, either (1) whatever goes, goes—sloth, willful ignorance, sexual degradation, drug abuse,[53] even suicide—or (2) whatever goes, does not go to the extent that it violates the moral interests of others to whom you owe duties of care and respect.[54] One's actions may be stupid, imprudent, unwise, self-defeating, and so on, but not morally wrong in the special sense as violative of any moral duties to oneself.

Consistent with the denial of a robust set of nonderivative, first-order duties to oneself may be the postulation of derivative, second-order duties respecting oneself implied by first-order duties to others. We might think of parents as having second-order duties to take care of themselves so they can comply with first-order duties to take care of their children. Lifeguards at the beach may have a second-order duty to remain physically fit so that they are prepared for the toughest acts of first-order dutiful ocean rescue. Applied to privacy, in order for there to be second-order duties to protect one's own privacy as a duty of self-care and respect, we would need to identify a first-order duty whose performance it furthers. Perhaps I have a moral duty to protect my online data only because if I do not, secrets and sensitive data about my friends and family that I am morally bound to protect would be disclosed to their detriment.

## Can Morality Be Self-Regarding?

The view contrary to the axiom of moral philosophy that duties are other-regarding only is strongly associated with Kantian ethicists and interpretations of the writings of Immanuel Kant.[55] As previously explained, Kant maintained that persons have duties to themselves.[56] But the notion is far from clear-cut, since, as with many of Kant's most central ideas, "rather than shedding light on [the concept of duties to oneself, he] puts it under a cloud."[57] The allure and repulsion of the concept has led to a vast exegetical literature among Kantian scholars and moral philosophers.[58] Policy and legal implications may attach to whether we think we can ascribe duties to oneself and hold people accountable for failure to perform them.[59]

Kant famously argued that we ought to treat humanity, whether in our own persons or the person of others, always as an end in itself, never merely as a means.[60] As one commentator has put it, "[H]ow one treats oneself is as much a moral question as how one treats others."[61] Commentators have argued that Kant understood duties to self as logically and morally prior to duties to others, the *sine qua non*, the foundation of duties to others.[62]

The self-regarding duties, like the other-regarding duties Kant ascribes, are not merely matters of utility, happiness, or prudence. They are matters of respect for the dignity of rational, autonomous human persons. Duties to oneself relate to the mandates of respect for our autonomy and rationality. These mandates include self-respect and entail a degree of self-esteem. For Kantians, our duties include the duty "constantly" to perfect our humanity and characters.[63]

A Kantian argument from the idea of duties to self against using drugs[64] might be that drug use undermines one's rationality and autonomy.[65] A Kantian argument from the idea of duties to self against publication of sensitive facts about oneself might be that it suggests a lack of self-respect or that it undermines freedom and autonomy by truncating future options or opportunities of the sort that foster autonomy and freedom.

## REJECTING PRIVACY AS A DUTY TO SELF: TWO TACKS

The claim that there are first-order, nonderivative privacy duties to ourselves might be rejected on the ground that ascribing *privacy* duties fundamentally misunderstands something about the nature of our privacy. Our privacy, the argument goes, is amenable to rights protection but not the protection of self-regarding duties. Other people must respect my privacy, and I must respect other people's privacy, but I don't have to respect my own privacy. For me, as to myself, privacy is optional. Now, one might back up this argument from two vantage points—I will call them the conceptual and the libertarian. The conceptual tack denies, along the lines of philosopher Marcus G. Singer,[66] that there are duties to oneself of any coherent kind, including duties to protect one's own privacy. The libertarian tack portrays as moral injustice failing to treat the choices a person makes about her own life as her own acts of rational autonomous decision making, properly immune from moral mandate.

## The Conceptual Tack

As commentators have pointed out, Kant himself recognized that the concept of duties to oneself generates a kind of contradiction or "antinomy." How can the binder be the bound?[67] Some critics suggest that the idea of a duty to oneself is indeed contradictory and nonsensical because individuals can surely release themselves at will from any duties they owe only to themselves.[68] Kant's resolution of the antinomy is, from the lawyer's perspective, obscure; his interpreters have been left to struggle. But some readers of Kant believe the notion of duties to oneself is indeed a self-contradiction.

Marcus G. Singer argued that rights are claims which can be waived and that rights and duties are correlative.[69] If D has a duty to P, then P has a right against D. But suppose D and P are identical. Now we say P has a duty to P. But to say that P has a duty to P is also to say that P has a right against P, which amounts to P having a claim against P. But, Singer argued, it makes no sense to say that anyone has a claim against himself. And it makes even less sense to say that the rights against oneself can be waived at will, for that would make the idea of duties to ourselves silly and incoherent. Singer asks, "What could it mean to have a right or a claim against oneself? (Could one sue oneself in a court of law for return of the money one owes oneself?)"[70]

One way to maneuver around Singer's objection would be to postulate that the self is actually two ontologically distinct entities: a present and future self. When I owe a duty to myself, I am really owing a duty to the future person I will become—the one who stands to benefit from the good reputation, employment, friendships, credit, and other advantages that flow from the present self's willingness to limit her disclosures. The philosophical problems attendant to this move to bifurcate the self render it unattractive as the main response to Singer, if avoidable. So, I set it aside.

Singer assumes without arguing that all moral rights are claims that can be waived and that are correlative to duties. Singer's critics have suggested,[71] and I agree, that he conflated moral and legal conceptions of morality, ignoring aspects of the moral point of view which cannot be reduced to rights and claims.[72] Moreover, it is by no means clear that all rights should be understood as claims that can be waived in the first place.[73]

There is a second problem. Singer's position requires him to explain the common use of the expression, "I owe it to myself to do X." Why do we talk this way? Are we not presupposing duties to ourselves? The idea of duties to self is common and entrenched in whole genres of discourse. An example advanced by Joan Straumanis is the genre of fiction in which all-suffering female characters set aside apparent duties to family in order to comply with felt duties to themselves.[74] They set out to make a change, to "do something for themselves"—to behave in self-enhancing ways, such as seeking independence, education, a craft, a job or a career.[75]

Singer suggests that when we say "we owe X to ourselves," we do not mean what we say. He suggests that such familiar statements are not literal, that what they really mean is that "I have a right to, am allowed to, and am determined to do X."[76] Or they mean that "I think it would be imprudent or foolish not to do X."[77] Because Singer interprets "duty to self" talk as pragmatic talk about self-interests, he claims the entire notion of duties to the self confuses morality with prudence. Figures of speech abound in language. But in the case of statements about duties to oneself, why suppose we do not mean exactly what we say? A moral theory should explain rather than discount inconvenient moral discourse. What needs explaining is the belief some moral agents have that, in addition to prudence and self-interest, they are ethically bound to act in a certain way with regard to their own lives.

Singer offers a response to the objection that his view is inconsistent with the common notion that people have a duty to preserve their own lives and develop their own talents. He argues that such duties are not well understood as duties to oneself.[78] They are best understood as duties owed to others who suffer if we fail to live and flourish.[79] They are, in effect, second-order duties to others that imply derivative responsibilities. A Kantian counterview invites us to see that each person's flourishing matters and that each moral agent's humanity has equal worth and merits moral regard. We are more than a tool for others' flourishing. We are agents and beneficiaries of our own flourishing.

Singer further argues that the recognition of vices and bad character traits in no way commits one to the notion of duties to oneself. The reason one should not be lazy or deceitful or a chain smoker is both that these habits and traits may be harmful to society and that they are not in one's prudent self-interest.[80] Quoting John Stuart Mill, "Self-regarding faults . . . are not properly immoralities, and to whatever pitch they may be carried, do not constitute wickedness."[81] While bad habits and poor character do have prudential and other-regarding consequences, it does not follow that they do not have self-regarding moral consequences as well.

Mill's words need to be understood in context. Mill's intent in distinguishing "wickedness" from "self-regarding faults" was to persuade readers accustomed to thinking that "wickedness" is an automatic ground for civilized Christian society to step in and take charge of people's lives instead to embrace the contingent utility of individual liberty. Once it is grasped that public regulation is not usually and necessarily the best (utility maximizing) response to self-regarding fault, there is no need to set self-regarding faults outside bounds of ethical discourse. Self-regarding faults may or may not amount to failure of individuals to do what utility demands. A utilitarian could consistently hold that the principle of utility obligates persons to act in certain ways with respect to others and in certain ways with respect to themselves, both in pursuit of the greatest happiness for the greatest number. Towards justifying substantial control over our own lives, Mill argues that the individual is usually the ideal arbiter of his own good because he is generally in the best position to ascertain what will further his own good. This epistemological assumption is completely consistent with a utilitarian interpretation of duties to oneself as duties to do, regarding one's own life and interests, what the principle of utility demands. A person could be ascribed a duty to protect information about him- or herself from disclosure for the sake of his or her own happiness, because his or her own happiness is part of the utilitarian calculus, too.

## The Libertarian Rejection

Introducing John Stuart Mill brings me to a very different sort of reason one might have for rejecting privacy protection as a duty to oneself. Political theorists traditionally describe as libertarians those who take personal responsibility and the free choices of individuals to be of paramount importance to moral justice. The moral position I am about to outline understands privacy in a libertarian fashion as a strongly, if not entirely, personal matter, as follows. There are moral duties. Moral duties include duties to others and may include duties to self. However, among duties to self, there surely is no duty to protect one's own privacy. Given ideals of human freedom, privacy is not the sort of thing that could be obligatory. Privacy is purely personal. Privacy could be obligatory but is not because, in our (free) world, privacy is a take-it-or-leave-it condition/value, or in our (free, interdependent) world, publicity and disclosure are superior to privacy. If a person chooses to protect his or her privacy, that is fine and dandy. It is never morally wrong or unethical for an individual to choose privacy, other than where doing so violates someone else's rights. By the same token, if a person chooses publication and sharing, living a transparent life in which he or she freely shares information about what he or she does, says, and thinks, that is nearly always fine and dandy too. It is not *prima facie* morally wrong or unethical to choose publicity over privacy.

A libertarian might agree with Singer and maintain that duties to oneself do not make sense. Consistently, such a libertarian would claim that there is no duty to protect one's own privacy. Yet, while denying a duty to protect one's own privacy (because of something about privacy), a libertarian might posit duties to or duties regarding oneself of other sorts, such as the sort egoists are famous for: *prima facie* duties to preserve one's life and aggressively to pursue one's own interests.

The libertarian finds the protection of privacy to be an unsuitable basis for the ascription of rights of self-care and self-respect. People don't have a duty to protect their privacy (whether or not they have other duties of self-care or self-respect). Some other moral goods may be inalienable—life and basic liberty, for example. Privacy, though, is inherently a matter of choice. Accordingly, the libertarian continues, it would likely be wrong for persons or governments to unduly constrain or coerce the privacy choices of competent adult individuals. Public policy should be premised on the principles that government should protect privacy as it protects ordinary liberties and that individuals should be free to waive any such protections should they not wish them.

Suppose a privacy libertarian were presented with the following realistic scenarios: (1) the thirty-five-year-old who publishes an opinion editorial in a mass-circulated newspaper critical of the administration's economic policies and in it reveals his good college grades, paltry current income, and the banks owed money for college loans and a condominium purchase; (2) the man or woman who discusses the details of an ugly divorce with any coworker who will listen; (3) the breast cancer patient who announces her diagnosis on a popular social networking vehicle and then, after a partial mastectomy, uploads "before and after" photographs of her affected breasts; and (4) the prominent man or woman who opts to have his whole genome sequenced and made public for use by researchers and encourages others to do the same. The privacy libertarian would say that none of the disclosures in these or similar cases involving educational, financial, sexual, interpersonal, or medical information amounts to an unethical or morally wrong act on the part of the discloser. The disclosures are personal choices that may involve risk, bad judgment, or bad taste but implicate no violations of any duties persons have to themselves (even if they may violate duties they have to others whose information is disclosed as an incident). [82]

The conceptual and the libertarian rejection of privacy as a duty to or regarding ourselves is consistent with the recognition of *prudential* grounds for safeguarding our own privacy so as to protect ourselves from the reputational, financial, or other harm that occurs when we live in the public eye or when our enemies or our well-meaning friends use otherwise secret information against us. In this vein, one could cite, as I have, a passage from the diary of John Adams. In 1770, the patriot urged that we protect ourselves from "damage, danger and confusion," and "loss, disgrace or mortification," by the policy of shielding "our sentiments, actions, desires, and resolutions."[83] It is open to a privacy libertarian to insist that Adams was wrong or that he was right as a practical matter for the eighteenth century, not for the twenty-first.

Perhaps I am overstating the strength of the libertarian threat. The moral case I would ultimately make for protecting my own privacy is not just about what I may owe myself but also about how my choices may harm others—the relevance of which no moral libertarian can ignore. Hence, a sufficient response to the libertarian might be to point out the negative externalities associated with individuals choosing to disregard their own privacy. Indeed, libertarians must recognize the possibility that recklessness and carelessness about one's own privacy can have adverse consequences for others. I may have an obligation to safeguard my own privacy because, if I don't, I contribute to methods of business (e.g., persistently weak privacy policies) and lines of business (e.g., data mining) that seriously harm the interests of others. There are facts to excavate in mounting this response to privacy libertarians and concerns about public choice that I cannot delve into here.[84]

### "No Moral Duty" Perspectives

As we can see from the foregoing discussion, there are several negative positions one might take respecting whether information privacy protection is a duty to oneself, including these:

1. *No moral duty to or regarding oneself.* There are no moral duties to oneself or regarding oneself, and therefore, no duty to protect one's own privacy. We may (or may not) have reasons of prudence and self-interest to protect our own privacy.
2. *No moral privacy protection duty.* There are moral duties to oneself, but they do not include a duty to protect one's own informational privacy. We may (or may not) have reasons of prudence and self-interest to protect our own privacy.
3. *No first-order moral duty to or regarding oneself.* There are no first-order moral duties to oneself (and therefore there is no such duty to protect one's own privacy), but there are first-order duties to others that may entail derivative second-order duties to protect one's own privacy.
4. *Prudence only.* We may have reasons of prudence and self-interest to protect our own privacy, and commonly do. There are no moral duties

to oneself, and therefore no duty to protect one's own privacy. Nor is there any primary duty to others that entails a derivative duty to protect one's own privacy.

5. *No reason to protect.* There are no general reasons of prudence and self-interest to protect one's own privacy. There are no moral duties to oneself, and therefore no duty to protect one's own privacy. Nor is there any primary duty to others that entails a derivative duty to protect one's own privacy.

I reject 1–5 above and subscribe to duties to oneself as an obligation to act in ways that protect one's welfare and promote self-respect. Moreover, I believe that among our duties to ourselves are duties of privacy protection. We ought—in the ethical sense—to protect our own privacy. I have not in this chapter exhausted the full analysis that ascriptions of privacy responsibilities require. I have, however, pointed the direction toward an expanded agenda of theorizing about the ethics of privacy in the information society's Age of Revelation.

## "Some Moral Duty" Perspectives

Privacy is a requirement of our freedom, dignity and good character. It is a foundational good, suitable for enshrining as a fundamental human right. [85] In my view, people do indeed have a moral or ethical obligation to protect their own privacy (the same way they have a moral or ethical obligation not to lie, cheat, or steal) where privacy is understood as conditions of partial or complete observational and informational inaccessibility to others. Informational privacy requires limits on disclosure, limits on access, and data security. Favouring privacy over publicity is not a matter of taste alone, like the choice between a white or blue breath mint. On the contrary, there will be situations in which it can be morally imperative to choose privacy and obligatory not to forgo privacy.

When Congressman Weiner included suggestive pictures in a Twitter message sent to a virtual stranger met online, [86] he violated his moral duty to himself to protect his own privacy as a matter of self-care and self-respect. I also believe there are occasions when one is obligated to choose publicity about oneself over privacy. One may have an obligation to disclose one's STD to one's lovers out of other-regarding care and respect. But information privacy appears to have the weighty status of a presumptive, essential, foundational moral good for persons, whereas publicity might not, at least not in a strictly analogous respect. (This is another philosophical question worthy of careful probing—is privacy or publicity the default value, or perhaps are they on equal *prima facie* footing?)

We should make a habit and virtue of protecting our own privacy.[87] Duties to protect one's own privacy can be articulated in admixtures of deontological, utilitarian, and aretaic frameworks, to name the most routinely discussed. The duty to protect one's own privacy is akin to a duty to promote the happiness, autonomy, and character of one's current and future self.[88] (I note that Kant himself did not maintain that individuals have a duty to promote their own happiness, as I would.[89]) A modern deontological morality might understand privacies of modesty and reserve as modes of self-esteem, self-respect, or spirituality. An aretaic or perfectionist morality might treat a degree of modesty and reserve as favourable character traits conducive to the best life. Imagine a man with colon cancer who tells his coworkers in a limited distribution email that he has colon cancer and is about to take some time off from work to begin treatment. Such a sensitive disclosure is not one that I would characterize as unethical. But now imagine that this same man emails, unsolicited, to his same coworkers a detailed electronic diary about his cancer that includes photographs of his surgical wounds, MRIs, and X-rays, along with emotional accounts of his feelings before, during, and after months of chemotherapy, radiation, and recovery. Now we have "oversharing" that raises ethical concerns. Why? Because of the discomfort he causes others, but also, critically, for the damage to his own reputation, his loss of dignity, and his departure from good judgment and temperate character.

To provide another example of virtue-ethics grounds for keeping information about oneself private, in *Unpopular Privacy* I referred to a well-known passage from the book of Matthew in the Christian Bible commending secrecy concerning our acts of charity, prayers, and piety.[90] What would otherwise be pious virtue devolves into approval-seeking performance when flamboyantly disclosed to others. It seems to take something away from the good of what we do if we do it primarily in public spaces to score points with others. The culture of disclosure and self-disclosure that recognizes no meaningful limit to showing off and exhibitionism is ethically flawed, whatever its practical rewards. And the limits prescribed may be moral limits on one's own conduct properly viewed as duties to self or second-order duties to self, implied by first-order duties to others.

## CONCLUSION

Towards concluding, I should emphasize my intention to avoid two implications: the implication that people have a duty to do the impossible and the implication that personal responsibility for one's own privacy precludes government and corporate responsibility for privacy protection. There are practical limits to how much people can do to protect their own privacy. Many of us are not sophisticated about the use of electronic technologies or the data-gathering practices that are now commonplace. Some of us cannot avoid cultural and economic pressures to engage in transactions that result in information disclosures. As individuals we have limited ability to negotiate with cloud service providers, Internet browser providers, telecommunications carriers, app developers, and the government over privacy-related "terms and conditions." Protecting our information privacy is hard. But we are not completely helpless. We can disclose less or differently. That said, nothing I am arguing here should be interpreted as letting Big Data or government or others off the hook. As I stated in my introduction, I am suggesting a new, richer way to think about the moral relationship of consumers to business and government—as partnerships in ethical goodness.

If moral philosophers can tell lawyers and policy makers what we must and may do, we have to take on the very significant and tedious challenge of listening to what they say. Like many normative philosophical questions affecting public policy, when taken seriously, the question I have presented here is difficult to answer, and answers difficult to defend.

A lot depends, in the first instance, on how one understands the concepts of privacy and moral or ethical goodness. But, definitional issues aside, it is clear that, with respect to a variety of contexts, points-of-view favouring privacy clash with points-of-view favouring publicity; and among the philosophical questions implicated by these perspectival differences is whether and when individuals may have a moral obligation to favour their own privacy over publicity about themselves, or, in the alternative, publicity about themselves over their own privacy.

## NOTES

1. Annabelle Lever, *On Privacy* (New York: Routledge, 2012), 1.
2. Ibid., 85.
3. Anita L. Allen, *Unpopular Privacy: What Must We Hide?* (Oxford: Oxford University Press, 2011), 21–22; Anita L. Allen, *Why Privacy Isn't Everything: Feminist Reflections on Personal Responsibility* (Lanham, MD: Rowman & Littlefield, 2003), 5–7.
4. Julie E. Cohen, "Configuring the Networked Citizen," in *Imagining New Legalities: Privacy and Its Possibilities in the 21st Century*, ed. Austin Sarat, Lawrence Douglas, and Martha Merrill Umphrey (Stanford, CA: Stanford Law Books, an imprint of Stanford University Press, 2012), 129, 144.
5. See Anita L. Allen, "Natural Law, Slavery, and the Right to Privacy Tort," *Fordham Law Review* 81, no. 3 (2012): 1187.
6. In asking this question, I mean to use the paired terms "duty" and "obligation" synonymously and also the terms "moral" and "ethical" synonymously as academic philosophers often do. Yet, "duty" and "ethical" sometimes connote specific social roles. And "ethical" is sometimes understood to designate a more cosmopolitan system of norms than "moral." Questions of ethical duty differ in key respects from questions of ethical moral virtue. The former center around concerns of conduct, the latter concerns of character.
7. Allen, *Unpopular Privacy*, 195–97.
8. See Jean Cohen, *Regulating Intimacy: A New Legal Paradigm* (Princeton, NJ: Princeton University Press, 2004). It would not follow from the ascription of self-regarding information

privacy obligations that the information people are obliged to keep quiet is all and only the information that makes other people uncomfortable and whose suppression reinforces prejudice and inequality.

9. Anita L. Allen, *Privacy Law and Society*, 2nd ed. (St. Paul, MN: West Academic, 2011), 4–6.

10. Anita L. Allen, "What Must We Hide: The Ethics of Privacy and the Ethos of Disclosure," *St. Thomas Law Review* 25, no. 1 (2012): 1.

11. See Allen, *Unpopular Privacy*, 156, 162. I also refer to a privacy "take away."

12. See Eric Posner, "Liberalism and Concealment," *New Republic*, December 13, 2011, http://www.tnr.com/book/review/unpopular-privacy-anita-allen. See, e.g., Judith Wagner DeCew, review of "Unpopular Privacy: What Must We Hide?," *Notre Dame Philosophical Reviews*, June 31, 2012, http://ndpr.nd.edu/news/31588-unpopular-privacy-what-must-we-hide/.

13. Presidential Commission for the Study of Bioethical Issues, *Privacy and Progress in Whole Genome Sequencing* (2012), http://bioethics.gov/sites/default/files/PrivacyProgress 508_1.pdf.

14. For example, Bradley E. Manning is a US soldier in his twenties currently awaiting trial to determine whether he violated federal law when, while stationed in Iraq and without authorization, he turned over volumes of diplomatic cables to WikiLeaks, which then released them to the general public. Archive of articles on Bradley Manning, *New York Times*, http://topics.nytimes.com/top/reference/timestopics/people/m/bradley_e_manning/index.html.

15. Center for Professional Responsibility (American Bar Association), *Model Rules of Professional Conduct* (Chicago: Center for Professional Responsibility, American Bar Association, 2003). (Rule 1.6: "Confidentiality Of Information. (a) A lawyer shall not reveal information relating to the representation of a client unless the client gives informed consent, the disclosure is impliedly authorized in order to carry out the representation or the disclosure is permitted by paragraph (b). (b) A lawyer may reveal information relating to the representation of a client to the extent the lawyer reasonably believes necessary. . . . (c) A lawyer shall make reasonable efforts to prevent the inadvertent or unauthorized disclosure of, or unauthorized access to, information relating to the representation of a client.")

16. See Tony Doyle, review of *Privacy in Context : Technology, Policy, and the Integrity of Social Life*, by Helen Nissenbaum in the *Journal of Value Inquiry* 45, no. 1 (2010): 97, 99–100.

17. See Patricia Sanchez Abril, "A (My)Space of One's Own: On Privacy and Online Social Networks," *Northwestern Journal of Technology & Intellectual Property* 6, no. 1 (2007): 73.

18. Eric Posner, supra note 12, making (without express attribution) arguments made by Richard Posner in his early work on privacy.

19. *Haynes*, 8 F.3d 1222, 1229 (7th Cir. 1993).

20. Ibid.

21. "Big Brother," IMDb.com, http://www.imdb.com/title/tt0251497.

22. See Kathryn Abrams, "Disenchanting the Public/Private Distinction," in Sarat et al., *Imagining New Legalities*, 25, 25–26.

23. See *Loving v. Virginia*, 388 U.S. 1, 2 (1967).

24. Dropbox, https://www.dropbox.com.

25. Foursquare, https://foursquare.com.

26. Tumblr, http://www.tumblr.com.

27. Jennifer Preston, "Weiner Confirms He Sent Private Messages to Girl, 17," *New York Times*, June 10, 2011, http://www.nytimes.com/2011/06/11/nyregion/weiner-says-he-sent-private-messages-to-girl-17.html.

28. Ibid. See also Ashley Parker and Michael Barbaro, "In Reckless Fashion, Rapid Online Pursuits of Political Admirers," *New York Times*, June 8, 2011, http://www.nytimes.com/2011/06/09/nyregion/weiners-pattern-turning-political-admirers-into-online-pursuits.html.

29. Parker and Barbaro, supra note 28; see also Brian Stelter, "Upending Anonymity, These Days the Web Unmasks Everyone," *New York Times*, June 20, 2011, http://www.nytimes.com/2011/06/21/us/21anonymity.html.

30. See Anne Cheung and Rolf H. Weber, "Internet Governance and the Responsibility of Internet Service Providers," *Wisconsin International Law Journal* 26, no. 2 (2008): 403.

31. "Fair Information Practice Principles," Federal Trade Commission, www.ftc.gov/reports/privacy-online-fair-information-practices-electronic-marketplace-federal-trade-commission.

32. American Institute of Certified Public Accountants, Inc. and Canadian Institute of Chartered Accountants, *Generally Accepted Privacy Principles* 1, no. 13(2009), http://www.aicpa.org/InterestAreas/InformationTechnology/Resources/Privacy/GenerallyAcceptedPrivacyPrinciples/DownloadableDocuments/GAPP_BUS_%200909.pdf.

33. Ann Cavoukian, "Privacy by Design: The 7 Foundational Principles" (2011), 1, http://www.privacybydesign.ca/content/uploads/2009/08/7foundationalprinciples.pdf.

34. I am not suggesting that the policies are adequate, only that they are on the right track.

35. "FTC Halts Computer Spying," Federal Trade Commission, September 25, 2012, http://www.ftc.gov/opa/2012/09/designware.shtm.

36. Anita L. Allen, "The Virtuous Spy: Privacy as an Ethical Limit," *Monist* 91, no. 3 (2008): 3.

37. The Electronic Communications Privacy Act of 1986, 18 U.S.C. §§2510–22 (2006), regulates access to communications and stored communications. The federal courts have found that there is a constitutionally protected interest in anonymous Internet use. See Anita L. Allen, "First Amendment Privacy and the Battle for Progressively Liberal Social Change," *University of Pennsylvania Journal of Constitutional Law* 14, no. 4 (2012): 885, 925n229–30. Citing *Mobilisa, Inc. v. Doe*, 170 P.3d 712, 717 (AZ Ct. App. 2007); *Doe v. Cahill*, 884 A.2d 451, 456 (DE 2005); *Indep. Newspapers, Inc. v. Brodie*, 966 A.2d 432, 438–41 (MD 2009); *Dendrite Int'l, Inc., v. Doe* No. 3, 775 A.2d 756, 760, 765 (NJ Super. Ct. App. Div. 2001); *Deer Consumer Prods., Inc. v. Little*, 938 N.Y.S.2d 767 (NY Sup. Ct. 2012); *In re Does 1–10*, 242 S.W.3d 805, 819–20 (TX Ct. App. 2007).

38. *R.S* ex rel. *S.S. v. Minnewaska Area Sch. Dist.* No. 2149, No. 12-588(MJD/LIB), 2012 WL 3870868, at *16–17 (D. Minn. Sept. 6, 2012). The court held that a juvenile may proceed on a claim that her school violated her First and Fourth Amendment speech and privacy rights by punishing her based on what were intended to be limited access Facebook postings from a home computer related to her dislike of a school employee. Ibid. at *9–13.

39. Lara Denis, *Moral Self-Regard: Duties to Oneself in Kant's Moral Theory* (New York: Garland, 2001), 36.

40. Henry Richardson suggested to me that certain philosophical problems can be avoided if we speak of duties "regarding the self" rather than duties "to the self."

41. Immanuel Kant, *Practical Philosophy*, trans. and ed. Mary J. Gregor (Cambridge: Cambridge University Press, 1996), 80.

42. Ibid., 73.

43. Allen W. Wood, *Kant's Ethical Thought* (Cambridge: Cambridge University Press, 1999), 43.

44. Ibid., 44.

45. Denis, *Moral Self-Regard*, 36–43.

46. Ibid, 37, 43.

47. Ibid., 37. Both duties come from the same categorical principle, but their content differs since according to Kant we have no duty to perfect others or to promote our own happiness, but we do have a duty to promote others' happiness and perfect ourselves, which, to Jeske, seems backward. See Diane Jeske, "Perfection, Happiness, and Duties to Self," *American Philosophical Quarterly* 33, no. 3 (1996): 263. But see also Keith Bustos, "Defending a Kantian Conception of Duties to Self and Others," *Journal of Value Inquiry* 42, no. 2 (2008): 241, 251–52.

48. See, e.g., Marcus G. Singer, "On Duties to Oneself," *Ethics* 69, no. 3 (1959): 202. (Hereinafter Singer, *On Duties to Oneself*.) ("[I]t is actually impossible . . . for there to be any duties to oneself."). See also Marcus G. Singer, "Duties and Duties to Oneself," *Ethics* 73, no. 2 (1963): 133, 142.

49. Lara Denis, "Kant's Ethics and Duties to Oneself," *Pacific Philosophical Quarterly* 78, no. 4 (1997): 321, citing Kurt Baier, *The Moral Point of View: A Rational Basis of Ethics* (Ithaca, NY: Cornell University Press, 1958), 215, 231.

50. See, e.g., Denis, *Moral Self-Regard*, 225–30, elaborating on duties to self. See also Bustos, supra note 47; Paul D. Eisenberg, "Duties to Oneself: A New Defense Sketched," *The*

*Review of Metaphysics* 20, no. 4 (1967): 602; Daniel Kading, "Are There Really 'No Duties to Oneself'?," *Ethics* 70, no. 2 (1960): 155; Mary Mothersill, "Professor Wick on Duties to Oneself," *Ethics* 71, no. 3 (1961): 205, 208.

51. Joan Straumanis, "Duties to Oneself: An Ethical Basis for Self-Liberation?," *Journal of Social Philosophy* 15, no. 2 (1984): 1.

52. A "sub-axiom" of the view might be an antipaternalism ethic and even libertarianism.

53. See Paul Smith, "Drugs, Morality and the Law," *Journal of Applied Philosophy* 19, no. 3 (2002): 233, 238.

54. Ibid., 233.

55. See Straumanis, "Duties to Oneself: An Ethical Basis for Self-Liberation?," 5.

56. See generally Denis, *Moral Self-Regard*.

57. Andrews Reath, "Self-Legislation and Duties to Oneself," in *Kant's Metaphysics of Morals: Interpretative Essays*, ed. Mark Timons (Oxford: Oxford University Press, 2002), 349, 350.

58. Denis, *Moral Self-Regard*, 39; Eisenberg, *A New Defense*, supra note 50, 602; Paul D. Eisenberg, "Duties to Oneself and the Concept of Morality," *Inquiry* 11 (1968): 129, 129–33; Jeske, "Perfection, Happiness, and Duties to Self," supra note 47, 263–64; George I. Mavrodes, Jan Narveson, and J.W. Meiland, "Duties to Oneself," *Analysis* 24, no. 5 (1964): 165, 165–67; Margaret Paton, "A Reconsideration of Kant's Treatment of Duties to Oneself," *Philosophical Quarterly* 40, no. 159 (1990): 222–23; Nelson Potter, "Duties to Oneself, Motivational Internalism, and Self-Deception in Kant's Ethics," in Timons, *Kant's Metaphysics of Morals*, 371; Reath, "Self-Legislation and Duties to Oneself," supra note 57; Rolf Sartorius, "Utilitarianism, Rights, and Duties to Self," *American Philosophical Quarterly* 22, no. 3 (1985): 241, 247–48.

59. Heike Baranzke, "Does Beast Suffering Count for Kant: A Contextual Examination of Section 17 in the Doctrine of Virtue," *Essays in Philosophy* 5, no. 2 (2004): 1, 3–5; Ruth F. Chadwick, "The Market for Bodily Parts: Kant and Duties to Oneself," *Journal of Applied Philosophy* 6, no. 2 (1989): 129; Lara Denis, "Animality and Agency: A Kantian Approach to Abortion," *Philosophy and Phenomenological Research* 76, no. 1 (2008): 117; Lara Denis, "Kant on the Wrongness of 'Unnatural' Sex," *History of Philosophy Quarterly* 16, no. 2 (1999): 225–26; Susan Feldman, "From Occupied Bodies to Pregnant Persons: How Kantian Ethics Should Treat Pregnancy and Abortion," in *Autonomy and Community: Readings in Contemporary Kantian Social Philosophy*, ed. Jane Kneller and Sidney Axinn (Albany: State University of New York Press, 1998), 265; Thomas A. Mappes, "What Is Personal Ethics, and Should We Be Teaching More of It?," *Teaching Philosophy* 11, no. 1 (1988): 33–35; Debika Saha, "'Duties to Oneself'—A Reflection," *Indian Philosophical Quarterly* 27, no. 4 (2000): 439, 441–43; Thomas Schramme, "Should We Prevent Non-Therapeutic Mutilation and Extreme Body Modification?," *Bioethics* 22, no. 1 (2008): 8, 11–12; Smith, "Drugs, Morality and the Law," supra note 53, 233; Charles Taliaferro and Michel Le Gall, "The Great Escape," in *Cannabis: Philosophy for Everyone: What Were We Just Talking About?*, ed. Dale Jacquette (Malden, MA: Wiley-Blackwell, 2010), 77, 87–88.

60. Kant, *Practical Philosophy*, 41, 79–81.

61. Smith, "Drugs, Morality and the Law," 238.

62. Denis, *Moral Self-Regard*, 188–94.

63. James A. Gould, "Kant's Critique of the Golden Rule," *New Scholasticism* 57, no. 1 (1983): 115–17.

64. See Samuel Freeman, "Liberalism, Inalienability, and Rights of Drug Use," in *Drugs and the Limits of Liberalism: Moral and Legal Issues*, ed. Pablo de Greiff (Ithaca, NY: Cornell University Press, 1999), 110, 114.

65. Smith, "Drugs, Morality and the Law," 238.

66. See supra note 48 and accompanying text.

67. Reath, "Self-Legislation and Duties to Oneself," 350–51.

68. Ibid., 351.

69. Singer, *Duties and Duties to Oneself*, 141.

70. Singer, *On Duties to Oneself*, 202.

71. Singer sought to answer his critics. Singer, *Duties and Duties to Oneself*, supra note 48.

72. See Warner Wick, "More about Duties to Oneself," *Ethics* 70, no. 2 (1960): 158; Warner Wick, "Still More about Duties to Oneself," *Ethics* 71, no. 3 (1961): 213.

73. See, e.g., Leo Katz, *Why the Law Is So Perverse* (Chicago: University of Chicago Press, 2011), 55.

74. Straumanis, "Duties to Oneself: An Ethical Basis for Self-Liberation?," 1.

75. Ibid.

76. Singer, *On Duties to Oneself*, 203.

77. Ibid.

78. Ibid., 204.

79. Ibid.

80. Ibid., 205.

81. Ibid.

82. Disclosing my financial status also discloses my children's and spouse's financial statuses. Disclosing my marital problems also discloses my spouse's marital problems. Disclosing my genome also partly or wholly discloses my biological relatives' genomes.

83. Allen, *Unpopular Privacy*, 195.

84. See Lior Jacob Strahilevitz, "Toward a Positive Theory of Privacy Law," *Harvard Law Review* 126, no. 7 (2013). See also my response, Anita L. Allen, "Privacy Law: Positive Theory and Normative Practice," *Harvard Law Review Forum* 126, no. 7 (2013).

85. E.g., The Treaty of Lisbon of the European Union established data protection as a fundamental right. See Treaty of Lisbon Amending the Treaty on European Union and the Treaty Establishing the European Community, art. 2, Dec. 13, 2007, 2007 O. J. C 306/1, at 52 ("Everyone has the right to the protection of personal data concerning them").

86. Ashley Parker, "Congressman, Sharp Voice on Twitter, Finds It Can Cut 2 Ways," *New York Times*, May 30, 2011, http://www.nytimes.com/2011/05/31/nyregion/for-rep-anthony-weiner-twitter-has-double-edge.html.

87. Allen, *Unpopular Privacy*, 195.

88. See Jeske, supra note 47, employing a Kant-inspired analysis of a duty to promote the perfection of others, a duty to promote the happiness of only our own intimates such as our friends and family members, and a duty to promote the happiness of our future selves.

89. Ibid., 265.

90. Allen, *Unpopular Privacy*, 195–96.

*Chapter Two*

# Respect for Context as a Benchmark for Privacy Online

*What It Is and Isn't[1]*

## Helen Nissenbaum

In February 2012, the Obama White House unveiled a "Privacy Bill of Rights" embedded in a comprehensive report, entitled "Consumer Data Privacy in a Networked World: A Framework for Protecting Privacy and Promoting Innovation in the Global Digital Economy."[2] In addition to the bill of rights, the report's framework for protecting privacy laid out a multistakeholder process, articulated foundations for effective enforcement, pledged to draft new privacy legislation, and announced an intention to increase interoperability with international efforts.[3] The White House report was but one among several governmental studies and reports in the United States and elsewhere[4] responding to increasingly vocal objections to information practices above and below the radar so out of control that in 2010 the *Wall Street Journal*, sentinel of business and commercial interests, launched a landmark investigative series, "What They Know," which doggedly revealed to readers remarkable and chilling activities ranging from ubiquitous online monitoring to license plate tracking and much in between.[5] The dockets of public-interest advocacy organizations were filled with privacy challenges. Courts and regulatory bodies were awash with cases of overreaching standard practices, embarrassing gaffes, and technical loopholes that enabled surreptitious surveillance and the capture, aggregation, use, and dispersion of personal information.

As awareness spread, so did annoyance, outrage, and alarm among ordinary, unsophisticated users of digital and information technologies as they learned of practices such as web tracking, behavioural advertising, surveillance of mobile communications, information capture by mobile apps (including location), capture of latent and revealed social network activity and big data.[6] (It bears mentioning that although rhetoric often names the technologies themselves as sources of concern, e.g., "big data" or "biometrics," the sources of privacy threats are sociotechnical systems: that is to say, technologies embedded in particular environments shaped by social, economic, and political factors and practices and put to specific purposes.[7]) Most salient to individuals are practices of familiar actors with which they are directly acquainted, such as Facebook, Google, Amazon, Yelp and Apple. More informed critics point to information brokers, back-end information services, ad networks, voter profilers, "smart grids," surveillance cameras and biometric ID systems, to name a few, which relentlessly monitor and shape lives in ways neither perceptible nor remotely comprehensible to the public of ordinary citizens.

Acknowledging the problem, governmental bodies in the United States have kept citizens' privacy on the active agenda, pursuing cases against specific activities.[8] They have conducted studies, public hearings, and multistakeholder deliberations on specific practices, such as commercial uses of facial recognition systems, surreptitious uses of personal information by mobile apps, and applications of big data.[9] Such initiatives are also underway in Europe in governmental as well as nongovernmental sectors, including, for example, the World Economic Forum, the Organization for Economic Cooperation and Development (OECD), and the European Commission.[10]

For those who have followed academic and public deliberations, these cycles of revelation and protest are not new. A more pointed source of incredulity, however, is that this panoply of information practices, for the most part, proceeds under the halo of legality, quite literally evoking gasps of disbelief among the newly informed. For privacy scholars and activists, the level of indignation about these perfectly lawful practices adds strength to their position that something is amiss in the relevant bodies of law and regulation—the status quo needs correction. In the recent history of privacy, the present moment resembles others in which new technologies, practices, or institutions are seen to cross a threshold, setting off a cry that "something has to be done!"[11]

This chapter focuses on the White House Consumer Privacy Bill of Rights and within it, the Principle of Respect for Context.[12] It argues that how this principle is interpreted is critical to the success of the Privacy Bill of Rights as an engine of change—whether it succeeds in its mission of change or devolves to business as usual.

# WHITE HOUSE REPORT AND RESPECT FOR CONTEXT

Until the Department of Commerce took up its study of privacy, a prelude to the 2012 White House report, the Federal Trade Commission had been the key government agency spearheading important privacy initiatives in the commercial arena with rulemaking and legal action. The report signaled direct White House interest in contemporary privacy problems and buoyed hopes that change might be in the air. The report and bill of rights were cautiously endorsed by a range of parties who have disagreed with one another on virtually everything else to do with privacy. The Electronic Frontier Foundation, for example, which had proposed its own Bill of Privacy Rights for Social Network Users, conceded that "this user-centered approach to privacy protection is a solid one."[13] The Electronic Privacy Information Center likewise "praised the framework and the President's support for privacy, and said that the challenge ahead would be implementation and enforcement,"[14] and the Center for Democracy and Technology "welcome[d] the Administration's unveiling," endorsing the report's "call for the development of consensus rules on emerging privacy issues to be worked out by industry, civil society, and regulators."[15] On the industry front, Google declared itself "on board with Obama's Privacy Bill of Rights," and Intel affirmed the Administration's "calls for U.S. federal privacy legislation based upon the Fair Information Practices."[16] Chris Civil, in an overview of the bill and reactions to it, cited *Time*'s observation that "the most 'remarkable' element of the new framework is that it has not been greeted with outrage from Silicon Valley companies, who have previously opposed similar privacy legislation efforts led by the California State Senate."[17]

Of the seven principles proposed in the Consumer Privacy Bill of Rights, six are recognizable as kin of traditional fair information practice principles, embodied, for example, in the OECD Privacy Guidelines. However, the third principle of "Respect for Context," the expectation that "companies will collect, use, and disclose personal data in ways that are consistent with the context in which consumers provide the data,"[18] is intriguingly novel and, in part, a reason the report suggested that something beyond business as usual was its aim. How far the rallying cry around respect for context will push genuine progress, however, is critically dependent on how this principle is interpreted. Context is a mercilessly ambiguous term with potential to be all things to all people. Its meanings range from the colloquial and general to the theorized and specific, from the banal to the exotic, the abstract to the concrete, and shades in between. If determining the meaning of context were not challenging enough, determining what it means to respect it opens further avenues of ambiguity. In short, the positive convergence of views held by long-standing antagonists may be too good to be true if it rests on divergent interpretations. Whether the Privacy Bill of Rights fulfills its promise as a watershed for privacy, whether the principle of respect for context is an active ingredient in the momentum, will depend on which one of these interpretations drives public or private regulators to action.

## MEANINGS OF CONTEXT

Setting aside general and colloquial uses, as well as idiosyncratic ones, this chapter takes its cues from specific meanings and shades of meanings embodied in recorded deliberations leading up to the public release of the report, and in action and commentary that has followed it, all clearly influential in shaping the principle. My purpose, however, is not purely semantic; it does not involve judging some of these meanings to be "correct" while others "incorrect." Instead, it is to highlight how different meanings imply different policy avenues, some seeming to favour the entrenched status quo, others to support progressive, if limited, improvement. Ultimately, I argue that the interpretation that opens doors to a genuine advancement in the policy environment is embodied in the theory of contextual integrity; it heeds the call for innovation, recognizes business interests of commercial actors, and at the same time places appropriate constraints on personal information flows for the sake of privacy. The chapter does not argue that it is incorrect to use context in the myriad ways we do—merely that only a subset of uses systematically favour certain policy directions over others, and, more important, not all those among this subset promise a productive departure from "business as usual."

In the subset of interpretations with systematic implications for policy, four are of particular interest because they reflect persistent voices in discussions leading up to and following the White House report: context as technology platform or system, context as sector or industry, context as business model or practice, and context as social domain. Although within each of the four there are nuances of meaning and subtleties of usage, for purposes of this discussion they have been set aside or, where possible, absorbed into the core. One example of this is *the context of a relationship*, which is more general and abstract than the four listed. In deciding whether this framing warranted a separate analysis, I examined comments from the Online Publishers Association introducing this phrase. Finding that it was referring specifically to the relationship between publishers and their clients (readers, viewers, etc.), I was comfortable absorbing this understanding of context within that of business practice.

There are many ways context may be relevant to those modeling human behaviour. Contextual factors are considered external to a given model but might increase its descriptive or predictive accuracy. In explaining online behaviour, for example, contextual factors such as geo-location, time, stage in a series or myriad other possibilities may be external to a given model but may serve to refine a model's performance, its descriptive or predictive accuracy, helping to explain and predict at finer grain behaviours such as web search, receptiveness to advertising, and even to vulnerability to malevolent overtures, such as phishing attacks.[19] In this manner, contextual factors could be cited in explanations of varying privacy expectations. Thus, one may observe that expectations are affected by the context of a promise, a relationship, a conversation, or an event. Place—geospatial or physical location such as home, office, café, supermarket, park, corner of Broadway and Bleecker—is a particularly salient contextual refinement.[20] Context as place is of natural interest not only because it reflects common English usage but also because, historically, it has served to qualify privacy expectations, such as in distinguishing the home from public space.[21]

I have not given independent consideration to context abstractly conceived because I have not seen systematic ties to specific expectations of privacy. Although place is a significant factor in accounting for privacy expectations, it was not singled out in the White House report. The importance of place in affecting privacy expectations is not necessarily *as an independent factor* (that is, whether an activity takes place inside a building or outside, at one particular geo-location or another), but rather as it functions in social terms, as, say, a church, home, or hospital—as will be clarified later in this chapter.

## Context as Technology System or Platform

Many of the privacy issues we are confronting emerge from the realm of digital networks—the Internet, and the myriad platforms and systems sitting atop (or below) it, such as mobile systems, email, social networks, cloud providers, and the web itself. For most of us, these disparate technical substrates, systems, and platforms are experienced indistinguishably from one another and, though technical experts give a more rigorous account of their differences, they are akin from the perspective of user experience and political economy. We talk of communication and transactions taking place *online* or *in* cyberspace and the privacy problems emerging from them are associated with these electronically mediated contexts without a clear sense that they may emerge in different ways because of the different architectures and protocols. They become the problems of online privacy—problems of a distinctive domain requiring a distinctive approach. It is a short distance to conceive of this technological substrate as a context, one that makes a difference to privacy; we readily conceive of talking in the context of, say, a phone call, acting in the context of an online social network, expressing ourselves in the contexts of Twitter, Facebook and Wikipedia, or in the contexts of a mobile app, or location-based services. In such expressions, contexts are defined by the properties of respective media, systems, or platforms whose distinctive material characteristics shape—moderate, magnify, enable—the character of the activities, transactions, and interactions they mediate. They also shape the ways information about us is tracked, gathered, analyzed, and disseminated. If properties of technical systems and platforms define contexts, then a principle that supports respect for contexts presumably implies that policies should be heedful of these defining properties of systems and platforms.

The idea of context as technical system or platform is suggested in the foreword of the White House report:

> Privacy protections are critical to maintaining consumer trust in networked technologies. When consumers provide information about themselves—whether it is in the context of an online social network that is open to public view or a transaction involving sensitive personal data—they reasonably expect companies to use this information in ways that are consistent with the surrounding context. Many companies live up to these expectations, but some do not. Neither consumers nor companies have a clear set of ground rules to apply in the commercial arena. As a result, it is difficult today for consumers to assess whether a company's privacy practices warrant their trust. [22]

Comments by others reflect a similar interpretation. AT&T, for example, notes that diverse technical platforms generate distinctive challenges to privacy: "Indeed, the power of Web 2.0 inter-related media is precisely that content can be used in ways that were not expected or understood when they were collected." [23] Google encourages enforceable codes of conduct that "reflect changing practices, technologies and shifting consumer expectations," [24] and Intuit observes that "collecting information for use in routing a request on the Internet should have different standards for transparency, acceptable uses, protection, and retention than the information collected to describe a patient's visit to a physician." [25] Finally, the idea that technology defines context is suggested in the framing of the National Telecommunications and Information Administration's (NITA) July 2012 kickoff multistakeholder process around mobile applications, suggesting that mobile apps define a normative category. [26]

## Context as Business Model or Business Practice

In the discourse surrounding the report, the interpretation of context as prevailing business model or business practice was evident in various comments, particularly those offered by incumbents in the IT and information industries—for example, "Technology neutral and flexible legislation can actually aid small business growth as it provides a clear set of 'rules of the road' for everyone, while at the same time allowing those rules to be adapted to each business' unique situation."[27] This comment from Intel suggests that technology per se does not define privacy rules of the road but that these should be guided by the needs of distinctive business models aimed at promoting growth. Similarly, "TRUSTe supports the continued role of industry in defining purpose specifications and use limitations based on the unique needs of a company's business model."[28] According to Google, "The fast-paced introduction of new Internet services drives equally rapid shifts in consumer expectations and preferences. An effective privacy regime must allow for realtime reactions to address changes in consumer privacy preferences resulting from the introduction and adoption of new tools and services."[29] AT&T urges, "This flexibility should also allow companies to describe the use of data within broad categories, such as 'for marketing purposes,' without the need [to] specify the particular purpose for the collection of each piece of data. Indeed, the power of Web 2.0 inter-related media is precisely that content can be used in ways that were not expected or understood when they were collected."[30] Asserting a special privilege for the business practices of online publishers, the Online Publishers Association (OPA), with members including WebMD, Fox News, and the *New York Times*, claims, "Online publishers share a direct and trusted relationship with visitors to their websites. In the context of this relationship, OPA members sometimes collect and use information to target and deliver the online advertising that subsidizes production of quality digital content."[31]

Interpreted as the model or practice of a particular business, context is established according to that business's aims and the means it chooses to achieve these aims. There is nothing surprising about merchants orienting their buying and selling practices around profitability, so we should not be surprised that information service providers orient their models around growth and competitive edge. According to this understanding, contexts are defined by particular business models, in turn shaping respective information flow practices. Taking Google's comment above as a concrete case in point, this interpretation suggests that contexts generated by its business-driven Internet services, for example, shape consumer expectations of privacy, and not the other way around. Similarly, AT&T speculates that the privacy assumptions users hold will bend flexibly to the contours of "marketing purposes," defined as whatever is needed to strengthen a business model.[32]

## Context as Sector or Industry

Endorsing the sectoral approach that the United States has taken to privacy protection, TRUSTe notes that "the regulatory frameworks currently in place in the United States reflect this inherently contextual nature of privacy, e.g., FCRA/FACTA (information used in 'consumer reports'), Gramm-Leach-Bliley (information sharing between financial institutions and affiliates), HI-

PAA (transactions involving protected health information by 'covered entities')."[33] In a similar vein: "Intuit's experience in multiple sectors has taught us that providers and consumers of information in the health sector, for example, have different requirements and expectations for protection than do those in financial services. . . . Subject matter experts could help inform the development of appropriately balanced codes."[34]

I have placed "industry" in the same category as "sector," not because they have identical meanings, but because, in practice, these terms are used interchangeably in the commentaries from which I rendered the category. Adopting the interpretation of context as sector or industry, respect for context would amount to adherence to the set of rules or norms developed by, for, and within respective sectors or industries.

## Context as Social Domain

This interpretation, supported by the theory of contextual integrity, presents contexts as social spheres, as constituents of a differentiated social space. As such, they serve as organizing principles for expectations of privacy. Although contextual integrity relies on an intuitive notion of social sphere, covering such instances as education, health care, politics, commerce, religion, family and home life, recreation, marketplace, work, and more, scholarly works in social theory and philosophy have rigorously developed the concept of differentiated social space, though with diverse theoretical underpinnings and terminology (e.g., sphere, domain, institution, field[35]). In intuitive as well as academic accounts, spheres generally comprise a number of constituents, such as characteristic activities and practices, functions (or roles), aims, purposes, institutional structure, values and action-governing norms. Contextual norms may be explicitly expressed in rules or laws or implicitly embodied in convention, practice or merely conceptions of "normal" behaviour. A common thesis in most accounts is that spheres are characterized by distinctive internal structures, ontologies, teleologies and norms.

From the landscape of differentiated social spheres, the theory of privacy as contextual integrity develops a definition of informational privacy as well as an account of its importance. Taking context to mean social sphere, respect for context would mean respect for social sphere. To explain what this means and why it opens new and significant avenues for the proposed White House policy framework requires a brief excursus into the theory of contextual integrity.

### A Detour: Theory of Contextual Integrity

Other accounts of the profound anxiety over privacy, fueled by the steep rise in capture, analysis, and dissemination of personal information, point to the loss of control by data subjects and sheer increased exposure. Although these factors are part of the story, the theory of contextual integrity holds the source of this anxiety to be in neither control nor secrecy, but appropriateness. Specifically, technologies, systems, and practices that disturb our sense of privacy are those that have resulted in *inappropriate* flows of personal information. Inappropriate information flows are those that violate context-specific informational norms (from here on, "informational norms"), a subclass of general norms governing respective social contexts.

Aiming at descriptive accuracy, the theory articulates a model wherein informational norms are defined by three key parameters: information types, actors, and transmission principles. It postulates that whether a particular flow, or transmission of information from one party to another, is appropriate depends on the following parameters—namely, the type of information in question, about whom it is, by whom and to whom it is transmitted, and conditions or constraints under which this transmission takes place. Asserting that informational norms are context-relative, or context-specific, means that within the model of a differentiated social world, they cluster around and function according to coherent but distinct social contexts. The parameters, too, range over distinct clusters of variables defined, to a large extent, by respective social contexts.

*Actors*—subject, sender, recipient—range over context-relevant functions, or roles (that is, actors functioning in certain capacities associated with certain context). These capacities (or functional roles) include the familiar—physician, nurse, patient, teacher, senator, voter, polling station volunteer, mother, friend, uncle, priest, merchant, customer, congregant, policeman, judge, and, of course, many more. In complex, hierarchical societies, such as the contemporary United States, actors governed by informational norms might also be collectives, including institutions, corporations, or clubs.

The parameter of *information type*, likewise, ranges over variables derived from the ontologies of specific domains. In health care, these could include symptomologies, medical diagnoses, diseases, pharmacological drugs; in education, they may include cognitive aptitude, performance measures, learning outcomes; in politics, party affiliations, votes cast, donations; and so forth. There are, in addition, types of information that range across many contexts: name, address, and gender, to give a few basic examples.

*Transmission principle*, the third parameter, designates the terms, or constraints under which information flows. Think of it as a sluice gate. Imagine that you are applying for a bank mortgage on a new home and have signed a waiver allowing the bank to obtain a copy of your credit report from Equifax. To map this transaction onto the structure of context-specific informational norms: (1) actors: you, the applicant, are the data subject; the bank is the data recipient; and the credit bureau is the sender; (2) information type includes the various fields of information that are provided in a credit report; and (3) transmission principle—"with the information subject's signed waiver." The transmission principle, abstractly conceived, has not been explicitly recognized in scholarly or policy deliberations even though, in practice, its implicit role in social convention, regulation, and law can be pivotal. Isolating the transmission principle as an independent variable also offers a more general account of the dominant view of privacy as a right to control information about ourselves. Through the lens of contextual integrity, this view mistakes one aspect of the right for the whole, since control over information by the information subject is but one among an extensive range of options, including, "in confidence," "with third-party authorization," "as required by law," "bought," "sold," "reciprocal," and "authenticated," among others.

A feature of informational norms that bears emphasizing is that the three parameters—actors, information types, and transmission principles—are independent. None can be reduced to the other two, nor can any one of them carry the full burden of defining privacy expectations. This is why past efforts to reduce privacy to a particular class of information—say "sensitive" information—or to one transmission principle—say, control over information—are doomed to fail and, in my view, for decades have invited ambiguity and confusion, hindering progress in our understanding of privacy and attempts to regulate its protection. Control over information is an important transmission principle, but always with respect to particular actors and particular information types, all specified against the backdrop of a particular social context. Although much could be said about each of the parameters, the scope of this chapter limits us.

Contextual integrity is achieved when actions and practices comport with informational norms. But when actions or practices defy expectations by disrupting entrenched, or normative, information flows, they violate contextual integrity. As such, informational norms model privacy expectations. When we find people reacting with surprise, annoyance, and indignation, protesting that their privacy has been compromised, the theory would suggest as a likely explanation that informational norms had been contravened, that contextual integrity had been violated. Conversely, informational norms may serve as a diagnostic tool with *prima facie* explanatory and predictive capacities. From observations of technical systems or practices that result in novel patterns of information flow according to actors, information types or transmission principles, the theory would predict that people may react with surprise and possibly annoyance. Contextual integrity provides a more highly calibrated view of factors relevant to privacy than traditional dichotomies such as disclose/not disclose, private/public.

The diagnostic or descriptive role of contextual integrity is not the full story, but before turning to the ethical dimension, two quick implications bear mentioning. One is that when it comes to the nuts and bolts of privacy law, policy, and design, area experts in respective contexts—education, health care, and family and home life—are crucial to understanding roles, functions and information types. They, not privacy experts, are best equipped to inform processes of norm discovery, articulation, and formation. A second implication is that though practices in well-circumscribed social institutions may be thickly covered by informational rules, only a fraction of all possible information flows in daily life are likely to be covered by explicit norms. Compare, for example, a court of law, a stock exchange, and a hospital with an informal social gathering, a shopping mall, a beauty parlor—picking a few at random. The lens of contextual integrity provides a view of emerging digital (sociotechnical) information systems in terms of radical disruptive information flows, in turn an explanation of contemporary anxiety and acute concern over privacy. But many novel information flows are disruptive, not because they contravene explicit norms, but because they open up previously impossible (possibly unimaginable) flows. In these instances, consternation follows because flows are unprecedented, and may or may not expose new vulnerabilities and hazards. How to cope with these puzzling cases, in addition to the ones in which existing norms are violated, is a challenge for the prescriptive dimension of contextual integrity.

## Contextual Integrity: Ethics and Policy

Novelty and disruption are not problematic even if they result in direct contraventions of entrenched informational norms. Even a superficial survey reveals many welcome alterations in flows brought about by adoption of information and network technologies—for example, enhanced health indicators, robust and cheap new forms of communication and association, such as through social networks, and information search tools online. In many of these instances, novel flows have replaced suboptimal ones that had become entrenched in particular contexts due to the limits of past technologies, media, or social systems. Questions must be addressed, however. How to evaluate disruptive information flows brought about by novel technologies, media, and social systems; how to distinguish those that embody positive opportunities from those that do not, and those that violate privacy from those that do not—all important challenges for any theory of privacy. When AT&T asserts, "Consumers approach the Internet with a consistent set of expectations, and they should be able to traverse the Internet having those expectations respected and enforced,"[36] it endorses the normative clout of our privacy expectations. And because we may not agree that all expectations deserve to be met, we can reasonably require a theory of privacy to account for the difference between those that do and those that do not. This is the challenge any normative theory of privacy should address, and it is the challenge for which a normative dimension of contextual integrity was developed.

A fundamental insight of contextual integrity is that because information flows may systematically affect interests and realization of societal values, these can be used as touchstones for normative evaluation. Where novel flows challenge entrenched informational norms, the model calls for a comparative assessment of entrenched flows against novel ones. An assessment in terms of interests and values involves three layers. In the first, it requires a study of how novel flows affect the interests of key affected parties: the benefits they enjoy, the costs and risks they suffer. These may include material costs and benefits as well as those less palpable, including shifts in relative power. Beyond this largely economic analysis frequently followed in policy circles, the normative analysis directs us to consider general moral, social, and political values. These would include not only costs and benefits but also considerations of fairness, the distribution of these costs and benefits, who enjoys the benefits and who endures the costs. Thus, for example, where new flows involve power shifts, this second layer asks whether the shifts are fair and just. Other core ethical and societal values that have been identified in a deep and extensive privacy literature are democracy, unfair discrimination, informational harm, equal treatment, reputation, and civil liberties. This literature has shone light particularly on the connections between privacy and aspects of individual autonomy including moral autonomy, boundary management, and identity formation.[37]

The third layer introduces a further set of considerations—namely, context-specific values, ends, and purposes. This layer sets contextual integrity apart from many other privacy theories. It offers a systematic approach to resolving conflicts among alternative patterns of information flow, which serve competing interests and values respectively. In a particular context, one pattern of flow might support individual freedom, an alternative, safety, and security. The additional analytic layer may resolve the conflict. In some, freedom will trump, and in others, security will trump, depending on facts on the ground and respective goals and values. Although privacy is often pitted against the interests of business incumbents, or is viewed as conflicting with values such as national security, public safety, and freedom of expression, contextual integrity allows us to unravel and challenge such claims. This layer insists that privacy, as appropriate information flows, serves not merely the interests of individual information subjects but also contextual social ends and values.

In the context of health care, for example, where the integration of electronic patient records has radically altered flows of information, it is crucial to ask how these have affected the attainment of ends and purpose of health care and whether the values associated with health care are sustained. In the United States, these aims might include curing and preventing disease, repairing bodily injury, and minimizing physical pain, while values include patient autonomy, frugality, equal access, and nondiscrimination. Thus, when assessing terms of access to medical records, patient interests (including freedom from embarrassment and shame) are an important consideration, as are the interests of other stakeholders, and an analysis must also consider the purposes and values of the health care context. If individuals avoid diagnosis and treatment because of access rules that are too lax, not only do they suffer, but others, too, pay the price. Consequently, ends and values of health care are undermined. A similar argument explains why ballot secrecy, or privacy, is crucial in democratic elections: it not only protects individual voters against intimidation, and possibly retribution, but also promotes democracy itself, which is based on autonomous preferences of individual citizens.[38]

The claim of this article is that context, understood as social sphere, is far more likely to yield positive momentum and meaningful progress in privacy law and policy than understood as technology, sector, or business model. With context-specific informational norms establishing the link between context and privacy, *respect for context* amounts to respect for contextual integrity. To flesh out this claim, a fresh look at the White House Privacy Bill of Rights will be instructive.

## RESPECT FOR CONTEXT AND
## THE CONSUMER PRIVACY BILL OF RIGHTS

The White House Privacy Bill of Rights embodies "fair information practice principles" (FIPPs), as have many codes of privacy before it, in the United States and internationally. Appendix B of the report accounts for its debt to FIPPs and other codes in a table that lines up respective principles of the Consumer Privacy Bill of Rights (CPBR) alongside respective principles in the OECD Privacy Guidelines, the Department of Homeland Security (DHS) Privacy Policy, and Asia-Pacific Economic Cooperation (APEC) Principles.[39] The CPBR principles of Transparency, Security, Access and Accuracy, and Accountability have relatively straightforward counterparts in the other sets of guidelines, each worthy, in its own right, of in-depth critical analysis. Respect for Context, the focus of this article, is aligned with Purpose Specification and Use Limitation Principles. The White House's CPBR principles of Focused Collection and Individual Control, whose counterparts in the OECD guidelines are listed as Collection and Use Limitation principles, would therefore also be affected by the interpretation of Context.

Let us zoom in for a closer look at the right of Respect for Context, which is "a right to expect that companies will collect, use, and disclose personal data in ways that are consistent with the context in which consumers provide the data."[40] Its close kin are given as (1) Purpose Specification and (2) Use Limitation, requiring that (i) "The purposes for which personal data are collected should be specified not later than at the time of data collection and the subsequent use limited to the fulfillment of those purposes or such others as are not incompatible with these purposes and as are specified on each occasion of change of purpose"[41]; and (ii) "Personal data should not be disclosed, made available or otherwise used for purposes other than those specified in accordance with Paragraph 9 (i.e., purpose specification) except . . . (a) with the consent of the data subject; or (b) by the authority of law."[42]

Speaking philosophically, we can say that the Purpose Specification and Use Limitation principles have only indexical meaning, emerging in particular, concrete instances of use. Once purposes are specified, uses, too, are limited accordingly. But what these purposes are, or may be, is not given in the principles themselves. One could admire the adaptability of these principles—a virtue of FIPPs, by some counts—or point out, as has Fred Cate, that FIPPs themselves do not provide privacy protection—merely procedural guidance whose substantive clout is indeterminate.[43] According to Cate, the FIPPs purpose specification principle offers some traction for privacy protection. He points out, however, that unless constraints are placed on what purposes are legitimate (and why), a purely procedural Purpose Specification Principle opens a glaring loophole in FIPPs.[44] This point is crucial for my argument about context.

Use Limitation, in turn, is compromised by the wild card character of Purpose Specification, as is the principle of Collection Limitation (often called Data Minimization), which restricts information collection to that which is necessary for specified purposes. Talk about a vicious circle! Other principles that may seem to be inoculated against this indexicality are also affected, albeit indirectly. Take Security and Data Quality requirements. Although no explicit mention is made of purpose in these principles, they are implied, as what counts as reasonable standards for both is surely a function of the purposes for which information is gathered and for which it is earmarked—for example, whether the information in question is being collected for purposes of national security versus consumer marketing. The meaning of these principles is dependent on purpose, and purpose may be specified by the data collector, at will. Unless and until purposes are shaped by substantive requirements, FIPPs constitute a mere shell, formally defining relationships among the principles and laying out procedural steps to guide information flows. Given the centrality of FIPPs in virtually all privacy (or data protection) policies throughout the world, it is surprising to find that privacy is elusive, and even that fairness itself can be questioned in the contemporary regimes of privacy policies.[45]

## A QUESTION OF INTERPRETATION

The rhetoric surrounding the White House release of the Consumer Privacy Bill of Rights was of a new page, ambitious and optimistic. The principle of Respect for Context offered a salient departure from FIPPs' Purpose Specification and Use Limitation principles. Herein lay the promise of something materially different, something better. But whether the promise can be fulfilled and not devolve to business as usual will depend on how we interpret context. In the previous section, we saw that the interpretation of Respect for Context is important not only in its own right but also for fixing meanings for other key principles, including Access and Accuracy, Focused Collection, and Security. Fixing meanings *correctly*—that is, in a such way that the innovation embodied in Respect for Context materially advances the state of privacy protection in the United States—is, therefore, critical. Below, I will explain why, among the four alternatives, context understood as social domain is the most viable basis for progress.

Consider context as a business model or practice. Under this interpretation, context would be determined by the exigencies of a particular business and communicated to individuals via general terms of service. In the context of an online purchase of physical goods, for example, it is reasonable for a merchant to require a consumer's address and valid payment information. But if business purpose is a blank check, we are in trouble. Even in this simple illustration, questions remain: What happens to the information after delivery is completed? With whom can this information be shared, and under what terms, and for how long? Who is responsible if harm follows its unintended leakage, or theft by criminals? With the ever-growing thirst for data, questions such as these have multiplied by orders of magnitude, and while our intuitions are robust when it comes to merchants of physical goods, reasonable purpose for businesses *in* the information business is murkier still.

If business model and practice define context, political economy would shape the relationship between the information collector and information subject, allowing no recourse to standards beyond business expedience (except in the few sectors where privacy legislation exists). By definition, each business entity determines what is and is not expedient. Other standards, such as security, use limitation, collection minimization, and access, which all are defined in terms of purpose, will be defined accordingly. Defining context as business model leaves the door wide open to anything reasonably conceived as profitable for respective businesses—buying up information resources, extracting information resources from transactions, and using them in any manner (limited only by positive law and regulation). This is not to say that business models are irrelevant to context and informational norms, only that the promise of change will not be fulfilled if business interests are the sole arbiters of context.[46] Although business needs are an important consideration, they do not form a sound basis for privacy's moral imperative.

What about context as technology platform or system? First, consider what this means. It is quite sensible to refer to a Facebook profile, a Bing search, a Fitbit group, the web, an email exchange, and a Google+ Hangout as contexts. The question here, however, is not whether it is *sensible* to use the term context in these ways but whether these ways can form the reference point for Respect for Context. Answering affirmatively means technological affordance would determine moral imperative; it means accepting that whatever information flows happen to be afforded by a social network, a web search engine, a health-tracking device, and so forth, not only determine what *can* happen but also what *ought* to happen. In these stark terms, the thesis may seem absurdly counterintuitive; yet it is embodied in familiar practices and reasoning. Take, for example, controversies surrounding online tracking. After conceding that there was strong support for providing individuals with the means to delete third-party cookies, various workarounds emerged, such as Flash cookies and browser fingerprinting that reinstated cross-site tracking functionality. If technological affordance defines moral imperative, there are no grounds for critiquing the workarounds. Similarly, when Mark Zuckerberg said Facebook had altered norms because the system had altered actual flows, he was right, by definition, because whatever flows are enabled by platforms simply *are* the flows that context legitimates.

Denying that technological affordance defines respect for context does not mean it is irrelevant to it. Practices are changed and sometimes they pull norms and standards along with them. The explosive growth of (socio)technical information systems, the source of much consternation over privacy, is responsible for radical disruptions in information gathering, analysis and distribution in the types of information that are accessed, analyzed and distributed, the actors sending and receiving information, and in the constraints or conditions under which it flows. These disruptions not only divert information flows from one path to another and one recipient to another (or others) but also may reconfigure ontologies yielding new categories of information, and new types of actors and modes of dissemination. Such changes may call for the reconsideration of entrenched norms and development of norms where none previously may have existed.

The "old" technologies of the telephone, for example, introduced novel flows of voice dissemination, including new classes of actors, such as telecommunications companies, in the early days, human operators, and later on, mechanical and electronic switches. Existing norms of flow governing communications and, say, eavesdropping, may provide initial models for new conditions afforded by the telephone. As novel systems cause increasing divergence from pre-existing affordances, novel challenges demand deeper examination of what is at stake in a social world, conversations, and relationships that have been reconfigured by telephonic media. A pair of famous U.S. Supreme Court cases, roughly forty years apart, reveal this progression: *Olmstead v. United States*, 277 U.S. 438 (1928), and *Katz v. United States*, 389 U.S. 347 (1967). Landmark Fourth Amendment cases involving a historical reversal of law, these cases have been endlessly analyzed and taught. The common lesson drawn from them, which I have no cause to challenge, is that the 1967 court finally "got it right." Shifting attention from the foreground of what counts as a legitimate expectation of privacy to the background of how the world had changed, we note that as telephones became normalized, phone-mediated conversations became integral to social life. In my view, this is key to explaining *why* the court "got it right" in the *Katz* case. The ascent of telecommunication in social, political, and economic life also meant addressing head-on the status of newly emerging actors, forms of information, and constraints on flow. To this day (underscored by the Snowden revelations) we are living with the consequences of legislation that attempted to define duties of phone companies, and the varied access they (and others) would have to new forms of data, from pen register data to the content of phone calls.[47]

Technical systems and platforms shape human activity by constraining and affording what we can do and say; in this sense, they are rightly conceived as contexts and deserve to be objects of attention and regulation. Allowing that people act and transact in contexts shaped by technical systems does not mean, however, that these systems fully account for the meaning of Respect for Context. So doing allows material design to define ethical and political precepts; it allows the powers that shape the technical platforms of our mediated lives not only to affect our moral and political experiences through built constraints and affordances but also to place them beyond the pale of normative judgment.

The practical implications of this distinction can be seen in relation to the first National Telecommunications and Information Administration (NTIA) multistakeholder process. No fool's errand, its mission was to establish a code of conduct for mobile applications developers. The NTIA process, which (1) identified a new class of actors, including mobile app developers, among others, and (2) articulated baseline constraints on appropriate behaviours in the ecologies of mobile information services, concluded with a set of guidelines.[48] In my view, respect for context should not stop with these. Beyond the baseline, it would require that distinct sets of informational norms be fleshed out for mobile app developers according to the social meaning, or function, of their specific apps. Although developers of, say, Yelp, Google Maps, Foursquare, Fitbit, and Uber should fulfill these baseline obligations in their collection, use, and disclosure of personal information, their obligations do not stop with these. One could reasonably expect Fitbit to treat the information it gathers differently from, say, Uber or Foursquare.

Mobile app developers do not escape additional obligations of social context any more than physicians are relieved of duties of confidentiality when information is shared with them over the phone rather than during an office visit. Where technical platforms mediate multiple spheres of life, the need to distinguish technological affordance from moral imperative is acute. Doubtless, technologies shape contexts, may even constitute them, but where Respect for Context is a bellwether for privacy, it is a mistake to confuse technological contexts with those that define legitimate privacy expectations.

Interpreting context as sector or industry overcomes some of the drawbacks of context as business model, because instead of devolving to the self-serving policies of individual businesses, norms of information flow could be guided by a common mission of the collective—ideally, collective best practice. This interpretation also aligns with the US sectoral approach to privacy regulation and legislation, which, at its best, allows for the generation of rules that are sensitive to the distinctive contours of each sector. Extracting a Principle of Respect for Context, carrying moral weight, from a descriptive notion of sector requires a bridge. One is to recognize explicitly that sectors include more than industries, which range over a limited set of, primarily, business sectors. Existing practice in the United States goes partway in this direction, in talk of education and health care, for example, as sectors. Extending the range to politics, family, or religion could deepen the appreciation of appropriate informational rules even further. Expanding and qualifying the scope of sectors in these ways, however, brings them close to the construct of social spheres around which the theory of contextual integrity is oriented.

Interpreting the Principle of Respect for Context as respect for contextual integrity means, first, that any significant disruption in information flows triggers a call for analysis and evaluation in terms of types of information, actors, and transmission principles. Because shifts and changes characteristic of these disruptions may correspond to shifts and changes in the balance of interests as well as achievement and abatement of values, identifying them is a crucial first step. Second, an evaluation of disruptive flows extends beyond conventional measures of stakeholder interests and even beyond general moral and political values. It brings to the fore context-specific functions, purposes and values. Context is crucial to privacy, and not merely as a passive backdrop against which the interests of affected parties are measured, balanced, and traded off; rather, it contributes independent, substantive landmarks for *how* to take these interests and values into account. It makes the integrity of the contexts *themselves* the arbiter of privacy practices—vibrant marketplace, effective health care, sound education, truly democratic governance and strong, trusting families and friendships.

## SUMMARY OF ARGUMENT

For the Consumer Privacy Bill of Rights to advance privacy protection beyond its present state, a great deal depends on how the Principle of Respect for Context is interpreted. Acknowledging the pivotal place context holds in the White House vision, commentaries have converged around four primary contenders: business model, technology, sector, and social domain. I have argued that respecting context as *business model* offers no prospect of advancement beyond the present state of affairs. Citing innovation and service as the drivers behind this interpretation, its proponents seem to expect individuals and regulators to sign a blank check to businesses in collection, use, and disclosure of information based on exigencies of individual businesses.

Respecting context as *sector* (or industry) fares slightly better, as it offers a framework beyond the needs of individual businesses for establishing standards and norms. How well this approach meaningfully advances privacy protection beyond the present state depends on how sectors are defined. If it follows the contours of industry, it might yield improvements in "best practices," but the interests of dominant incumbents may still prevail. This problem is particularly acute where the sector or industry in question is the "information sector," where the proverbial fox would be guarding the henhouse. Further, if industry dominates the construction of sectors, the influence of sectors such as health care, education, religion, and politics will be diminished, or the commercial aspects of these industries may play a disproportionate role. Correcting for these distortions brings sector-as-context closer to context as social domain. Understanding context in purely *technological* terms implies that legitimate expectations should be adjusted to reflect technical affordances and constraints. But so doing drains respect for context of moral legitimacy, getting things exactly backwards. Our morally legitimate expectations, shaped by context and other factors, should drive design and define the responsibilities of developers, not the other way around.

Interpreting context as *social domain*, as characterized in the theory of contextual integrity, avoids many of the problems associated with the other three. To respect context under this interpretation means to respect contextual integrity and, in turn, to respect informational norms that promote general ethical and political values, as well as context-specific ends, purposes, and values. Informational norms constitute the substantive cornerstone of policy and practice and replace both the serendipity of design and arbitrary policies serving dominant parties. The ultimate contribution of contextual integrity does not rest with the concept of context per se, but with two fundamental ideas behind it. One is the idea that privacy (or informational) norms require all relevant parameters to be specified, including actors (functioning in roles), information types, and transmission principles. Omitting any one of these yields rules that are partial and ambiguous. The second fundamental idea is of context-specific ends, purposes, and values, which extend the significance of privacy beyond the balancing of interests, harms, and benefits. Contextual integrity reveals the systematic dependencies of social values on appropriate information flows, once and for all challenging the fallacy of privacy as valuable for individuals alone.

## CONCLUSION: IMPLICATIONS FOR PRACTICE

I have argued that how context is interpreted in Respect for Context makes more than a semantic difference. To demonstrate the significance of this difference, let us consider how it might play out in practice by returning to 18 U.S.C. § 2511 (2)(a)(i), which, as we saw, prohibits telecommunications providers from intercepting, disclosing, or using the content of communications except in limited circumstances, which include rendering service or protecting their property, with further exceptions for legitimate needs of law enforcement and national security. For the sake of argument, assume that no such legislation existed and, based on the Principle of Respect for Context, regulation for this slender part of the landscape must be newly designed. What difference does interpretation make?

Let us begin with the interpretation of *context-as-technology*—not merely technology influencing context, but *defining* it. Under this interpretation, we would conclude that whatever interception, disclosure, or use of content is enabled by the mediating technologies should be "respected." Expectations of parties utilizing these technologies could not extend beyond what the technologies allow—for affordance defines legitimacy. Interpreted as *business model*, respect for context would allow individual providers to pursue whatever practices and policies they believe will promote profitability and an edge over competitors. These might include scanning conversations to pick out customers' commercially relevant interests, or providing access to interested parties willing to pay handsomely for access to conversations. I am not suggesting these particular outcomes are likely, merely the reasoning towards practice that this interpretation allows. Interpreting context as *sector* is likely to follow a slightly different track, if only because individual businesses, unless they collude, will seek to entrench practices that appeal to customers and level the playing field with competitors. Moreover, it is clear that how the boundaries, contours, and definition of sectoral groupings are set would affect the policies and principles respective sectors support.

According to contextual integrity, interpreting context as social domain would focus attention on the role of telecommunications providers as communications' mediators. In this light, the tailored access rights devised by 18 U.S.C. § 2511 (2)(a)(i), allowing surveillance of conversations for the express purpose of assuring quality of service and protection of property, was a brilliant compromise. Laxer policies, as supported by the other interpretations, may discourage intimate or political conversation, as well as other sensitive conversations, such as strategic business planning or path-breaking scientific collaborations, creating disadvantage for those needing to communicate or benefiting from it. But beyond these impacts on various parties, they would reduce the utility of communications networks to individuals as well as their service of respective contextual ends, purposes, and values. Context as social domain draws attention to these higher-order considerations, also reflected in the drafting of 18 U.S.C. § 2511 (2)(a)(i).

As a brief aside, contextual thinking could have averted the Google Buzz fiasco.[49] Technological thinking may have suggested an alluring opportunity to leapfrog into social networks based on Google's holdings from its email network. A business argument might have supported Buzz, in light of Facebook's success and Google's proprietary access to Gmail content and metadata. But failure to recognize that email serves multiple, disparate social contexts yielded an unappealing system and provoked outrage and indignation.

Contexts are shaped by technology, business practice, and industry sector. They may also be constituted by geographic location, relationship, place, space, agreement, culture, religion, and era, and much more besides. In individual cases, any of these factors could qualify and shape people's expectations of how information about us is gathered, used, and disseminated. No one of them, however, provides the right level of analysis, or carries the same moral and political weight as social domain. This is the thesis I have defended here. In light of it, I offer an amendment to the Consumer Privacy Bill of Rights' Principle of Respect for Context:

> Respect for Context means consumers have a right to expect that companies will collect, use, and disclose personal data in ways that are consistent with the [social] context in which consumers provide the data.

## NOTES

1. "Respect for Context as a Benchmark for Privacy Online: What It Is and Isn't" by Helen Nissenbaum originally appeared in *Social Dimensions of Privacy: Interdisciplinary Perspectives*, edited by Beate Roessler and Dorota Mokrosinska (Cambridge: Cambridge University Press, 2015), pp. 278–302. Copyright 2015 Cambridge University Press. Reprinted by permission of Cambridge University Press.

2. White House, "Consumer Data Privacy in a Networked World: A Framework for Protecting Privacy and Promoting Innovation in the Global Digital Economy" (February 2012), https://www.whitehouse.gov/sites/default/files/privacy-final.pdf, 9.

3. Chris Civil, "President Obama's Privacy Bill of Rights: Encouraging a Collaborative Process for Digital Privacy Reform," *The Bolt* (blog), *Berkeley Technology Law Journal*, March 12, 2012, accessed June 11, 2013, http://btlj.org/?p=1712.

4. E.g., World Economic Forum, *Rethinking Personal Data: Strengthening Trust* (May 2012), http://www3.weforum.org/docs/WEF_IT_RethinkingPersonalData_Report_2012.pdf;

Federal Trade Commission, *Protecting Consumer Privacy in an Era of Rapid Change: Recommendations for Businesses and Policymakers* (March 2012), http://www.ftc.gov/os/2012/03/120326privacyreport.pdf.

5. Julia Angwin and Jennifer Valentino-Devries, "New Tracking Frontier: Your License Plates," *Wall Street Journal*, September 29, 2012, http://on.wsj.com/1w2G8gB; Jeremy Singer-Vine and Jennifer Valentino-Devries, "Sites Sharing Personal Details: The Journal's Test," *Digits* (blog), *Wall Street Journal*, December 7, 2012, http://blogs.wsj.com/digits/2012/12/07/sites-sharing-personal-details-the-journal-methodology/#.

6. Anxiety over the digital age, and, more specifically, big data, is a major theme in mainstream tech and business journalism as of 2013. For more information, see the *New York Times* special section "Big Data 2013," http://bits.blogs.nytimes.com/category/big-data-2013/.

7. Helen Nissenbaum, *Privacy in Context: Technology, Policy and the Integrity of Social Life* (Stanford, CA: Stanford Law Books, 2010).

8. E.g., *Google Inc. v. Joffe*, 729 F.3d 1262 (9th Cir. 2013), *cert. denied*, 134 S. Ct. 2877 (2014); Opinion, *Fed. Trade Comm'n v. Wyndham Worldwide Corp.*, No. 13-01887 (D. N.J. April 7, 2014); Amended Order Granting Motion for Preliminary Approval of Class Action Settlement, In re Netflix Privacy Litigation, No. 11-00379 (N. D. Cal. July 5, 2012).

9. National Telecommunications and Information Administration, "Privacy Multistakeholder Process: Mobile Application Transparency," November 12, 2013, www.ntia.doc.gov/other-publication/2013/privacy-multistakeholder-process-mobile-application-transparency; see also http://www.ntia.doc.gov/category/privacy.

10. World Economic Forum, *Rethinking Personal Data*; Organization for Economic Cooperation and Development, *The OECD Privacy Framework* (2013), http://www.oecd.org/internet/ieconomy/privacy-guidelines.htm; Jan Philipp Albrecht, European Parliament, Committee on Civil Liberties, Justice and Home Affairs, *Report on the Proposal for a Regulation of the European Parliament and of the Council on the Protection of Individuals with Regard to the Processing of Personal Data and on the Free Movement of Such Data (General Data Protection Regulation)*, COM(2012)0011–C7-0025/2012–2012/0011(COD) (2013).

11. Jacques Ellul, *The Technological Society* (New York: Knopf, 1964); Willis H. Ware, *The Computer in Your Future* (Santa Monica, CA: Rand Corporation, 1967); Harvey Brooks, "Technology, Evolution, and Purpose," *Daedalus* 109 (1980); Priscilla M. Regan, *Legislating Privacy: Technology, Social Values, and Public Policy* (Chapel Hill: University of North Carolina Press, 1995).

12. An early version of this chapter was presented at the "Privacy Law Scholars Conference 2013" where James Rule, Mike Hinze, and other participants provided excellent commentary. I have benefited from deep insights of many colleagues and from opportunities to present the work at the Amsterdam Privacy Conference, University of Washington, Foundation Télécom Seminar on The Futures of Privacy, and the EU JRC Ispra Workshop on Emerging ICT for Citizen Veillance. Funding from the NSF—CNS-1355398 and DGE-0966187—and Intel Science and Technology Center for Social Computing provided crucial support for this work. Thanks to Solon Barocas for assembling key materials and sharpening central ideas. Without it, this article could not have gotten off the ground. To Emily Goldsher-Diamond, thanks are due for outstanding research and editorial assistance, without which it could not have been completed.

13. Marcia Hoffman, "Obama Administration Unveils Promising Consumer Privacy Plan, but the Devil Will Be in the Details," *Deeplinks* (blog), Electronic Frontier Foundation, February 23, 2012, https://www.eff.org/deeplinks/2012/02/obama-administration-unveils-promising-consumer-privacy-plan-devil-details.

14. "White House Sets Out Consumer Privacy Bill of Rights," Electronic Privacy Information Center, February 23, 2012, https://epic.org/2012/02/white-house-sets-out-consumer-.html.

15. "White House Unveils 'Consumer Privacy Bill of Rights'; Industry Embraces 'Do Not Track,'" Center for Democracy & Technology, February 23, 2012, https://cdt.org/press/white-house-unveils-consumer-privacy-bill-of-rights-industry-embraces-do-not-track/.

16. David Hoffman, "White House Releases Framework for Protecting Privacy in a Networked World," *Policy@Intel* (blog), February 23, 2012, http://blogs.intel.com/policy/2012/02/23/white-house-privacy.

17. Civil, "Privacy Bill of Rights."

18. White House, *Consumer Data Privacy*, 47.

19. Julia Kiseleva et al., "Discovering Temporal Hidden Contexts in Web Sessions for User Trail Prediction," in *Proceedings of the 22nd International Conference on World Wide Web Companion* (International World Wide Web Conferences Steering Committee, Geneva, Switzerland, 2013); Julia Kiseleva et al., "Predicting Current User Intent with Contextual Markov Models," in *Data Mining Workshops (ICDMW), 2013 IEEE 13th International Conference* (IEEE, 2013).

20. See, e.g., Cynthia Dwork and Deirdre K. Mulligan, "It's Not Privacy, and It's Not Fair," *Stanford Law Review Online* 66 (September 3, 2013): 35–40, http://www.stanfordlawreview. org/online/privacy-and-big-data/its-not-privacy-and-its-not-fair.

21. U.S. Const. amend. VI; Andrew D. Selbst, "Contextual Expectations of Privacy," *Cardozo Law Review* 35, no. 2 (2013).

22. White House, *Consumer Data Privacy*, ii.

23. Alan Charles Raul et al., *Comments of AT&T Inc. Before the Department of Commerce Internet Policy Task Force in the Matter of Commercial Data Privacy and Innovation in the Internet Economy: A Dynamic Policy Framework* (January 28, 2011), 17, http://www.ntia.doc. gov/files/ntia/comments/101214614-0614-01/attachments/ACF320.pdf.

24. Pablo L. Chavez, *Comments of Google Inc. to U.S. Department of Commerce* (January 28, 2011), 9, http://www.ntia.doc.gov/files/ntia/comments/101214614-0614-01/attachments/ FINALCommentsonDepartmentofCommercePrivacyGreenPaper%20%283%29.pdf.

25. Barbara Lawler, *Comments of Intuit Inc. Before the Department of Commerce, Office of the Secretary, National Telecommunications and Information Administration* (January 28, 2011), 8–9, http://www.ntia.doc.gov/files/ntia/comments/101214614-0614-01/attachments/ Intuit.pdf.

26. *Multistakeholder Process to Develop Consumer Data Privacy Code of Conduct Concerning Mobile Application Transparency*, July 2012. Symposium conducted at the open meeting of the National Telecommunications and Information Administration, Washington, D.C.

27. Intel, *RE: FTC Staff Preliminary Report on Protecting Consumer Privacy*, comments to Federal Trade Commission (January 26, 2011), 4, https://www.ftc.gov/policy/public-comments/comment-00246-0.

28. Fran Maier, *TRUSTe's Comments in Response to the Department of Commerce's Green Paper—Commercial Data Privacy & Innovation in the Internet Economy: A Dynamic Policy Framework* (January 28, 2010), 2, http://www.ntia.doc.gov/federal-register-notices/2010/ information-privacy-and-innovation-internet-economy-notice#comment-28878.

29. Chavez, *Comments of Google, Inc.*, 2.

30. Raul et al., *Comments of AT&T Inc.*, 17.

31. Pam Horan, Comments from Online Publishers Association, *Re: FTC Preliminary Staff Report on "Protecting Consumer Privacy in an Era of Rapid Change: A Proposed Framework for Businesses and Policymakers"—File No. P095416* (February 17, 2011), 4, http://www.ftc. gov/policy/public-comments/comment-00315-0.

32. Raul et al., *Comments of AT&T Inc.*, 17.

33. Maier, *TRUSTe's comments*, 2.

34. Lawler, "Comments of Intuit, Inc.," 9.

35. For a further discussion on spheres, see Nissenbaum, *Privacy in Context*, 80, 131, 166–69, 198–200, 240–41.

36. Raul et al., *Comments of AT&T Inc.*, 10.

37. See Nissenbaum, *Privacy in Context*, especially Part II.

38. For longer, more elaborate discussion, see Helen Nissenbaum, "A Contextual Approach to Privacy Online," *Daedalus* 140, no. 4 (2011): 32–48; Nissenbaum, *Privacy in Context*.

39. White House, *Consumer Data Privacy*, 49–52.

40. Ibid., 47.

41. Ibid., 50.

42. Ibid.

43. For Cate's cogent analysis, see Fred H. Cate, "The Failure of Fair Information Practice Principles," in *Consumer Protection in the Age of the Information Economy*, ed. Jane K. Winn

(Aldershot, Hants, England: Ashgate, 2006), 343–79, http://papers.ssrn.com/sol3/papers.cfm? abstract_id=1156972. See another astute discussion in Ira Rubinstein, "Privacy and Regulatory Innovation: Moving Beyond Voluntary Codes," *I/S, a Journal of Law and Policy for the Information Society* 6, no. 3 (2010): 356–423.

44. In fairness, others in the policy arena have noted the indeterminacy of the linchpin purpose specification and use limitation principles and are attempting to set substantive standards. For example, the EU Article 29 Working Party in Opinion 03/201d on purpose limitation and aspects of the problem discussed in Judith Rauhofer, "One Step Forward, Two Steps Back: Critical Observations on the Proposed Reform of the EU Data Protection Framework," *Journal of Law and Economic Regulation* 6, no. 1 (2013): 57–84.

45. Nissenbaum, "Contextual Approach."

46. Milton Friedman, "The Social Responsibility of Business Is to Increase Its Profits," *New York Times Magazine*, September 13, 1970.

47. 18 U.S.C. § 2511(2)(a)(i) (2011): "It shall not be unlawful under this chapter for an operator of a switchboard, or an officer, employee, or agent of a provider of wire or electronic communication service, whose facilities are used in the transmission of a wire or electronic communication, to intercept, disclose, or use that communication in the normal course of his employment while engaged in any activity which is a necessary incident to the rendition of his service or to the protection of the rights or property of the provider of that service, except that a provider of wire communication service to the public shall not utilize service observing or random monitoring except for mechanical or service quality control checks." Thanks to Chris Hoofnagle for calling attention to this crucial point.

48. National Telecommunications and Information Administration, *Short Form Notice Code of Conduct to Promote Transparency in Mobile App Practices* (July 25, 2013), http://www.ntia. doc.gov/files/ntia/publications/july_25_code_draft.pdf.

49. Thanks to Ira Rubinstein for suggesting Google Buzz as an illustration of the different thinking generated by different interpretations of context. Also, see Ira Rubinstein and Nathan Good, "Privacy by Design: A Counterfactual Analysis of Google and Facebook Privacy Incidents," *Berkeley Technology Law Journal* 28, no. 2 (2013): 1333–414.

## Chapter Three

# Privacy and the Dead

## James Stacey Taylor

In recent years there has been a wealth of discussion on the nature and value of privacy. In addition to these perennial and foundational question concerning privacy, the question of whether a respect for privacy holds any special value for a democratic society, the question of the relationship between privacy and security, the question of whether persons have duties to protect informational privacy (either their own or that of others), and the question of the relationship between informational privacy and freedom of speech have all attracted considerable academic attention.[1] Yet, despite this blossoming interest in privacy, very little attention has been focused on the issue of whether we should respect the privacy of the dead. This is unfortunate, for many people desire that their private affairs remain private even after they are dead, and so the question of whether these desires should be respected is important. In this chapter I argue that we owe no duty to the dead to respect their privacy, for we have no reason to believe that they can be either harmed or wronged by its violation. However, my conclusion is not that we can thereby violate the privacy of the dead with impunity. Instead, I argue that while we owe no duty to the dead to respect their privacy, we should still respect it out of concern for the interests of the living.

### PRIVACY AND POSTHUMOUS HARM

It is common to claim that there is a duty to respect the privacy of the dead. This claim has been invoked to argue that the DNA of the Pharaoh Tutankhamen should not be extracted and analyzed,[2] that the gender identity of Queen Christina of Sweden should not be determined and disclosed,[3] and that the psychiatric records of the Nazi war criminals tried at Nuremburg be kept confidential.[4] More prosaically, the duty to respect the privacy of the dead has been invoked by health care professionals in refusing to release medical information about their deceased patients,[5] by family members objecting to the release of autopsy findings, and by relatives of deceased persons objecting to certain information about them being revealed by their biographers.[6] But why should one believe that there is a duty to protect the informational privacy of the dead? One possible answer to this question is that abiding by this duty is required to prevent harming the persons whose privacy would be violated, through thwarting their interests in keeping certain information about themselves private.

The view that persons can be harmed by actions or events that occur after they are dead has respectable historical antecedents. Aristotle, for example, famously recognized that "a dead man is popularly believed to be capable of having both good and ill fortune. . . . In exactly the same way as if he were alive but unaware . . . of what was happening."[7] And this Aristotelian view of the possibility of posthumous harm is widely held by persons who work on the metaphysics of death. The orthodox account of how such harm is possible is that which has been independently developed by Joel Feinberg[8] and George Pitcher.[9] To establish intuitively the Aristotelian point that the dead can be harmed just as could a person who was "alive but unaware" of the harms that had befallen her, Feinberg offers two hypothetical cases. In Case A, "a woman devotes thirty years of her life to the furtherance of certain ideals and ambitions in the form of one vast undertaking."[10] A month before she dies, the "empire of her hopes" collapses and she is disgraced—but she learns of neither of these things, as her friends conceal the facts from her. In Case B, precisely the same events transpire as in Case A, but this time the "empire of her hopes" collapses within a year of her death.[11] Feinberg holds that since it "would not be very controversial" to say that the woman had been harmed in Case A, it should similarly be held that the woman in Case B was harmed, since the same interests that were set back in Case A were set back in Case B.[12] Having thus established to his own satisfaction that persons can be harmed after their deaths, Feinberg turns to consider the obvious disanalogy between Case A and Case B: that in Case A the woman whose interests were thwarted existed at the time of their thwarting, whereas in Case B she did not. In response to this, Feinberg explicitly follows Pitcher, holding that the person who was harmed by the thwarting of the interests in Case B was the woman as she was when alive; the antemortem person whose interests were thwarted after her death.[13] Yet this response raises another difficulty: that it appears that an event that occurs after the woman's death in Case B (the collapse of the "empire of her hopes") causes her to be harmed prior to her death. Feinberg wisely disavows such retroactivity, instead again following Pitcher in holding that the relationship between the posthumous collapse of the woman's enterprise and the harm that befell her was not a *causal* relationship but a *conceptual* relationship. The collapse of the woman's enterprise thus did not *cause* her to be harmed, but, instead, merely *made it true* that she was harmed.[14] To illustrate this, Pitcher provides the example of the world being "blasted to smithereens during the next presidency after Ronald Reagan's," with this event making it true that "even now, during Reagan's term, he is the penultimate president of the United States."[15] Pitcher's point here can be further supported by the recognition that there are many other properties that can be ascribed to individuals after their deaths without invoking retroactive causation. A woman who dies before her daughter gives birth will still become the grandmother of her grandchild (G) when he is born. Similarly, a man who shoots another, who shoots back, killing him, will become the killer of his victim once she dies as a result of his shooting, even if this occurs after the original shooter's death.

If Feinberg and Pitcher (and Aristotle) are correct, and it is possible for a person to be harmed by an event or action that occurs after her death, then it would be possible for a person to be harmed as a result of her privacy being violated after her death. Thus, if, as seems to be the case, Queen Christiana of Sweden had an interest in her gender identity being kept secret from others, its revelation would harm her through thwarting this interest, and this would be true whether this occurred prior to her death or after it. This line of reasoning appears to support the view that the putative (defeasible) duty to respect the privacy of the dead is an instance of the more general (defeasible) moral duty to avoid harming persons.

Despite the initial plausibility of the Feinberg–Pitcher line of argument in favour of the possibility of posthumous harm, it should not be accepted.[16] Feinberg and Pitcher are correct to note that the (putative) subject of posthumous harm must (if such harm exists) be the antemortem person whose interests were posthumously thwarted. That the person whose interests are at stake no longer exists at the time of their thwarting—and hence her interests do not exist, either—is no bar to their being thwarted. Although a person's interests die with her, their intentional objects can extend beyond the scope of her (and their) own existence. Since an interest is thwarted when the action or event that was its intentional object fails to transpire, the thwarting of a person's interests can occur after they have ceased to exist. Like a person who acquires the property of "the grandmother of G" as a result of an event that occurs after her death, an interest can acquire the property of "being thwarted by event E" as a result of an event that occurs after it has ceased to exist. But this explication of how persons and interests can acquire new properties (e.g., the property of being a grandmother, or the property of being thwarted) as a result of actions or events that occur after they have ceased to exist—and hence how a person can acquire the property of being harmed as a result of events that occur after her death—carries with it the seeds of destruction for the Feinberg–Pitcher account of posthumous harm. The properties that can be attributed to persons ("grandmother," "killer,") or interests ("thwarted" or "fulfilled") on the basis of actions that take place or events that occur after the persons or interests in question have ceased to exist are all properties that satisfy two conditions. First, they are properties whose criteria for ascription are uncontroversial. There is no doubt that a woman whose daughter has given birth to a live child is a grandmother, and there is no doubt that when X did not transpire a person's interest in X transpiring has been thwarted. Second, they are properties that can be legitimately ascribed to their subjects on the basis of certain Cambridge changes that they (the subjects) undergo. A woman, W, whose daughter gave birth to a live child after she (W) had died underwent no Oxford change on the basis of her daughter's giving birth, only a Cambridge change—but this sufficed for her to become the grandmother of her daughter's child. Similarly, an interest can acquire the property of "being thwarted" on the basis of a Cambridge change that it undergoes when its intentional object is precluded from ever transpiring. The property of "harm," however, does not satisfy the first criterion—and it does not satisfy it precisely because the issue of whether it satisfies the second condition is contested. A person can be harmed by actions that occur after her death if Feinberg's interest-based account of well-being is accepted. However, a hedonist who holds that harm is constituted by adverse mental states would deny that a person could be harmed by anything that occurs after her death. That properties that satisfy both of the conditions outlined above can be predicted of subjects on the basis of actions or events that occur after they have ceased to exist does not thereby show that properties that fail to meet either one or both of these conditions (e.g., harm) could similarly be so predicated. The Feinberg–Pitcher account of posthumous harm is thus importantly incomplete. As such, it provides us with no reason to believe that persons can be harmed by events that occur after their deaths. It therefore cannot support the claim that we should respect the privacy of the dead on the grounds that to do otherwise would be to harm the antemortem persons that they were when they were alive.

## PRIVACY AND WRONGING THE DEAD

Of course, to show that the Feinberg–Pitcher account of posthumous harm is incomplete and thus cannot be used to support the claim that the duty to respect the privacy of the dead exists as an instance of the general moral duty to avoid the infliction of harm is not to show that the dead cannot be harmed. It is possible that an alternative account of how posthumous harm is possible could be forthcoming.[17] And it is possible that the Feinberg–Pitcher view could be revised in such a way that it is clear that the property of harm does indeed satisfy both of the conditions outlined above. But instead of focusing on establishing the possibility of posthumous harm, a proponent of the view that we have a duty to respect the privacy of the dead might try a different tack. It is possible that persons can be wronged without being harmed. For example, if Hardcastle promises to give Sebastian a lift but maliciously fails to show up, Sebastian would have been wronged by Hardcastle's breaking of this promise. But if Sebastian received a lift from Charles instead, and was not in the slightest bit inconvenienced by Hardcastle's omission, he would not have been harmed by Hardcastle's breaking of the promise.[18] Instead of arguing that the dead would be harmed by a failure to respect their privacy, then a proponent of the view that we owe a moral duty to the dead to respect their privacy might argue that even though they would not be *harmed* by a failure to abide by this duty, they would be *wronged* by this.

Just as the "dead" who would be the subjects of (putative) posthumous harms would be the antemortem persons whose interests were thwarted, so too would the subjects of (putative) posthumous wronging be the antemortem persons who were wronged by the violation of their privacy. But how could the posthumous violation of a person's privacy wrong her? One initially plausible explanation is that in violating a person's privacy after she is dead, one is compromising her autonomy by accessing information that she desired that one did not access, and that to compromise her autonomy in this way would be to wrong her. But this initial account of how violating a person's privacy after she is dead would be to wrong her is mistaken on two counts. First, it can, at best, only explain how some posthumous violations of privacy (putatively) compromise the autonomy of the persons subject to them. It cannot explain how posthumous violations of privacy that the antemortem persons subject to them would not be concerned about would be wrong. To see this, note that some item of information I that a person P possesses is private relative to some other persons (Q, R, S . . .) just in case P is justified in precluding (Q, R, S . . .) from accessing I. But it is possible that P would care not a whit about other persons accessing I even though she would be justified in precluding them from accessing it. In such a case, for example, Q's accessing of I would violate P's privacy, but since P would not care about Q's accessing of I, and so took no steps to preclude him from doing so, Q's accessing of I would not compromise P's autonomy at all. At best, then, this initial account of how violating a person's privacy after she was dead would compromise her autonomy could provide only a partial explanation of why such violations would be to wrong the person whose privacy was violated (if there are persons who are wronged by the violation of their privacy even though this did not compromise their autonomy), or else its proponents would have to accept that some privacy violations do not wrong the person whose privacy is violated. But things get worse for this initial account of how a posthumous violation of a person's privacy would wrong her. It was implicitly accepted in the first response that if P had taken steps to preclude Q

from accessing I, and yet Q had done so anyway, Q would have compromised P's autonomy. But there is no reason to believe this. A person is
autonomous with respect to her decisions to perform particular actions to the
degree that it is she, and not someone else, who is the font of them. Thus, if a
person is manipulated into making a decision (for example, to smother his
wife with a pillow in punishment for perceived infidelity), then, to the extent
that it was not he, but another, who was the origin of that decision, his
autonomy with respect to it would be compromised. But if this is so, then the
postmortem violation of a person's privacy would not compromise her antemortem autonomy at all. This is because the person who violated her privacy
after her death could not in so doing have affected her (antemortem) decisions in any way. Thus, the violation of a person's privacy postmortem
would not compromise her autonomy at all.

Yet while this second objection demonstrates that what appeared to be an
initially plausible explanation of how the posthumous violation of a person's
privacy would wrong her through compromising her autonomy is mistaken,
it indicates an avenue that is likely to prove fruitful in providing an account
of how violating a person's privacy after her death could wrong her. While it
is correct to note that the posthumous violation of a person's privacy could
not compromise the autonomy of the antemortem person whose privacy was
violated, it would also be correct to note that a violation of a person's privacy
*while she is alive* could not, on this understanding of autonomy, compromise
her autonomy. To see this, assume that Queen Christiana took steps to keep
her gender identity secret, but one of her maids took steps to discover it and
was successful. Even though this was a violation of the queen's privacy, it
would not have compromised her exercise of her autonomy. It would still
have been she, and not her maid, who was the font of her decisions. However, although the maid's violation of the queen's privacy would not have
compromised the Queen's autonomy *simpliciter*, it would have thwarted her
*successful* exercise of it, for the steps that she would have taken to safeguard
it would have been in vain. And this would be true whether the violation of
her privacy would have occurred either pre- or postmortem.

Perhaps, then, a person who is now dead can be wronged by the posthumous violation of her privacy insofar as this would thwart her successful
exercise of her autonomy; that is, such a violation would have thwarted her
autonomous attempts to keep the information that the violator accessed private, and such a thwarting would wrong her. The first point to note about this
possible explanation of how the posthumous violation of a person's privacy
could wrong her is, again, that it would only apply to those violations of
privacy that the person in question sought to prevent. If Queen Christiana had
taken no steps to ensure that her gender identity remained secret, the intentional discovery of the truth about it, though violating her privacy, would not
have thwarted the successful exercise of her autonomy. As with the first

attempt to account for how the posthumous violation of a person's privacy could wrong her, then, this account provides only a partial explanation of why such violations would be to wrong the person whose privacy was violated; barring that, its proponents must accept that some privacy violations do not wrong the person whose privacy is violated. Second, and more important, the claim that to thwart the successful exercise of a person's autonomy is to wrong her raises the question of why this is so. It might be argued that such a thwarting would wrong the person whose successful exercise of her autonomy (e.g., in maintaining her privacy) was thwarted, as this would undermine the instrumental value that her autonomy held for her. The instrumental value that a person's autonomy would have for her would be derived from the value of the goods that its exercise would increase her chances of securing. Such goods would either be those that, once secured, contributed to her well-being, or those whose acquisition would further a project that had value for her even though its success would not contribute to her well-being. As the above discussion of the relationship between posthumous violations of privacy and posthumous harm showed, there is no reason to believe that persons can be harmed (or benefitted) by events that occur after their deaths. Given this, if the posthumous thwarting of a person's successful exercise of her autonomy would be to wrong her, it must be because it would thwart a project that had value for her independent of her well-being. Yet on the face of it this seems odd, for there is no general moral duty to refrain from thwarting the projects of other persons. If I make a better widget than my competitor and she consequently goes out of business, I have certainly thwarted her business project, but I have not wronged her. It thus seems that the wrongfulness of thwarting another person's projects lies not in the thwarting itself, but in the *reasons* that motivated such thwarting. To see this, consider the difference between a person who builds a fence to spite his neighbour by obstructing her much-loved view of the ocean, and a person who builds an identical fence, obstructing an identical much-loved view, to keep his goats in check. The former act would be blameworthy while the latter would be blameless.[19] The reason for this lies in the attitude that the fence-builder took towards his neighbor: In the former case he deliberately set out to thwart (one of) her projects, while in the latter this thwarting was merely a by-product of his pursuit of his own legitimate interests. Putting this in terms of privacy and autonomy, then, a person who deliberately aims to violate the privacy of another would wrong her by giving the instrumental value of her autonomy (and hence her interests) less weight in his decision-making than a proper respect for them would morally require. And this would be true whether the violation occurred before the death of the victim or after it.

At this point, then, it seems that the deliberate violation of a person's privacy after she is dead could wrong her insofar as it was performed without due regard for the instrumental value of her autonomy. That is, a person could be wronged by the posthumous violation of her privacy because this resulted from her violator adopting an inappropriate attitude towards the value of her autonomy. (Note that according to this analysis, the wrong of the privacy violation was derivative from the wrongful attitude that its violator adopted towards the instrumental value of her autonomy.) But despite appearances, it is not clear that such a violation of a person's privacy would wrong her in this way. To see this, consider a person who believed that Harry Flashman, the fictional antihero of George MacDonald Fraser's series of "Flashman" epistolary novels, was a real person and that the novels were in fact his diaries. Motivated by spite, this person publicizes the most scandalous aspects of Flashman's intimate life as revealed in the "diaries." This act—intended to violate Flashman's privacy—was performed without due regard for the instrumental value of Flashman's autonomy, had Flashman been a real person. However, since Flashman is merely a fictitious character, this act cannot wrong him, as he does not exist. Note that this does not commit one to holding that the would-be revealer of the intimate details of Flashman's life does nothing wrong. It is perfectly compatible with the claim that he did not *wrong Flashman* to hold that he *did wrong* by attempting to violate Flashman's privacy. But just as Flashman does not exist, so too do the dead not exist. Thus, just as the would-be revealer of Flashman's secrets would not wrong him, so too is it the case that persons who violate the privacy of the dead do not wrong them, either.

One might object at this point and note that, unlike Flashman, the dead *did* exist; they, unlike Flashman, had projects to be thwarted, and autonomy whose instrumental value should be respected. But while these claims are true, if one uses them to justify the claim that the dead can be wronged by the violation of their privacy, one will be committed implausibly to asserting that a person who believes that he violates the privacy of a dead person will do more wrong than a person who mistakenly believes that he does this (as the person whose privacy he believes he is violating was fictitious). Not only will the person who violated the privacy of a dead person have done wrong by adopting an inappropriate attitude towards the instrumental value of the autonomy of a person he believed existed, but he will *also* have wronged that person if he happened to have existed. To see this—and to see how implausible the view that this is the case is—consider two cases, Actual and Fictitious. In Actual, the privacy violator violates the privacy of an actual person. In Fictitious, he attempts to violate the privacy of a fictitious person he believes to be real. According to the view that the dead can be wronged by violations of their privacy, the privacy violator would have done more wrong in Actual than he would in Fictitious. He would have done wrong by adopting a morally inappropriate attitude towards the value of the autonomy of the person whose privacy he believed he was violating, *and* he would have wronged her. In Fictitious, however, he would merely have done wrong by adopting a morally inappropriate attitude towards the value of the autonomy of the person whose privacy he believed he was violating. Thus, if one holds that the dead can be wronged by violations of their privacy, one will be committed to holding that the wrongdoing in Actual was greater than that in Fictitious, *even though* in both cases the attitudes adopted by the violator were identical, and *even though* we have no reason to believe that the effects of her actions were anything but identical.[20] (Recall that we have no reason to believe that persons can be harmed by events that occur after their deaths, and so the fact that in Actual, actual interests were thwarted can give us no reason to distinguish these cases on the basis of posthumous harm.) But this is implausible. As such, then, while we could hold that it would be wrong to violate the privacy of the dead on the grounds that this would evince a morally inappropriate attitude towards the instrumental value of personal autonomy, persons are not themselves wronged by any violation of their privacy that might occur after death.

## CONCLUSION

I have argued that we have no reason to believe that persons can be harmed by any violations of their privacy that might occur after they die, and I have argued that the violation of a person's privacy after her death would not wrong her. I have, however, also argued that this latter claim is compatible with holding that it would be wrong to violate a person's privacy after her death, if such a violation evinced a morally inappropriate underevaluation of the instrumental value of the autonomy of the person whose privacy was thus violated. Thus, even if persons cannot be harmed by events that occur after their deaths, and even if they cannot be wronged by the posthumous violation of their privacy, we should still respect the privacy of the dead. But the reason why we should respect persons' privacy after their deaths is not grounded in any claims concerning the effects that its violation would have on the antemortem persons subject to this. Instead, the reason why we should be concerned about the privacy of the dead is because the living will (often) be concerned that their privacy be respected after they die. Thus, to safeguard the concern of the living that their privacy will remain intact after their deaths, we should respect the privacy of those who are now dead.

## NOTES

1. Along with the articles found in this anthology, see Anita L. Allen, *Unpopular Privacy: What Must We Hide?* (Oxford: Oxford University Press, 2011).
2. Soren Holm, "The Privacy of Tutankhamen—Utilizing the Genetic Information in Stored Tissue Samples," *Theoretical Medicine and Bioethics* 22, no. 5 (2001): 437–49.

3. Malin Masterton, Mats G. Hansson, and Anna T. Höglund, "In Search of the Missing Subject: Narrative Identity and Posthumous Wronging," *Studies in History and Philosophy of Biological and Biomedical Sciences* 41, no. 4 (2010): 340–46.

4. Noted by Jack El-Hai in "Full Disclosure: Do Individuals Have a Right for Their Medical Records to Remain Private after Death, or Can Public Interest pPrevail?," *Aeon Magazine*, September 1, 2014, http://aeon.co/magazine/philosophy/a-writers-duty-overrides-the-ethics-of-patient-privacy. See also Malin Masterton, Mats G. Hansson, Anna T. Höglund, and Gert Helgesson, "Can the Dead Be Brought into Disrepute?" *Theoretical Medicine and Bioethics* 28, no. 2 (2007): 137–49.

5. See, for example, Jessica Berg, "Grave Secrets: Legal and Ethical Analysis of Postmortem Confidentiality," *Connecticut Law Review* 34, no. 1 (2001): 81–122.

6. See Craig Howes, "Afterword," in *The Ethics of Life Writing*, ed. John Paul Eakin (Ithaca, NY: Cornell University Press, 2004), 245.

7. Aristotle, *Nicomachean Ethics*, trans. J. A. K. Thomson (Baltimore, MD: Penguin Books, 1953), 1.10.

8. Joel Feinberg, "Harm to Others," in *The Metaphysics of Death*, ed. John Martin Fischer (Palo Alto, CA: Stanford University Press, 1993), 171–90.

9. George Pitcher, "The Misfortunes of the Dead," *American Philosophical Quarterly* 21, no. 2 (1984): 183–88.

10. Feinberg, "Harm to Others," 181.

11. Ibid., 182.

12. Ibid.

13. Ibid., 183.

14. Ibid., 185.

15. Pitcher, "The Misfortunes of the Dead," 188.

16. An earlier version of the following argument has been developed in James Stacey Taylor, *Death, Posthumous Harm, and Bioethics* (New York: Routledge, 2012), chap. 1.

17. Alternative accounts of how posthumous harm is possible are outlined and rejected in Taylor, *Death, Posthumous Harm, and Bioethics*, chaps. 2–3.

18. I owe a version of this example to Paul Tudico.

19. Note that the blameworthiness of an act such as this need not justify its legal prohibition.

20. Note that since the effects of the attempted violation of privacy in Fictitious and the actual violation of privacy in Actual were identical, to hold that the privacy violator did no more wrong in Actual that he did in Fictitious does not commit one to endorsing an equivalence thesis concerning the blameworthiness of attempted wrong acts versus successful wrong acts in standard cases. Note, too, that to claim that the effects of the (attempted) privacy violation in Actual were different from those in Fictitious since in Actual one of the effects of this violation was to wrong the dead person whose privacy was violated would be to beg the question.

## Chapter Four

# Connecting Informational, Fourth Amendment and Constitutional Privacy

## Judith Wagner DeCew

Much philosophical and legal discussion of the scope and value of privacy is quite recent, and until 1890 privacy protection may have been taken for granted. Nevertheless, the concept of privacy is not new. In this chapter, I describe early discussions as well as legal protections of privacy in three areas: tort law protection of informational privacy, Fourth Amendment protection of privacy through protection against unreasonable searches and seizures, and more recent protection of what the US Supreme Court has termed "constitutional privacy." I argue that despite claims to the contrary, there are important historical, conceptual, and philosophical connections between these three interests. [1]

Historical evidence that privacy has been discussed and valued for centuries is not difficult to find. Perhaps most famous is Aristotle's distinction in the "Politics" between the *polis*, or political realm, and the *oikos*, the domestic realm. [2] The political realm of governing, open to men only, was deemed by Aristotle to be a public arena, whereas the domestic realm of home and family was viewed by him to be a private arena. This Aristotelian distinction between public and private spheres of life has continued to influence and dominate much of the scholarship on privacy. John Locke provides another well-known example of a historical reference to a public/private distinction. Locke invokes the distinction in the chapter on property in his *Second Treatise on Government*. [3] In the state of nature, he argues, one owns one's own body and yet other property is held in common, or deemed public. When one mixes one's labour with property—harvesting grain or catching fish, for example—that which was held in common becomes one's private property.

Although individuals are cautioned to leave "enough and as good" for others, private property acquisition is heralded by Locke as an appropriate goal. These are two reminders that the concept of privacy has played a prominent role in major philosophical works since ancient times.

As Alan Westin has pointed out, while human beings like to think that their desire for privacy is distinctively human, studies have shown that virtually all animals share a need for privacy by seeking individual seclusion, territoriality, or small-group intimacy.[4] Moreover, Westin argues persuasively that anthropological, sociological, and biological literature demonstrates that most cultures around the world mirror these behaviours, and use distance-setting mechanisms to protect a private space to promote individual well-being and small-group intimacy, thereby exhibiting both the value of privacy and the need to preserve it. Although not all societies protect privacy in the same way, in virtually every society individuals engage in patterns of behaviour and adopt avoidance rules in order to seek privacy. Cultures that rely on communal living often have religious or other ceremonies where privacy through isolation is provided. When privacy cannot be attained by individuals through physical isolation, people demonstrate ways of finding privacy by turning away or averting their eyes, or by finding psychological ways to protect their private thoughts and sentiments. Westin concludes that privacy is a cross-species and cross-cultural value, and that claims to individual privacy in some form are universal for virtually all societies.

The first serious discussions of the meaning of privacy in the United States developed in the law, as legal protection for privacy was granted and expanded. The initial legal protection of privacy was introduced in tort law. Warren and Brandeis[5] argued that privacy protection should be established as a legal right to give individuals the right "to be let alone" to protect their "inviolate personality." They urged that protection of individual rights over the person and one's property were already established in common law, and that political, social, and economic changes demanded recognition of new rights. Protection against actual bodily injury had been extended to protect against injury attempts, and protection for physical harm was expanded to protect human emotions through slander and libel. Similarly, they thought, new inventions and technology such as the printing press and camera called for a new step to curtail invasions of privacy by newspapers and photography to protect a general right to the immunity of the person and the right to one's personality, and also to guarantee one's right to control information published in the media about oneself and one's family. Thus they argued that privacy protection was already implicitly protected; could fill gaps left by other remedies such as nuisance, trespass, and intentional infliction of emotional distress; and thus should be explicitly recognized as a right to privacy. Arguing that this would not be the addition of a new right, or judicial legislation, they urged it was reasonable to explicitly acknowledge individual rights to keep publicity about oneself and one's likeness unavailable to others—as long as privacy protection did not prohibit publications of general interest protected by freedom of the press, or data on a "public figure" about whom the public might have a right to know some personal information. By 1905, this privacy right to control information about oneself was affirmed and expanded.

Legal theorists worked to articulate the meaning and scope of this tort informational privacy protection. William L. Prosser[6] defended privacy but was troubled about the difficulty of such unresolved questions as whether one could have a reasonable expectation of privacy in public spaces, whether information part of the public record could still deserve privacy protection many years later, and who should count as a "public figure" deserving a lesser expectation of privacy than normal citizens. Later cases and analysis suggest answers to the first two questions are affirmative,[7] and the last question remains a matter of debate. Edward J. Bloustein argued that all privacy wrongs were similar and conceptually linked as ways of protecting an individual's inviolate personality, including an individual's independence, human dignity, integrity and freedom from emotional distress.[8] Privacy protection formed the essence required for an individual to be a unique and self-determined being and was the tool needed for protection against intrusions demeaning to individuality and affronts to personal human dignity that can occur in manifold ways.

Other commentators concurred that tort privacy protection could be meaningfully seen as a unitary right protecting one's ability to control information about oneself; yet they provided alternative accounts of the moral value of this type of privacy. Some argued that the right protected one's integrity as a person, as an essential context for the fundamental relations of respect, love, friendship, and trust.[9] According to this view, being able to control how much personal information one shares with others is necessary to define oneself and one's values free from undesired impingement by others, and gives one the ability to determine one's distance from others—namely, with whom one remains a mere acquaintance, with whom one becomes a friend, and with whom one becomes an intimate companion. Philosophers including Stanley I. Benn, Robert Gerstein, James Rachels, Jeffrey Reiman and Richard A. Wasserstrom generally agreed. Benn focused on the need for privacy to protect respect for persons, human dignity and personal relations free from being the object of scrutiny, and autonomy from social pressures to conform—a sphere of privacy as a necessary condition for one's personality to bloom and thrive.[10] Gerstein emphasized privacy as required for intimacy, without uninvited intrusions that would lead to a chilling effect.[11] He argued that one cannot "lose" oneself in an intimate relationship if one is constantly worried about being overheard or put under surveillance. Rachels[12] and Wasserstrom[13] endorsed the view that privacy is necessary for the development of different relationships, and Reiman[14] developed privacy as fundamental for intimacy and personhood, as a social ritual by which an individual's moral title to existence is confirmed.

Despite the well-established protection of tort privacy to control information about oneself in the courts, and the almost universal acceptance of the value of informational privacy by the populace, it has been persuasively argued that the United States (and many countries in Asia) have developed limited systems of privacy protection that focus on self-regulation within industry and government so that personal information is readily available. By contrast, the European Union (EU) and others have adopted an alternative vision highlighting consumer protection and individual privacy against the economic interests of firms and public officials.[15] The European Union's Data Protection Directive of 1995, now adopted in some form by all twenty-seven EU nations, contains comprehensive rules with privacy commissioners or agencies empowered to enhance individual privacy protection, requiring that personal information not be collected or used for purposes other than those initially intended without individual consent, and so on, despite the challenges of the September 11, 2001, terrorist attacks. This contrasts sharply with the US approach allowing entities such as insurance companies and employers ample access to personal information, given a lack of governmental support for privacy legislation and a patchwork of privacy guidelines. The United States has generally stood behind efficiency and laissez-faire arguments that business and government need unfettered access to personal data to guarantee economic growth and national security. By contrast, the EU has sent a coherent signal that privacy has critical value in a robust information society because citizens will only participate in an online environment if they feel their privacy is guaranteed against ubiquitous business and government surveillance.

A second major way in which privacy protection has evolved in the United States is through the Fourth Amendment: "The right of the people to be secure in their persons, houses, papers, and effects, against reasonable searches and seizures, shall not be violated." This is clearly related to privacy in tort law, as an unreasonable search or seizure is one way of gaining personal information. Initial privacy protection under this amendment relied on the literal wording from the Bill of Rights. Thus information gained from wiretaps outside of houses involved no search and no seizure, and the language of the amendment could not be extended to wiretaps.[16] This interpretation was overruled in *Katz v. U.S.*,[17] judging that evidence obtained through an electronic listening and recording device in public was disallowed, even though there was no physical entrance into the area. The judgment favoured an expectation of privacy even in a public place; it argued that Fourth Amendment privacy is not just about physical intrusion, for it protects people and not places. Brandeis's famous privacy argument won the day: the Constitution recognizes the significance of one's spiritual nature, feelings and intellect, and seeks to protect Americans in their beliefs, thoughts, emotions, and sensations, prohibiting unjustifiable governmental intrusion on the privacy of the individual no matter what means are employed. This second type of privacy protection from the Fourth Amendment has endured but may become controversial. Recent cases involving new technologies such as thermal imaging devices allow more intrusive privacy intrusions and will continue to test staunch Fourth Amendment privacy safeguards.

A third type of privacy protection has developed in constitutional law. In *Griswold v. Connecticut*,[18] the majority opinion defended a married couple's right to get information and instruction about birth control, and in the process first announced that despite there being no word "privacy" in the Constitution, this concept could be defended as a constitutional right to privacy. The majority defended the right to privacy as being older than the Bill of Rights, defended marriage as an enduring, sacred, and intimate relation and association, and defended one's home as a special and private area. They cited famous cases that they viewed as precedents—concerning personal decisions about one's home, family, and marriage, including the right to association, rights to educate one's children as one chooses, rights to decide about a child's study in private school, protection against mandatory sterilization, and more. One can recognize an insight in the reasoning. There is no right not to be assaulted articulated in the Constitution, for example, but it is surely protected and deemed to be a basic right. There is good reason to believe that the Founding Fathers took privacy within marriage and family to be so fundamental that they saw no reason to mention it explicitly.

Nevertheless, the constitutional right to privacy has been harshly criticized by Judge Robert Bork,[19] philosopher William Parent,[20] and others. Perhaps most seriously, this third type of constitutional privacy protection has been viewed by some as not being about privacy at all. On the one hand, these critics reject defense of the right as having no justifiable legal grounds as a privacy right but only a defense of liberty or autonomy. On the other hand, the right has been characterized as being overly vague, so that it is unclear what exactly it protects and what it does not. With regard to the first complaint, it has been successfully argued in reply that while we have multiple individual liberties such as freedom of expression, many do not seem to be about anything particularly personal or related to the types of concerns we might be willing and able to see as privacy issues. If so, then liberty is a broader concept than privacy and privacy claims are a subset of claims to liberty. Many philosophical commentators have supported this view that privacy protects freedom or liberty, and that privacy protection gains for us freedom to define ourselves and our relations to others.[21]

A moving account of understanding privacy as a necessary and an indis-
pensable condition for freedom comes from a literary quotation from Milan
Kundera:

> But one day in 1970 or 1971, with the intent to discredit Prochazka, the police
> began to broadcast these conversations [with Professor Vaclav Cerny, with
> whom he liked to drink and talk] as a radio serial. For the police it was an
> audacious, unprecedented act. And, surprisingly: it nearly succeeded; instantly
> Prochazka *was* discredited: because in private, a person says all sorts of things,
> slurs friends, uses coarse language, acts silly, tells dirty jokes, repeats himself,
> makes a companion laugh by shocking him with outrageous talk, floats heret-
> ical ideas he'd never admit in public, and so forth. Of course, we all act like
> Prochazka, in private we bad-mouth our friends and use coarse language; that
> we act different in private than in public is everyone's most conspicuous
> experience, it is the very ground of the life of the individual; curiously, this
> obvious fact remains unconscious, unacknowledged, forever obscured by lyri-
> cal dreams of the transparent glass house, it is rarely understood to be the value
> one must defend beyond all others. Thus only gradually did people realize
> (though their rage was all the greater) that the real scandal was not Prochaz-
> ka's daring talk but the rape of his life; they realized (as if by electric shock)
> that private and public are two essentially different worlds and that respect for
> that difference is the indispensable condition, the sine qua non, for a man to
> live free; that the curtain separating these two worlds is not to be tampered
> with, and that curtain-rippers are criminals. And because the curtain-rippers
> were serving a hated regime, they were unanimously held to be particularly
> contemptible criminals. [22]

The analogies between Kundera's scenario and electronic surveillance and
street cameras common in society today are clear. There is further evidence
that privacy and liberty are distinct concepts, that liberty is a broader notion,
and that privacy is essential for protecting liberty. We have many forms of
liberty unrelated to what we might value as private and inappropriate for
government intervention for personal reasons. The right to travel from state
to state without a passport, for example, seems to be a freedom far different
from freedom to make choices about personal and intimate concerns about
one's body—for example, the use of contraception. The U.S. Supreme Court
has recognized this, calling the constitutional privacy cases those about an
"individual interest in making certain kinds of important decisions." [23]

However, this philosophical reply about the relationship between privacy
and liberty does not address the second critique about the vagueness of the
right. The constitutional right to privacy has protected information and access to birth control, the right of couples to choose the marriage partner of
their choice regardless of race, the right of an individual to view pornographic materials in the privacy of his or her home (as long as there is no production or distribution of the material), abortion rights, and ultimately the right

of individuals—gay or straight—to engage in consenting adult sexual intimacy in their own homes, striking down antisodomy statutes. While these sorts of decisions are admittedly somewhat varied, the question is what "kinds of important decisions" are worthy of being protected? The court at one point said that the constitutional right to privacy protects certain decisions about home, procreation, family, and marriage, and has added that it covers certain personal decisions about one's lifestyle.

The problem is trying to articulate what exactly are the interests protected by privacy concerns and how they may relate to concerns about freedom, intimacy, and self-development. Unfortunately, this is a serious and intransigent difficulty. One approach has been to dismiss privacy as a philosophically important concept. Judith Jarvis Thomson's famous critique of privacy in this sense is a reductionist view that there is no need for a right to privacy because all talk of privacy can be reduced to talk of rights to property and to bodily security (and perhaps other) rights.[24] Thomson's account, however, has been widely and amply criticized by Thomas Scanlon,[25] James Rachels, Jeffrey Reiman, Julie Inness,[26] and others who have argued that it is just as likely that the reverse is true, and rights to property and bodily security can be derived from a more fundamental right to privacy.

Yet it has not been easy for philosophers to provide clear guidelines on the positive side of understanding what privacy protects and why it is important. There has been consensus that the significance of privacy is almost always justified for the individual interests it protects, most importantly, protections of freedom and autonomy in a liberal democratic society.[27] Philosophers have argued that it does seem reasonable to view a subset of liberty cases as privacy cases—namely, those which involve choices or decisions about one's body, marriage, intimate relationships and lifestyle.[28] Ferdinand Schoeman[29] eloquently defended the importance of privacy for protection of self-expression and social freedom. More recent literature has extended this view and has focused on the value of privacy not merely for the individual interests it protects, but also for its irreducible social value. Concerns over the accessibility and retention of electronic communications and the expansion of camera surveillance have led commentators to focus attention on loss of individual privacy as well as privacy protection with respect to the state and society.[30]

Priscilla Regan writes, for example,

> I argue that privacy is not only of value to the individual, but also to society in general. . . . Privacy is a *common value* in that all individuals value some degree of privacy and have some common perceptions about privacy. Privacy is also a *public value* in that it has value not just to the individual as an individual or to all individuals in common but also to the democratic political system. Privacy is rapidly becoming a *collective value* in that technology and

market forces are making it hard for any one person to have privacy without all
persons having a similar minimum level of privacy.[31]

According to Daniel Solove, "By understanding privacy as shaped by the
norms of society, we can better see why privacy should not be understood
solely as an individual right. . . . Instead, privacy protects the individual
because of the benefits it confers on society." Moreover, "the value of privacy should be understood in terms of its contribution to society."[32] Solove
believes privacy fosters and encourages the moral autonomy of citizens, a
central requirement of governance in a democracy. One way of understanding these comments—that privacy has not only intrinsic and extrinsic value
to individuals but also instrumental value to society—is to recognize that
these views develop from the earlier philosophical writings (Charles Fried,
Rachels, Schoeman) on the value of privacy in that it heightens respect for
individual autonomy in decision making for self-development and individual
integrity and human dignity, and also enhances the value of privacy in various social roles and relationships that contribute to a functioning society.
According to this contemporary scholarship, privacy norms help regulate
social relationships such as intimate relations, family relationships, professional relationships including those between a physician and a patient, a
teacher and a student, a lawyer and a client, and so on. Thus privacy enhances social interaction on a variety of levels, and in this way enhances
intimacy, self-development, and the ability to present ourselves in public as
we wish. According to Solove, a society without respect for privacy for
oneself and others becomes a "suffocating society."[33]

It may be messy and difficult to find adequate words to express just what
privacy governs, and it is understandable that some still believe the term
"privacy" is too vague and not well enough articulated. Consider, however,
Ronald Dworkin's observation about another general concept: "Equality is a
popular but mysterious political ideal. People can become equal (or at least
more equal) in one way with the consequence that they become unequal (or
more unequal) in others. . . . It does not follow that equality is worthless as an
ideal."[34] Similarly, with the ambiguity and vagueness of liberty (positive
versus negative, freedom of expression, etc.): it may protect a range of different but related interests. It does not follow that it is worthless as an ideal.
These concepts, like privacy, are crucial for understanding our role as social
beings and for protecting values fundamental to living lives free from various
unacceptable governmental and individual intrusions and surveillance.

Nevertheless, the concern about just what privacy protects, and an understanding of privacy's value for individuals as well as society, leads to additional difficulties about understanding the boundaries between the private
and the public in problematic cases, and in particular the darker side of
privacy raised by feminist critiques of privacy. Here, the lingering effects of

Aristotle's distinction between the public political and private domestic spheres continue to be damaging. If privacy protects individual intimacy and family relationships, it is important to ask whether it is possible to defend privacy staunchly in the face of familiar objections to privacy protection based on feminist critiques that privacy has been used, and perhaps still is, to shield male dominance in family relations.

The reality of domination and abuse in private needs to be aired more fully and addressed, but collapsing the public/private distinction and leaving everything public is an unacceptable and dangerous alternative. Absent domestic violence and coercion, there is great value for women and men in preserving privacy—and a sanctuary where they can live free from scrutiny, the pressure to conform, free to express their identities through relationships and choices about their bodies and lifestyles. No one has yet explained how to understand the public/private dichotomy in a way that intertwines the two. But it may be possible that Mill's famous harm principle—despite its notorious ambiguities on types of harm, for example—can be invoked in important ways in some cases, often domestic ones, to help determine when government intervention can be justified in the private realm. Harm to others needs to be reported, not shrouded in private, and, following Mill, we may want to believe that adult voluntary and consenting behaviour is not the business of the state or the courts. Nevertheless, as for Mill, there are serious problems with drawing a clear line between cases leading to harm to others and those that are self-regarding or occur with the voluntary consent of others. Deeply entrenched cultural beliefs, in favour of female genital mutilation, for example, seem to lead to the conclusion that even with "consent" the state should not necessarily remain out of the affairs of individuals. Otherwise it would seem that a physician must honor a woman's rational, yet culturally entrenched, decision that the physician must perform genital mutilation surgery on her. Thus it seems there must be some constraints on what counts as significant and meaningful consent.

Nevertheless, the harm to others versus harm to self distinction can perhaps help with other cases where the public/private boundary is blurred. For example, one may wonder whether parents should have the power to withhold cancer or other medical treatments from children—for religious or other reasons—when such treatments are medically sound and have been shown to increase survival rates. While some may view this as a completely private family decision, it seems extremely difficult to justify in the face of clear harm to the children. As a family decision it may be viewed as presumptively private, but that it is also a situation where privacy is and should be overridden by considerations of harm to others. Privacy claims are not absolute, and the privacy considerations need to be taken seriously, but they can certainly be outweighed by other considerations such as harm to others, threats of harm and at times even paternalism (female genital mutilation, etc.) and more.

Returning to a clearer case, we can understand why private consumption of pornography, and ownership of pornography in the privacy of one's home, is self-regarding in Mill's sense and not appropriate for state intervention and regulation. Whereas production and distribution of pornography to others, where there are genuinely increased threats of violence against women and children, pose a serious enough threat of harm to justify either a ban or regulation, depending on the alternative which best controls the pornographic material in the face of a black-market value for such material. Determining and documenting the likelihood and extent of harm—and whether to consider not merely physical but also emotional harm and other considerations that may override privacy—will not be easy, but it may provide a rule of thumb that can be a starting guideline. Nevertheless, we have seen it also leads to further complications, especially in cases where different cultures and religions endorse gender roles and other aspects in family circles that are oppressive to women (female genital mutilation, the Muslim burka controversy, and such). If considerations of harm to others can override privacy, what other considerations can do so as well? It is classic for governmental agencies to cite national security concerns as adequate for overriding individual expectations of privacy, but clarifying which national security concerns are serious enough to justify privacy breaches can lead to an interminable tangle of arguments, as is clear from debates surrounding the PATRIOT Act.

Two relatively recent court cases on privacy help demonstrate the way in which thought about constitutional privacy, the public/private distinction, and the role of government as a public enforcer against individual claims to privacy are evolving. In *Bowers v. Hardwick*,[35] the US Supreme Court refused to strike down Georgia's antisodomy statute and the privacy argument lost by a narrow margin. Some have argued that the court failed to consider the privacy issue at all, but that is misleading. The majority did consider the privacy claim, even if summarily, and rejected it. They argued that no demonstration had ever been given that there was a connection between family, marriage, or procreation on one hand, and homosexual sodomy on the other. An enraged dissent condemned the majority's refusal to take into account the intimacy of the issue at stake, retorting that only the most willful blindness could prevent one from recognizing the right of individuals to conduct intimate consenting adult relationships within the privacy of their own homes as being at the heart of the Constitution's protection of privacy.

The decision in *Lawrence v. Texas*[36] overturned *Bowers*. The court was aided in *Lawrence* by the fact that the statute was worded as aimed solely at homosexuals and thus discriminatory. While the majority could have treated the issue merely as a liberty or autonomy case, it placed a major focus on privacy. Regarding the anti-sodomy statutes, the majority argued such restrictions touch

> upon the most private human conduct, sexual behavior, and in the most private of places, the home. The statutes do seek to control a personal relationship that, whether or not entitled to formal recognition in the law, is within the liberty of persons to choose without being punished as criminals.
>
> This, as a general rule, should counsel against attempts by the State, or a court, to define the meaning of the relationship or to set its boundaries absent injury to a person or abuse of an institution the law protects. It suffices for us to acknowledge that adults may choose to enter upon this relationship in the confines of their homes and their own private lives and still retain their dignity as free persons. When sexuality finds overt expression in intimate conduct with another person, the conduct can be but one element in a personal bond that is more enduring.[37]

Noting that punishing consenting adults for private acts had not been discussed much in the legal literature, the majority referred to precedents which confirmed that our laws and traditions afford constitutional protections to personal decisions relating to marriage, procreation, contraception, family relationships, child rearing, and education. The court quoted at length from *Planned Parenthood of Southeastern PA v. Casey*[38] about the most intimate and personal choices a person may make in a lifetime, choices central to personal dignity and autonomy and the right to define one's own concept of existence, of meaning, and so on. The majority concluded that the "petitioners are entitled to respect for their *private* lives. The State cannot demean their existence or control their destiny by making their *private* sexual conduct a crime" (emphasis added). It is significant that by using language continuing to support privacy as a grounding for the decision, the majority opinion makes clear that nothing can justify the statute's "intrusion into the personal and private life of the individual." This provides a strong general recognition and confirmation that with meaningful consent and the absence of harm to others or other overriding considerations, privacy must be protected.

Given that privacy protection has developed in three distinct areas of law—with separate introductions and historical developments in different decades for each—it is not surprising that both legal texts and many legal theorists (and a few philosophers) treat the privacy interests at stake as very different. The separate classifications of these three interests may be viewed by some as a historical coincidence or may provide some with a sense of order in the law. Let me close by emphasizing, to the contrary, that there are important historical, conceptual, and philosophical reasons for understanding all three interests in privacy developed in the law—informational (tort), Fourth Amendment and constitutional—as being closely related. First, note that the court majority in *Lawrence* adopted, in this recent crucial case, an understanding of constitutional privacy that is remarkably close to early descriptions of the value of affording protection for informational privacy as well as privacy protection under the Fourth Amendment. The wording echoes early writings by legal theorists and philosophers, as well as Milan Kundera, on the value and meaning of privacy as being central to human dignity, one's personhood, and at the heart of one's right to define one's own existence.

Second, historical uses of the term "privacy" are not solely focused on informational privacy. For Aristotle, the public and private spheres are realms of life, and the domestic or private sphere is located within the home and family, clearly distinct from the public realm of government. For Locke, one owns one's own body, and presumably thus has control over one's body, and then makes property one's own by mixing one's labor with it. Thus, historical references to privacy include references to a sphere surrounding one's body and family and personal property—echoing the current ordinary language use of "privacy" and the Supreme Court's invocation of the term "privacy" in the constitutional cases.

Third, it is noteworthy that the sweeping language from Warren and Brandeis's argument for protection of a right to privacy in tort law protecting information about oneself and one's reputation is echoed in the similar language in Brandeis's famous quote in the dissent of the *Olmstead* case:

> The makers of our Constitution undertook to secure conditions favorable to the pursuit of happiness. They recognized the significance of man's spiritual nature, of his feelings and his intellect. They knew that only a part of the pain, pleasure and satisfactions of life are to be found in material things. They sought to protect Americans in their beliefs, their thoughts, their emotions and their sensations. They conferred, as against the Government, the right to be let alone—the most comprehensive of rights and the right most valued by civilized men. To protect that right, every unjustifiable intrusion by the Government upon the privacy of the individual, whatever the means employed, must be deemed a violation of the Fourth Amendment. [39]

This language became part of the majority view in the Fourth Amendment *Katz* case later on, and it is reflected again in the groundbreaking 1965 *Griswold* decision announcing the constitutional right to privacy. This dissent is also quoted at length in a 1969 constitutional privacy case where it is called well-established and a fundamental right to be free from unwanted governmental intrusions into one's privacy. [40] The wording makes it clear that in all these varied cases, privacy protects both peace of mind and bodily integrity. It is, moreover, difficult to believe that it is a mere accident that Brandeis's quotation and language were used as a basis for all three types of privacy protection in the law.

Fourth, another way of seeing the close relationship and connections between the three types of privacy protected in law is to note the similarity of reasons appealed to in seeking privacy protection for tort and Fourth Amendment law as well as various interests now covered by constitutional privacy. There is a philosophical argument for connecting the three strands of privacy protection in the law, based on the range of similar reasons given in defense of their importance.

People have many different reasons for wanting to control information about themselves, and their motives range from freedom from libel and defamation to commercial gain. Often, however, freedom from scrutiny, embarrassment, judgment, and even ridicule are at stake, as well as protection from pressure to conform, prejudice, emotional distress, and the losses in self-esteem, opportunities, or finances arising from those harms. In such cases we are more inclined to view the claim to control information as a privacy claim. A tort privacy action to control information about oneself, and Fourth Amendment claims about unreasonable searches and seizures, are two mechanisms that society and the law have created to accomplish such protection. By themselves they are not wholly adequate, however, because the interests that justify the screen on information include the interest in being free to decide and make choices about family, marriage, and lifestyle absent the threat of the same problematic consequences that accompany an information leak. In other words, it is plausible to maintain that worries about what information others have about one are often *due* to worries about social control by government or others. What one can do to me, or what I can do free of the threat of scrutiny, judgment, and pressure to conform, may often depend on what information (personal or not) an individual, the state, or others have about me. Clearly my behaviour is also affected by the extent to which I can make my own choices. Therefore, both the threat of an information leak and the threat of decreased control over decision making can have a chilling effect on my behaviour. If this is correct, then the desire to protect a sanctuary for ourselves, a refuge within which we can shape and carry on our lives and relationships with others—intimacies as well as other activities—without the threat of scrutiny, embarrassment, and the deleterious consequences they might bring, is a major underlying reason for providing information control, protection from unreasonable search and seizure, and control over decision making.[41] Thus there are clear conceptual and philosophical connections between privacy interests and the values they protect in tort, Fourth Amendment, and constitutional law.

The point can be highlighted by noting cases where all the relevant privacy concerns seem importantly relevant and intertwined, as in recent cases about drug testing in public schools. Informational privacy was obviously relevant—in the *Lindsay Earls* case,[42] the results of student drug tests were strewn about at least one teacher's desk where anyone passing by could see them, and clearly the drug tests, though targeted at drug use, could also detect prescription medications a student might be taking, information about pregnancy, diabetes, and other medical conditions. The court clearly treated the *Earls* case and earlier ones as Fourth Amendment privacy cases—asking if the drug tests were a violation of prohibitions against unreasonable search and seizure. Furthermore, issues that go to the heart of constitutional privacy were also involved: concerns about whether or not students were being watched while urinating, puncturing one's skin for blood samples, and so on, especially if the drug tests were mandatory or random and not announced. In such cases the courts have been concerned about the role of public schools as guardians of students in attendance there. But the privacy issues are still significant, and the drug testing cases raise privacy questions about one's control over information about oneself, about whether drug tests are reasonable or not as a search and seizure, as well as concerns about the inviolability of the body.

I have argued that privacy interests protected in tort, Fourth Amendment, and constitutional law can be seen as historically, conceptually, and philosophically related, demonstrating that privacy may be considered a distinct and fairly coherent set of values and concerns. Privacy has been discussed since ancient times, appears to be a cross-species and cross-cultural value, and can be seen to be highly valuable despite important feminist concerns about its use to shield domination and abuse. While there are no clear guidelines for drawing boundaries between public and private domains, harm to others can be one of several considerations in differentiating borderline cases, particularly in domestic contexts. Privacy is not an absolute value, but can be viewed as the default, requiring government and others to justify their need to intrude. The digital age, and the scope of privacy post–9/11, far from leaving individuals caring less about their privacy, has increased interest in, and urgent pleas for, more careful and thoughtful privacy guidelines and controls, whether for the more extensive wiretapping of individuals and e-mail tracking justified using the PATRIOT Act, electronic medical records, airport scanners, or biometric identification. Facebook's lack of genuine privacy protection, for example, is accepted by many, but has drawn outrage from others. Tracking of Internet use has led to increased demand for "do not track" options analogous to "do not call" legislation protecting citizens from unwanted solicitation. As technology advances, new privacy challenges will proliferate, and both the courts and philosophical dialogue are having a difficult time keeping up with these changes. The current literature on privacy is massive, and the worries about privacy protection are becoming tougher and more numerous. But for the public, the desire and value and demand for privacy protection remains unabated.

# NOTES

1. This chapter is based on Judith Wagner DeCew, "Privacy," *Routledge Companion to Philosophy of Law* (New York: Routledge, 2012).

2. Aristotle, "Politics," in *The Basic Works of Aristotle*, ed. Richard McKeon, trans. Benjamin Jowett (New York: Random House, 1941).

3. John Locke, *Second Treatise on Government*, ed. Thomas P. Reardon (1690; repr., New York: Macmillan, Library of Liberal Arts, 1988).

4. Alan Westin, "The Origins of Modern Claims to Privacy," in *Philosophical Dimensions of Privacy: An Anthology*, ed. Ferdinand D. Schoeman (Cambridge: Cambridge University Press, 1984), 56–74.

5. Samuel Warren and Louis Brandeis, "The Right to Privacy," *Harvard Law Review* 4, no. 5 (1890).

6. William Prosser, "Privacy," *California Law Review* 48, no. 3 (1960).

7. Helen Nissenbaum, *Privacy in Context: Technology, Policy, and the Integrity of Social Life* (Palo Alto, CA: Stanford University Press, 2010); *Melvin v. Reid*, 112 Cal. App. 283, 1931.

8. Edward J. Bloustein, "Privacy as an Aspect of Human Dignity: An Answer to Dean Prosser," *New York University Law Review* 39 (1964): 962–1007.

9. Charles Fried, "Privacy," *Yale Law Journal* 77 (1968).

10. Stanley I. Benn, "Privacy, Freedom, and Respect for Persons," in *Philosophical Dimensions of Privacy: An Anthology*, ed. Ferdinand D. Schoeman (Cambridge: Cambridge University Press, 1984), 223–44.

11. Robert Gerstein, "Intimacy and Privacy," *Ethics* 89, no. 1 (1978): 76–81.

12. James Rachels, "Why Privacy is Important," *Philosophy & Public Affairs* 4, no. 4 (1975): 323–33.

13. Richard A. Wasserstrom, "Privacy: Some Arguments and Assumptions," in *Philosophical Dimensions of Privacy: An Anthology*, ed. Ferdinand D. Schoeman (Cambridge: Cambridge University Press, 1984), 317–32.

14. Jeffrey Reiman, "Privacy, Intimacy, and Personhood," *Philosophy & Public Affairs* 6, no. 1 (1976): 26–44.

15. Abraham L. Newman, *Protectors of Privacy: Regulating Personal Data in the Global Economy* (Ithaca and London: Cornell University Press, 2008).

16. *Olmstead v. U.S.*, 277 U.S. 438, 1928.

17. *Katz v. U.S.*, 389 U.S. 347, 1967.

18. *Griswold v. Connecticut*, 381 U.S. 479, 1965.

19. Robert Bork, *The Tempting of America* (New York: Free Press, 1990).

20. William Parent, "A New Definition of Privacy for the Law," *Law and Philosophy* 2, no. 3 (1983): 305–38; William Parent, "Privacy, Morality and the Law," *Philosophy & Public Affairs* 12, no. 4 (1983), 269–88.

21. Ferdinand D. Schoeman, ed., *Philosophical Dimensions of Privacy: An Anthology* (Cambridge: Cambridge University Press, 1984); Ferdinand David Schoeman, *Privacy and Social Freedom* (Cambridge: Cambridge University Press, 1992); Fried, "Privacy"; Reiman, "Privacy, Intimacy, and Personhood."

22. Milan Kundera, *Testaments Betrayed: An Essay in Nine Parts* (New York: HarperCollins, 1995), 260–61.

23. *Whalen v. Roe*, 429 U.S. 589, 1977.

24. Judith J. Thomson, "The Right to Privacy," *Philosophy & Public Affairs* 4, no. 4 (1975): 295ff–314.

25. Thomas Scanlon, "Thomson on Privacy," *Philosophy & Public Affairs* 4, no. 4 (1975): 315–22.

26. Julie Inness, *Privacy, Intimacy and Isolation* (Oxford: Oxford University Press, 1992).

27. Jeffrey Reiman, "Driving to the Panopticon: A Philosophical Exploration of the Risks to Privacy Posed by the Information Technology of the Future," in *Privacies: Philosophical Evaluations*, ed. Beate Rössler (Palo Alto, CA: Stanford University Press, 2004); Beate Rössler, *The Value of Privacy* (Cambridge, MA: Polity Press, 2005).

28. Schoeman, *Privacy and Social Freedom*; Judith Wagner DeCew, *In Pursuit of Privacy: Law, Ethics and the Rise of Technology* (Cornell: Cornell University Press, 1997).

29. Schoeman, *Privacy and Social Freedom*.

30. Reiman, "Driving to the Panopticon: A Philosophical Exploration of the Risks to Privacy Posed by the Information Technology of the Future"; Daniel Solove, *Understanding Privacy* (Cambridge, MA: Harvard University Press, 2008); Nissenbaum, *Privacy in Context: Technology, Policy, and the Integrity of Social Life*.

31. Priscilla Regan, *Legislating Privacy* (Chapel Hill: University of North Carolina Press, 1995), 213.

32. Solove, *Understanding Privacy*, 98 and 171fn.

33. Ibid., 15; see also Kundera, *Testaments Betrayed*, supra.

34. Ronald Dworkin, "What Is Equality: Part I: Equality of Welfare," *Philosophy & Public Affairs* 10, no. 3 (1981): 185.

35. *Bowers v. Hardwick*, 478 U.S. 186, 1986.

36. *Lawrence v. Texas*, 539 U.S. 558, 2003.

37. Ibid.

38. *Planned Parenthood of Southeastern PA v. Casey*, 505 U.S. 833, 1992.

39. *Olmstead v. U.S.*, 277 U.S. 478, 1928.

40. *Stanley v. Georgia*, 394 U.S. 557, 1969.

41. Cf. DeCew, *In Pursuit of Privacy*, 63–64.

42. *Board of Education v. Earls*, 536 U.S. 822, 2002.

## Chapter Five

# Privacy, Freedom of Speech and the Sexual Lives of Office Holders

## Dorota Mokrosinska

Last year the Dutch public was electrified by the news about Onno Hoes, Mayor of Maastricht. A local TV channel, PowNed, broadcast material presenting Hoes in sexually charged encounters in a gay bar and the national press published Hoes's erotic selfie from gay dating app Grindr. In the aftermath of the commotion brought about by the media revelations, Hoes resigned his post. Hoes's sexual scandal is a rather parochial one compared to French President Francois Hollande's love affair with actress Julie Gayet or U.S. President Bill Clinton's affair with his White House intern Monica Lewinsky. They all, however, raise the same question: Is the press entitled to print stories about extra-marital affairs of public office holders? On the one hand, the right to privacy, guaranteed by many democratic states, entitles citizens, including politicians, to protect their intimate affairs from the public gaze.[1] On the other hand, the right to free speech entitles citizens, including journalists, to say and print what they please.[2] Press stories about extramarital affairs of office holders are where the democratic rights to privacy and to free speech come to clash: what some want to say and print about others is what those others would rather keep private.[3] As Joshua Rozenberg puts it, "How can I enjoy my right to write about you, if you can require me to respect your privacy? How can you insist that I show respect for your family life if I have the right to say what I like about you in public?"[4] This chapter takes the conflict between privacy and freedom of speech as its focus and asks how it should be resolved in liberal-democratic states.

In current legal practice, conflicts between freedom of speech and privacy are usually resolved in favour of freedom of speech. Both European and American jurisprudence prioritize free speech when it conflicts with privacy.[5] The weaker status of privacy in comparison with freedom of speech has to do with the way these rights are construed in legal and political practice. When reflecting on freedom of speech, the courts invoke democratic values. As Eric Barendt points out, the argument from democracy has been the most influential theory in the development of contemporary free speech law.[6] In the courts' reflection on privacy, however, no broader political interests are invoked. Analyzing the jurisprudence of the European Court of Human Rights, Kirsty Hughes observes that the court associates the right to privacy with individual interests such as "physical and psychological integrity" and "the right to identity and personal development." It sees freedom of speech, on the other hand, as "fundamental to a democratic society."[7]

The political justification of free speech gives it more leverage in cases of conflict with privacy. When the courts confront a choice between restricting free speech for the sake of privacy on the one hand and restricting privacy for the sake of free speech on the other hand, the choice appears to be one between an infringement of the essential foundation of a democratic society and an incursion into the interests of an individual. A calculation is then easily made: when individual interests conflict with the broader political interests of a society, protecting individuals' privacy seems to be a luxury that society can ill afford. To insist on protecting individual interests in privacy at the cost of democratic interests in freedom of speech might even be seen as a threat to democratic government.[8]

Freedom of speech is given additional priority if construed as political speech—that is, speech that addresses "matters of public concern"[9] and is "relevant to the development of public opinion on the whole range of issues which an intelligent citizen should think about."[10] Information concerning politicians' sexual affairs belongs to the range of issues citizens take interest in. Arguably, its disclosure may contribute to public debate and to the assessment of politicians' performance in office; as Frederick Schauer noted, a significant part of the population in most countries considers having an extramarital affair as a disqualifying trait for holding public office.[11] From this perspective, media disclosures of sexual affairs of office holders can be seen as a form of political speech, in which case they may enjoy special protection even if, for reasons of privacy, individual office holders would rather keep intimate details of their sexual lives away from public gaze. This reasoning seems to guide jurisprudence dealing with cases of speech addressing the private lives of public office holders. Schauer observes that American jurisprudence dealing with privacy cases has progressively narrowed the scope of privacy rights and progressively insisted on the press's First Amendment rights to publish information concerning office holders' personal lives that is of public interest, regardless of the consequences to the individuals unwillingly brought into public view.[12] European jurisprudence adopts a similar approach. Ruling in the few privacy cases involving public figures, the European Court of Human Rights held that privacy rights are infringed *unless* the information is used to contribute to a story of public importance; on that approach, disclosures of the personal affairs of politicians may be protected if they can be seen as contributions to political debate.[13] Harm to individual interests following privacy violations is outweighed by political gains in democratic deliberation.

In this chapter I argue that the conceptual framework prevailing in current legal practice overlooks the political dimension of the right to privacy. I argue that privacy, just as freedom of speech, can be justified in terms of values foundational to liberal-democratic states. Once the political value of privacy is recognized, the prevailing legal and political approach to conflicts between freedom of speech and privacy should be revised.

## PRIVACY, FREE SPEECH, AND DEMOCRATIC EQUALITY

The thought that privacy is vital for liberal-democratic society has been present in privacy scholarship, but it has seldom received systematic treatment.[14] Annabelle Lever is one of the few scholars to analyze it in a comprehensive way. Lever develops a democratic conception of privacy that bases the value of privacy on the liberal-democratic principle of equality. "Privacy," she writes, "has intrinsic value . . . reflecting the importance that democracies attach to our ability to see and treat each other as equals."[15] She argues that under conditions of pluralism and disagreement, equality stands for the equal right of people to govern others without regard to their worldviews, social status, wealth, merits, qualifications, competencies, or education.[16] To illustrate that privacy is an integral part of the commitment to equality so understood, she resorts to the example of the secret ballot. Privacy built into the voting booth expresses the democratic commitment to equality in the sense that it prevents citizens from being forced to subject their voting choices to the judgment and criticism of others. Without privacy arrangements, individuals might be forced to defend their views to others and run the risk of being exposed to public ridicule, shame, or humiliation, which is inconsistent with the idea that they are equally eligible to decide matters of common concern.

Lever employs her democratic account of privacy to examine the conflict between privacy and freedom of speech.[17] She calls into question the prevailing view that any limitation of freedom of speech in the name of privacy is always an unacceptable threat to democratic government. Given that democratic commitments to equality commend keeping intimate information private, restricting the disclosure of such information serves rather than undermines democracy. This is the case, in her view, even if the publication of sensitive personal information has beneficial effects by drawing public attention to a legitimate moral or political cause. Lever insists that "people are entitled to keep some true facts about themselves to themselves, should they so wish, as a sign of respect for their moral and political status, and in order to protect themselves from being used as a public example in order to educate or to entertain other people ... or to advance a legitimate moral or political cause."[18] To publish personal information about people without their consent is to exercise power over them and subject them to others' judgment, which threatens their equal social standing.

Spelling out the interests in privacy in terms of interests in democratic equality, along the lines of Lever's argument, changes the outcome of weighing privacy against freedom of speech. But how? One difficulty is that a democratic justification of freedom of speech can proceed in terms of the democratic commitment to equality, too. In that case, it is not clear how we are to weigh the interests in equality involved in privacy against the interests in equality involved in freedom of speech.

Freedom of speech can be argued to advance democratic equality because, by offering every citizen the possibility to speak her mind and persuade others, it ensures that each citizen has an equal possibility to influence the political decision-making process.[19] Commonly the argument takes the following form: if every citizen is to participate equally in political debate, then every citizen must have an equal possibility to say and print in the public forum anything he or she considers relevant to political life and governance, and that may include information that others would rather keep private. For example, if I consider extramarital affairs of office holders a relevant factor in assessing their performance in office, I must be free to investigate and bring such private affairs to public attention. According to another version of this argument, freedom of speech advances democratic equality because it ensures that the democratic citizenry has the information it needs to participate in governance. Along these lines, Schauer has defended a claim that freedom of speech serves the equality of the voting power of democratic citizens. In his view, the idea that all citizens have an equal say in choosing their representatives commits us to giving equal weight to their informational preferences and providing them with information they judge relevant to their voting decisions. A voter who wishes to have information about an office holder's marital fidelity has a right to obtain such information because "the arguments that militate in favor of the right to vote . . . are likely to militate as well in favor of an interest in obtaining the information that is relevant to voting."[20] From this perspective, the interests in voting equality served by freedom of speech entitle the press to print stories about the extramarital affairs of politicians if citizens happen to find such stories relevant to their voting decisions.

In both versions of the account of free speech presented above, the scope of the claims to free speech depends on people's actual wishes to disclose information; freedom of speech protects disclosure of any material that either the speaker finds relevant to communicate in the political forum or the public actually takes interest in. When the scope of the material protected by freedom of speech depends on people's actual wishes to disclose information, we cannot exclude the possibility that some will wish to reveal what others wish to keep private. In that case, the interests in equality served by freedom of speech militate against privacy.

When both free speech and privacy rights are spelled out in terms of equality, then equality seems to pull in two opposite directions: on the one hand, it entitles some individuals to keep their intimate affairs private, should they so wish, and, on the other hand, it entitles others to make such intimate material public, should they consider it relevant to discuss it in the democratic forum. How should we weigh against each other the equality interests involved in each of these rights?

Booking progress here requires revisiting the scope of the claims to privacy and the claims to freedom of speech. I argue that to the extent that equality confers normative force upon the rights to privacy and the rights to free speech, it also determines the legitimate scope of each of these rights in the political domain. When the scope of freedom of speech, just as the scope of privacy, is determined by the same equity principle, rather than by people's preferences to disclose information, a tension between privacy and freedom of speech is resolved before it could ever arise.

I begin my argument by articulating the common denominator of the claims to privacy and free speech—that is, the liberal-democratic interest in equality. Drawing on previous work,[21] I place my argument in the framework of political liberalism: just as in Lever's argument, political liberalism takes pluralism and disagreement as its point of departure. From this perspective, equality between people who hold divergent views of the good life is expressed in the requirement of public justification in determining which moral principles are appropriate to govern the political domain. In the next sections I link the right to privacy and the right to free speech to equality so understood and explore the extent to which the commitment to equality inherent in public justification determines the boundaries of both privacy and freedom of speech.[22]

## PUBLIC JUSTIFICATION

Public justification is at the core of the liberal concept of political relations. The idea that "the social order must be one that can be justified to the people who live under it" is among the theoretical foundations of liberal political thought.[23] The lack of public justification deprives an association of political legitimacy and, indeed, of a political character because, for liberals, the lack of public justification characterizes the nonpolitical condition of a state of nature: "The moral flaw of the state of nature . . . is that we act without [public] justification."[24]

Public justification does not refer to just any set of beliefs supporting government action that may prevail among individuals in a given historical period. Public justification is a response to the disappearance of such widely shared beliefs and a way to bypass disagreement between individuals who hold competing views of the good life. As Charles Larmore puts it, public justification refers to "principles of association which individuals have reason to affirm together despite deep substantial disagreements setting them apart."[25]

Why seek public justification? Why bypass disagreement? Liberals point to two reasons. First, the diversity of private judgements poses a practical challenge to the stability of cooperation between individuals. From this perspective, public justification creates the conditions for peaceful coexistence and stable cooperation between individuals who profoundly disagree. More important, for the purposes of my argument, is the second reason for circumventing disagreement and seeking public justification. For liberals, disagreement is a moral problem because it undermines the equal moral status and moral sovereignty of individuals. When there are several competing conceptions of the good in the community, unilateral enforcement by an individual of her favoured view is inevitable. However, such a unilateral imposition infringes on the equal freedom of those who hold competing views.[26] From this perspective, public justification creates relations of equal freedom between individuals holding competing worldviews. In Rawls's words, "[P]ublic reason is characteristic of a democratic people: it is the reason . . . of those sharing the status of equal citizenship."[27]

Following political liberals, I have spelled out the liberal-democratic commitment to equality in terms of public justification. Below I argue that this model of liberal-democratic politics has important implications for the status and scope of privacy and freedom of speech.

## PRIVACY AND PUBLIC JUSTIFICATION

Liberals construe politics as "the final recourse for people who cannot agree";[28] they see politics as a common ground upon which people, despite deep differences setting them apart, can stand together in a way that enables equal freedom between them. Not every personal view of the good life, not every lifestyle, commitment, or action, and not every piece of personal information has a place in the political realm defined in this way. Some lifestyles and commitments, for example, sexual morality or religious beliefs, concern issues that are objects of irresolvable controversy. Bringing such contentious issues into the spotlight of public attention and judgement would provoke disagreement and, thereby, destroy rather than establish common ground. Information searches meant to bring such personal commitments to collective attention would have a similar effect. To establish common ground, the material brought under collective attention should allow the people concerned to find principles with which to conduct their lives together and bypass their disagreements. Therefore, the liberal commitment to public justification constrains the material that individuals and groups acting in their political capacity bring to the attention of others. Firstly, this commitment limits the considerations that individuals might wish to employ in deciding matters of mutual concern (e.g., when casting votes in elections or pressing group demands on common resources) to considerations that reasonable others could accept. Second, it requires that individuals engaged in the processes of decision making which concern the organization of their life together refrain from pressing claims in terms that others could not accept.

Based on the understanding of public justification outlined above, the commitment to public justification in politics rules out certain personal commitments and actions as objects of mutual interference among individuals acting in their political capacity. Similarly, it rules out certain personal information as an object of mutual scrutiny. On pain of endangering politics as a common ground between people who profoundly disagree about matters of worldviews, lifestyles, beliefs, and commitments, such material, and the corresponding information, should be withheld or, if known, left unacknowledged. In sorting out which material is appropriate and inappropriate for individuals to introduce into the political forum, public justification sets out rules of concealment and disclosure between individuals acting in their political capacity. Insofar as this requires that individuals withhold certain personal material, I submit, political association based on public justification involves privacy arrangements. Insofar as these rules prescribe withholding personal commitments, views of the good life and lifestyle, they are decisional privacy arrangements. Insofar as they prescribe withholding certain personal information, they are informational privacy arrangements.

A qualification is in order. The depoliticization and privatization of substantive views about which citizens disagree could be taken to suggest that all disagreement is relegated off liberal politics and privatized. This is not the case. What is relegated off politics is an appeal to reasons that others cannot accept and not all cases of disagreement are of that sort. Now it is possible that people disagree but appeal to mutually acceptable reasons. The disagreement arises here from what Rawls called the burdens of judgement: due to the complexity of evidence or the variety of life experiences that bear on judgement, individuals may interpret, apply and rank reasons differently.[29] Insofar as individuals formulate their conflicting positions in terms of reasons that all sides can accept, reasonable disagreement properly belongs to the political domain. A classic example is the discussion on abortion, in which both pro-life and pro-choice advocates formulate their claims in terms of reasons that their adversaries can accept—namely, the value of life and the value of freedom respectively.

Following political liberals, I have spelled out the liberal-democratic commitment to equality in terms of public justification. I have argued that privacy is implicated in the concept of public justification. As a flip side of public justification, privacy derives its moral force from the commitment to equality inherent in public justification. Its scope reflects the scope of the material that public justification relegates off the political realm. What is then private in liberal-democratic politics?

## THE SCOPE OF PRIVACY CLAIMS

Certain spheres of activity, such as the sphere of domestic life, have been traditionally marked as private.[30] The realm of privacy I have isolated in liberal-democratic politics is not defined in terms of any substantive concerns. The border between the political and the private is constructed out of reasons that people can and cannot reasonably accept as governing their life together—that is, reasons that meet and fail to meet the test of public justification. Public justification sorts out the material that falls in and out of the political realm. Failures to provide reasons that others can reasonably accept therefore identify the material that counts as private from the perspective of liberal-democratic politics.

What people can and cannot reasonably accept is a matter of well-known controversy among liberals. However, there is a consensus that one fails public justification if one rejects the aim of pressing one's claims on others in terms of reasons that others could accept. Claims that fail public justification in this way are, in the liberal idiom, unreasonable.[31] The unreasonable, then, outlines a domain that, on pain of violating the integrity of liberal politics, should be held back from the political forum and, if known, left unacknowledged.[32]

Failures of public justification are not confined to renouncing the aim of justification. One may strive to justify his or her claims to others but fail nonetheless. This is the case when the justification one offers appeals to beliefs that others, who adhere to different worldviews, cannot be expected to endorse. For liberals, substantive claims failing public justification in this way should not be invoked in the political decision-making process. Their proper place is the privacy of personal or associational life but not the realm of liberal citizenship. In effect, many substantive beliefs and commitments, important though they are to people's self-understanding, will be depoliticized and set aside as private issues. Exactly what material is depoliticized and set off as private depends on the model of public justification one endorses.

There are two general approaches to public justification.[33] In the first approach, public justification is a constraint on the content of reasons to which individuals can appeal in the political domain; it admits only those substantive views upon which all reasonable worldviews could converge.[34] The substantive views that divide individuals fail the public justification test and should be set aside as private:

> When you and I learn that we disagree about one or another dimension of the moral truth, we should say nothing at all about this disagreement and put the moral ideas that divide us off the conversational agenda of the liberal state. In restraining ourselves in this way, we need not lose the chance to talk to one another about our deepest moral disagreements in countless other, more *private* contexts.[35]

In this content-oriented model of public justification, in a society characterized by pluralism and disagreement, sexual morality or religious beliefs are granted the status of privacy: given that they are the object of disagreement, they fail the public justification test. Privacy insulates such matters from public exposure, scrutiny, and interference: they should be held back from the political forum and, if known, left unacknowledged. Appealing to views regarding sexual morality or religious beliefs in political arguments violates equal freedom and injects material into the political realm that undermines the integrity of the political realm as common ground. The same holds for probing into people's private lives with the aim of placing their sexual choices or religious beliefs in the spotlight of collective attention and judgment. To insist, like Schauer, that disclosure of such information may be relevant to citizens' voting decisions is to allow citizens to appeal in their political judgments to material that is dysfunctional to liberal politics. To vote for or against politicians on the grounds of their sexual choices or religious beliefs is to recognize that a particular sexual morality or religion can generate principles capable of governing the common life. This approach to politics violates the liberal commitment to equal liberty.

In the second approach, public justification, rather than being a restriction on the content of reasons, is a constraint on the process of reasoning whereby citizens arrive at substantive decisions. What material is excluded from the political forum depends on the manner in which people engage with each other's arguments and respond to them. As one exponent of this approach argues, what material is let in and out of the political forum depends on (1) whether objections based on public reasons are advanced against appealing to it in political decision-making processes and (2) whether there is any convincing way to answer these objections.[36] For example, "Citizens can publicly advocate for a ban on same-sex marriage on the basis of religious reasons against homosexuality," provided that they address "any objections against such policy based on the political value of equal treatment. Unless next time around they are willing to accept unequal treatment themselves, they must come up with a convincing explanation of how is it that 'separate but equal' is an acceptable policy as regards this group of citizens but not others."[37] In this procedure-oriented model of public justification, then, citizens cannot determine in advance what material is capable and incapable of justification; that depends on what reasons have survived the scrutiny of public deliberation. Thus, appeals to religious beliefs in advocating a ban on same-sex marriage are depoliticized and set off as private only if citizens advancing religious reasons against homosexuality fail to answer objections that such a policy violates the political value of equal treatment. If no objections are raised, or if the objections are answered convincingly, the political rationale for privatizing these issues is absent and no privacy considerations insulate them from the public gaze.[38]

Let me address a possible concern about the argument I have developed above. I have argued that to the extent that controversies regarding sexual morality reflect disagreements about substantive worldviews between individuals, views regarding sexual morality may fail public justification and, in that case, be depoliticized and set aside as private in liberal-democratic politics. One may wonder how this argument can deal with cases in which the sexual affairs of office holders engage them in violation of the law, engage them in practices involving abuse of power and harm to others, or otherwise affect their performance in office. Think of an extramarital affair between the then director of the Central Intelligence Agency and retired general David Petraeus and his biographer, Paula Broadwell, with whom he admitted to having shared classified material on the Afghan war. Silvio Berlusconi's affair with an underage dancer and the way he used his position as prime minister to cover it up is another relevant example, as are the sexual escapades of Dominique Strauss-Kahn, the former International Monetary Fund chief, which led to charges of rape and aggravated pimping. If sexual affairs are private, are the violations of the law, abuse of power and office, and the exploitation and harm of women that they involve private, too?

In response to this concern, recall that liberals, in the spirit of John Stuart Mill's harm principle, are prepared to allow intervention into people's private affairs in order to prevent harm that individuals cause to others. This position voids the private status of sexual affairs if their pursuit involves exploitation of and harm to women. The same holds for cases in which the pursuit of matters classified as private engages office holders in violation of the law or abuse of public office. Political institutions and the law specify and assign political rights and duties that correspond to principles adopted through the decision-making process governed by public justification. Given that liberals ascribe priority to political rights and duties over other commitments that individuals may have, abuse of office and violation of law involved in the pursuit of private affairs are never private.[39] Thus, to the extent, then, that the pursuit of sexual affairs engages office holders in harmful or illegal acts or involves abuse of office, the private status of sexual affairs is voided. As they are not private, no privacy considerations ban their public scrutiny and media reporting.

I have argued that the liberal model of political relations involves privacy arrangements. Privacy, as the flip side of public justification, derives its normative force from the commitments to equality inherent in public justification. The scope of privacy is determined in terms of reasons that people, who are motivated to justify to one another their claims to power, cannot reasonably accept. With respect to the scope of liberal privacy, three more comments are in order.

First, the circumstances in which the norms of liberal privacy obtain correspond to the range of application of public justification. In the classic Rawlsian approach, the requirement of public justification is limited to "constitutional essentials and questions of basic justice."[40] Others, like Larmore, claim that the rationale for public justification requires applying public justification to issues of daily politics, including, for example, issues such as education, the organization of health care or employment, or regulation of the entertainment industry. Given that the point of public justification is to legitimize the use of coercion to those subject to it, almost all state action is in need of public justification, since almost all state action is backed by coercive power.[41] Although I cannot discuss this position here, I endorse it for the remainder of the chapter. Adopted for the purposes of my argument, this position implies that the norms of privacy are binding across an equally broad political spectrum.

Second, as with public justification, the norms of liberal privacy do not bind individuals in the nonpolitical sphere of what Rawls called the "background culture" of civil society—that is, the culture of "daily life, of its many associations: churches and universities, learned and scientific societies, and clubs and teams" and professional groups.[42] As long as individuals act in civil society, unreasonable and comprehensive personal beliefs failing the public justification test need not be kept private (they may be public with respect to the members of a given group or association that share them). Their status in the nonpolitical domain of civil society is not determined by the political account of privacy I outline in this chapter. In that regard, the traditional theories of privacy (for example, those defending privacy in terms of individual autonomy) may apply.

Finally, within their domain of application, norms of privacy bind equally on all individuals acting in their political capacities, both citizens and representatives. This is because, following Rawls,[43] the requirement of public justification binds on all individuals equally; the norms of privacy implicated in public justification reflect that. Hence, insofar as sexual morality remains private in liberal-democratic politics, the media no less violates the privacy of office holders when disclosing their sexual affairs than it does when disclosing the sexual affairs of ordinary citizens. [44]

Let me now address the link between public justification and freedom of speech before turning to the question of balancing privacy and freedom of speech.

## FREEDOM OF SPEECH AND PUBLIC JUSTIFICATION

Freedom of speech is cherished as a democratic value because, among others, it serves democratic equality by offering every citizen an equal possibility to influence the political decision-making process by speaking her mind and persuading others. In the framework of political liberalism, political participation is governed by public justification. Public justification requires that citizens participating in political decision making restrict themselves to arguments formulated in terms of reasons that all concerned can accept—that is, public reasons. Adapted to this conceptual framework, the link between freedom of speech and equal political participation proceeds in the following way: freedom of speech serves the equality of political participation governed by public justification because it offers each citizen an equal chance to offer public reasons in support of the claims each makes in the political forum.

If freedom of speech serves the equality of political participation defined in terms of public justification, what does that imply about the scope of freedom of speech? Liberals are commonly seen as champions of freedom of speech. According to that conventional view, the scope of freedom of speech corresponds to people's actual wishes to disclose information; in effect, the scope of freedom of speech appears to be virtually unlimited. In the light of the liberal commitment to public justification, however, an unlimited scope of freedom of speech is not obvious. Public justification, as indicated in previous sections, requires filtering the material citizens introduce into the political realm. For example, insofar as considerations relating to sexual morality fail the public justification threshold, public justification requires that they be removed from the political realm and, if known, be left unacknowledged. Appealing to considerations relating to sexual morality in public debate violates equal freedom and threatens the integrity of liberal-democratic politics. The same holds for probing into people's private lives with the aim of placing such material in the spotlight of collective attention and judgment. Now the constraints that public justification imposes upon the material citizens introduce into the political realm, I submit, have implications for the scope of the right to free speech in the political domain. In particular, the scope of the right to free speech cannot protect speech that introduces material failing public justification.[45] On pain of violating the integrity of liberal-democratic politics, one cannot hold on to the requirement of public justification in the political realm and maintain at the same time that freedom of speech entitles citizens to say and print in the political realm what they please. In other words, the material that public justification relegates off the political domain cannot be reintroduced into the political domain by an appeal to freedom of speech. Hence, insofar as considerations relating to sexual morality fail the public justification threshold, an appeal to free speech does not justify disclosing them in the political realm.

## CONCLUSION

In the preceding sections I have made two points. I argued that (1) privacy is the flip side of public justification and that (2) public justification restricts the scope of freedom of speech. If we accept these arguments, then we are committed to conclude that (3) privacy, as the flip side of public justification, sets limits on freedom of speech in liberal-democratic politics. This conclusion reveals a double flaw in the prevailing legal approach to conflicts between privacy and freedom of speech.

First, the claim that privacy is the flip side of public justification calls into question the view of privacy prevailing in current legal practice. Current jurisprudence associates privacy with individual interests such as individual autonomy, integrity, and reputation. I have argued that this traditional view of privacy is incomplete and overlooks the political value of privacy. As a condition of public justification, respect for privacy advances the interests that public justification is meant to realize in the political realm of the liberal-democratic state: that is, equal freedom of individuals.

Second, my conclusion calls into question the priority that current jurisprudence grants to the claims to free speech over the claims to privacy. The legal practice of granting priority to freedom of speech over privacy rests on the assumption that freedom of speech serves democratic equality while privacy does not. Following Lever, I have shown this assumption to be unjustified by arguing that privacy serves the liberal-democratic commitment to equality just as freedom of speech does. I have spelled out the liberal-democratic commitment to equality in terms of public justification and argued that public justification determines the scope of each right—that is, it determines whether information may be disclosed as a matter of free speech or whether it is subject to the privacy norms. To the extent that public justification depoliticizes certain personal material and relegates it to the private domain, privacy, as the flip side of public justification, sets limits to freedom of speech.

How should we, then, approach the conflicting claims regarding disclosures of the extramarital affairs of office holders: the media appeals to free speech against the office holders' claims to privacy? In liberal-democratic societies characterized by pluralism, controversies regarding sexual morality reflect disagreements about substantive worldviews between individuals. To the extent that views regarding sexual morality fail public justification and are depoliticized and set aside as private in liberal-democratic politics, they are not to be appealed to and attended to in the political realm. Unless harm, violation of the law, or abuse of office are involved, then, irrespective of whether citizens happen to take an interest in the extramarital affairs of politicians, such matters are beyond the legitimate business of the liberal-democratic citizenry.[46] If sexual morality fails public justification, we cannot introduce sexual morality issues into the political domain by an appeal to freedom of speech. To the extent that in current political practice media revelations of the sexual affairs of office holders enjoy protection as a form of political speech, this practice, from the liberal-democratic perspective endorsed in this essay, is unjustified. Taking seriously the idea of public justification as a principle organizing the liberal-democratic political order commits us to accept that privacy, being the flip side of public justification, sets limits to free speech.

## NOTES

1. I discuss the privacy of office holders in Dorota Mokrosinska, "How Much Privacy for Public Officials?," in *Social Dimensions of Privacy: Interdisciplinary Perspectives*, ed. Beate Roessler and Dorota Mokrosinska (Cambridge: Cambridge University Press, 2015), 181–201.

2. Subject to legal exceptions, such as defamation, fighting words, incitement to crime or sedition.

3. Privacy and free speech do not always conflict; privacy may be a condition of free speech. See Eric Barendt, "Privacy and Freedom of Speech," in *New Dimensions in Privacy Law: International and Comparative Perspective*, eds. Andrew T. Kenyon and Megan Richardson (Cambridge: Cambridge University Press, 2010).

4. Joshua Rozenberg, *Privacy and the Press* (Oxford: Oxford University Press, 2004), 4.

5. With respect to European jurisprudence, see Eric Barendt, *Freedom of Speech* (Oxford: Oxford University Press, 2007); Kirsty Hughes, "The Social Value of Privacy, the Value of Privacy to Society and Human Rights Discourse," in Roessler and Mokrosinska, *Social Dimensions of Privacy*. With respect to American jurisprudence, see Adam D. Moore, *Privacy Rights: Moral and Legal Foundations* (University Park: Pennsylvania State University Press, 2010), chap. 7, referring to Andrew Jay McClurg, "Bringing Privacy Law Out of the Closet," *North Carolina Law Review* 73, no. 3 (1995); Barendt, *Freedom of Speech*, 155.

6. Barendt, "Privacy and Freedom of Speech," 18.

7. Hughes, "The Social Value of Privacy," 232, 237, 241.

8. See Annabelle Lever, "Privacy, Democracy and Freedom of Expression," in Roessler and Mokrosinska, *Social Dimensions of Privacy*, 162.

9. Barendt, *Freedom of Speech*, 159; Frederick Schauer, *Free Speech: A Philosophical Enquiry* (Cambridge: Cambridge University Press, 2001), 44.

10. Barendt, *Freedom of Speech*, 163.

11. See Frederick Schauer, "Can Public Figures Have Private Lives?," *Social Philosophy and Policy* 17, no. 2 (2000): 302.

12. Schauer, *Free Speech*, 225; see also Barendt, *Freedom of Speech*, 2; Moore, *Privacy Rights*, 2010, Cha. 7.

13. Barendt, "Privacy and Freedom of Speech," 19.

14. Spiros Simitis, "Reviewing Privacy in an Information Society," *University of Pennsylvania Law Review* 135, no. 3 (1987): 732; Ruth Gavison, "Privacy and the Limits of Law," *Yale Law Journal* 89, no. 3 (1980): 455; Priscilla M. Regan, *Legislating Privacy* (Chapel Hill: University of North Carolina Press, 1995).

15. Annabelle Lever, *On Privacy* (New York: Routledge, 2012), 13.

16. Ibid., 12.

17. Lever, "Freedom of Expression."

18. Ibid., 163, 172.

19. Schauer, *Free Speech*, 41–42.

20. Schauer, "Public Figures," 300–301; see also Barendt, "Privacy and Freedom of Speech," 17.

21. Mokrosinska, "How Much Privacy."

22. Moore offers another critique of the prevailing approach to conflicts between privacy and freedom of speech (Moore, *Privacy Rights*, chap. 7). Given that his approach does not fit the political liberalism framework, I do not address it here.

23. Jeremy Waldron, "Theoretical Foundations of Liberalism," in *Liberal Rights: Collected Papers, 1981–1991* (Cambridge: Cambridge University Press, 1993), 57–58; John Rawls, *Political Liberalism*, The John Dewey Essays in Philosophy, no. 4 (New York: Columbia University Press, 1996), 137.

24. Gerald F. Gaus, *Justificatory Liberalism: An Essay on Epistemology and Political Theory* (New York: Oxford University Press, 1996), 182.

25. Charles Larmore, "Public Reason," in *The Cambridge Companion to Rawls*, ed. Samuel Freeman (Cambridge: Cambridge University Press, 2003), 380.

26. Gaus, *Justificatory Liberalism*, 182–84.

27. Rawls, *Political Liberalism*, 213.

28. Stephen Macedo, *Liberal Virtues: Citizenship, Virtue, and Community in Liberal Constitutionalism* (Oxford: Clarendon Press, 1991), 53.

29. Rawls, *Political Liberalism*, 54–58.

30. Marking the domestic sphere as private has been the subject of feminist critiques (Catharine A. MacKinnon, *Toward a Feminist Theory of the State* [Cambridge, MA: Harvard University Press, 1989]; Carole Pateman, "Feminist Critiques of the Public/Private Dichotomy," in *The Disorder of Women: Democracy, Feminism, and Political Theory* [Stanford, CA: Stanford University Press, 1989], 118–40).

31. Rawls, *Political Liberalism*, 49.

32. For a detailed discussion, see Mokrosinska, "How Much Privacy."

33. Simone Chambers, "Theories of Political Justification," *Philosophy Compass* 5, no. 11 (2010): 893–903.

34. Bruce Ackerman, "Why Dialogue?," *Journal of Philosophy* 86, no. 1 (1989): 5–22.

35. Ibid., 16; emphasis added.

36. Christina Lafont, "Religion and the Public Sphere," *Philosophy and Social Criticism* 35, nos. 1–2 (2009): 132.

37. Christina Lafont, "Religious Citizens & Public Reasons," *The Immanent Frame* (blog), February 8, 2008, http://blogs.ssrc.org/tif/2008/02/08/religious-citizens-public-reasons.

38. Lafont, "Public Sphere," 132.

39. Christie Hartley and Lori Watson, "Is Feminist Political Liberalism Possible?," *Journal of Ethics & Social Philosophy* 5, no. 1 (2010): 20.

40. Rawls, *Political Liberalism*, 227–30.

41. Jonathan Quong, "Public Reason," in The Stanford Encyclopedia of Philosophy, ed. Edward N. Zalta, May 20, 2013, http://plato.stanford.edu/archives/sum2013/entries/public-reason, referring to Charles Larmore, "The Moral Basis of Political Liberalism," *Journal of Philosophy* 96, no. 12 (1999): 599–625.

42. Rawls, *Political Liberalism*, 220.

43. Ibid., 217.

44. Dennis Thompson has a different view of the strength of public justification. He argues that the binding force of public justification applies more strongly to individuals who exercise power over other people and have responsibilities to others on whose behalf they act (Dennis F. Thompson, "Public Reason and Precluded Reasons," *Fordham Law Review* 72, no. 5 [2004]: 2077–79). From this perspective, the strength of the norms of privacy will differ as between citizens and officials. This means that media's obligation to leave alone the personal lives of office holders will be less stringent than vice versa.

45. Langton argued that liberals are committed to restrict freedom of speech in the name of equality. Her argument addresses pornography speech. (Rae Langton, "Whose Right? Ronald Dworkin, Women, and Pornographers," *Philosophy and Public Affairs* 19, no. 4 [1990]: 311–59.)

46. There are complexities to this topic, which I discuss in Mokrosinska, "How Much Privacy."

## Chapter Six

# Democracy, Privacy and Security

## Annabelle Lever

This chapter is concerned with the role of democracy in preventing terrorism, identifying and apprehending terrorists, and in minimizing and alleviating the damage created by terrorism.[1] Specifically, it considers the role of democracy as a resource, not simply a limitation, on counterterrorism.[2]

I am mainly concerned with the ways in which counterterrorism is similar to more familiar forms of public policy, such as the prevention of crime or the promotion of economic prosperity, and so nothing that I say turns on being able sharply to distinguish terrorism from other bad things that democracies have to face. And I do not, then, address the extensive debate on the best way to define terrorism.[3] However, I assume that terrorists characteristically seek to terrorize people in order to secure their particular ends. What forms that terror takes, what people terrorists seek to terrorize, and what ends terrorists seek to promote I assume to be indeterminate, open to change, and a matter for empirical investigation. However, I take it that the Irish Republican Army (IRA), Baader Meinhoff, and the Red Brigade, as well as certain animal rights groups in the United Kingdom and certain anti-abortion groups in the United States, are examples of terrorist groups and individuals. In short, I assume that terrorism is principally characterized by the choice of means to given ends, rather than by the ends themselves, and that it is the choice of means, rather than the favoured ends, that makes terrorism so problematic from a democratic perspective.

However good the goal, terrorizing a population—whether or not it involves killing the innocent—is morally wrong and, from a democratic perspective, an abuse of power over the lives of others. While the use of terror may indicate that the ends sought by terrorists are such that people cannot be expected to support them voluntarily, there is no justification for supposing that the ends of terrorism must be morally or politically unacceptable simply because the means are both. It is a staple of ordinary life—not merely of philosophical examples—that people are sometimes unjustified in the means they use in order to accomplish perfectly acceptable ends. So, the ends terrorists seek are, or might become, morally or politically acceptable without in any way altering our objections to the use of terror as a tool for promoting them.

Before turning to the goals of counterterrorism and the role of democracy in achieving those goals, it may be helpful briefly to distinguish specifically democratic objections to terrorism from more familiar ethical objections to it. Most obviously, terrorism is generally wrong because it involves unjust killing, maiming and terrorizing. Utilitarians, for instance, will likely focus on the pain it creates in sentient beings (animal as well as human); Kantians will likely object to the ways that terrorism treats people simply as means to other people's ends, as though people are not also ends in themselves, however useful they may be to others. These both strike me as persuasive objections to terrorism. However, they are not intrinsically democratic—that is, they are the sorts of objections to terrorism you might make whatever your views of legitimate government. By contrast, the democratic objections to terrorism importantly turn on the unjust ascription of power over others implicit in terrorism. Arrogation of such power is at odds with the core democratic idea that people are entitled to govern themselves freely and as equals. No government is entitled to terrorize its citizens, whatever one thinks about the legitimacy of capital punishment, nor is the government entitled to exercise its powers arbitrarily, or in ways and for ends that have not been approved by citizens or their representatives. There are, therefore, distinctive ethical objections to terrorism from a democratic perspective that are not reducible to, although consistent with, more familiar objections.[4]

A comparison may be helpful. "Outing" involves the dissemination and publication, without consent, of sensitive personal information in order to achieve some particular moral or political purpose.[5] The typical case involves revealing that some well-known or influential figure is gay or HIV positive—but the fact that someone has cancer, that they had an abortion, that they were a victim of rape, that they were once communists or worked for the secret service are also examples of the phenomenon. Classic objections to "outing" involve claims that the relevant information is private or personal, and so should not be made public without consent; or that revealing this information is unlikely to achieve the desired ends, and may even prove counterproductive. A natural Kantian objection would be that outing treats someone simply as a tool for other people's purposes, and that this is morally wrong.

These strike me as good objections to "outing" as a general matter, although they are not always persuasive. However, these objections are rather different from the specifically democratic objection, which is is to the arbitrary ascription of power over others involved in the practice. Who decides to do the outing, who is chosen as victim, and how the costs and benefits of outing are determined are all decided in ways that deny victims the ability to influence a matter that may have serious implications for their lives, liberty, social standing, their prospects of employment, their marriage, and the custody of their children. Nor, of course, is there any scope for appeal, oversight, or compensation implicit in outing, as usually practiced.[6] The power involved, therefore, is fundamentally undemocratic, even if it is not absolute—or the power of life and death.[7] So, while outing, like terrorism, may be successful in achieving ends that are morally good, and potential objects of democratic consent, the means used are unacceptable and at odds with the reasons to value democratic government.

## THE GOALS OF COUNTERTERRORISM

I take the goals of counterterrorism centrally to involve the prevention of terrorism, the identification and capture of terrorists, and the minimization and alleviation of damage from terrorism. These are scarcely the only goals of counterterrorism, but I imagine that these must have a central place in democratic responses to terrorism, whatever the case with other political regimes.

If these are the central goals of counterterrorism, then the origin of terrorism (whether it is homegrown, imported or some combination of the two) is irrelevant to the legitimacy of the goals, though it may matter to the means used in realizing them. Moreover, the goals of counterterrorism are importantly similar to those characteristic of other forms of public policy, which typically seek to minimize or prevent the occurrence of bad things—whether or not the causes are human or intentional.[8]

The goals of fighting terrorism are importantly similar to the goals involved in fighting crime and, more generally, to the goal of preventing noncriminal sources of harm. So, many of the resources and constraints typical of these other cases will be useful and important in the case of terrorism—in part because the differences between terrorism and organized crime may be hard to determine (especially because terrorists are likely to fund themselves through various criminal activities)[9] and because the terror created by some diseases when first discovered (cancer/AIDS) or by certain events (floods, famines, eclipses, economic depressions) are all susceptible to manipulation by the unscrupulous for their own purposes. The *source* and particular *character* of the terror, therefore, does not matter to the legitimacy of trying to prevent it, to minimize the harms created by it, and to identify and apprehend those who seek to promote and to benefit from it. Finally, *rehabilitation and not just punishment* may be a legitimate goal of counterterrorism and, in some cases, may be obligatory, because the moral horror of an act does not automatically transfer to the person who committed it, as is clear from the case of child killers.

These theoretical points have practical relevance to counterterrorism. It is likely that fairly long-running terrorist organizations will have members who "want out" or who, with a little persuasion, can be brought to envisage and desire an alternative way of life. Handling such people involves complex moral, as well as practical, judgements about the appropriate punishment for their acts; the appropriateness of promising immunity from that punishment; and the appropriateness of demanding their active participation in the fight against their former comrades. Fear of public hostility to anything that looks like being "soft on crime"—let alone "soft on terrorism"—may well hamper efforts to be *open* about the bargains/promises made to former terrorists and to use the promise of rehabilitation and/or immunity from punishment as an inducement to desist from terrorism. Security forces therefore become vulnerable to the charge of acting illegitimately (undemocratically) and immorally if and when their bargains come to light.[10]

These are real practical handicaps in counterterrorism, as in efforts to diminish crime more generally. They arise from mistaken views about the nature of moral responsibility, desert and punishment; and it is as important to counterterrorism, as it is to other public policy objectives, to counter these. As we will see, debate and deliberation are, therefore, democratic resources for achieving security.

## DEMOCRACY

Democracy has many forms, but its key feature is that citizens are entitled to participate in government—in formulating, executing, and judging matters of public policy—and have intrinsically equal claims to do so. This claim to participate is different from the idea that citizens are entitled to be consulted by those who have responsibility for government—an ideal that characterized the medieval conception of kingship, for example. It is also different from the idea that governments should consider people's interests equally, or "govern in the interests of all." Attractive and important though these political ideals may be, they do not imply that ordinary people are entitled themselves to hold positions of public power and responsibility and, therefore, to do the consulting, considering, and governing themselves, or through agents who they have authorized.

Of course, there are different ways of ensuring democratic participation, and different ways of interpreting the ideal itself. However, a common feature of these is that people have moral and legal rights, liberties, opportunities, and resources to *enable* them to participate in politics freely and as equals. These rights, liberties, opportunities, and resources structure the *competitive* aspects of politics so that winners and losers are capable of, and motivated to seek, cooperation in the future. In short, in (modern) democracies, winners do not "take all"; losers "live to fight another day"; and words, arguments, and dialogue, rather than force, intimidation, and exclusion are the main tools of competition, as of government itself.[11] This helps to explain why religious, civil, and personal liberties are so critical to democratic government, even when they seem to be apolitical or, even antipolitical, and why their content and justification from a democratic perspective may be rather different from those characteristic of liberalism, even in its egalitarian forms.[12]

For example, the point of protecting privacy from a democratic perspective, is not that privacy is some preeminent individual good because of its connection to human dignity, intimate and familial relationships or to property ownership—as it would be from liberal perspectives. Privacy may or may not be justified on these grounds. The point, rather, is that protection for anonymity, confidentiality, seclusion, and intimacy—to name a few characteristics of privacy—helps to foster the freedom and equality necessary for democratic politics by structuring and limiting competition for power in ways that enable people to see and treat each other as equal despite incompatible beliefs, interests, and identities. Although there is likely to be considerable overlap between democratic and liberal accounts of people's rights to privacy—especially when we consider the more egalitarian forms of liberalism associated with John Rawls, Ronald Dworkin, or Thomas Nagel—these are not going to be identical, and there is no reason, offhand, why democratic ideas of privacy should be closer to liberal ones than to utilitarian, Marxist, communitarian, or feminist ones—which typically accord less importance to individual self-expression, sexual and romantic fulfillment, or private ownership than liberals.[13]

*The relevance of these points to counterterrorism* is that democratic government is not the same as liberal government, or even constitutional government, although many forms of democracy are liberal (in the sense that they place a premium on individual rather than collective goods and rights) and are constitutional (in that deciding upon, judging and carrying out formal laws is the preeminent way in which collectively binding decisions are made—in contrast to the more informal and *ad hoc* ways in which people often govern themselves).

It is only comparatively recently that philosophers have really started to probe the differences between democratic and allied moral and political ideals—in particular, the differences between democratic and liberal egalitarian ideas about people's rights, values and claims on scarce resources. It is therefore difficult to provide simple and concrete examples of the significance of these differences for counterterrorism. The point, rather, is to be aware that liberal objections to wiretapping, for example, may be rather different from democratic ones—so what would be unjustified from one perspective is not necessarily unjustified from the other. This is partly because the considerations determining what is and is not justified can differ—as we have seen—but partly that what counts as an invasion of privacy (whether justified or not) may be rather different in the two cases.

For example, liberals tend to think that there is something especially bad about constraining sexual and religious expression, compared to scientific or military expression.[14] This shapes their understanding of people's claims to secrecy in sexual and religious matters, compared to economic and scientific ones—where companies, for example, are typically accorded considerable freedom to determine what is secret and to deny their employees privacy, and in military matters, where the government is given a fairly free hand.[15]

It is unclear that we should accept these sorts of priorities—however familiar they may be—if what we are concerned with is the distribution of power amongst individuals. Hence, the importance we should attach to differences between various techniques for surveillance—closed circuit television (CCTV) cameras compared to policemen, say—and to their location in pubs and shops, not just train stations and airports. These differences may not be particularly significant from a liberal perspective, insofar as surveillance here can be described as occurring in public places, accessible to all, rather than in domestic or intimate settings. However, they may matter a great deal from a democratic perspective. These different tactics and locations of surveillance suggest rather different ways of distributing security and liberty among individuals and of conceptualizing the good of security itself. So the differences between democratic and liberal approaches to privacy can affect the ethics of counterterrorism, and of security more generally.[16] For instance, the differences between racial profiling, random searches, and universal searches shows that there are very considerable moral and political differences in the way we can scrutinize and monitor each other. Racial profiling places the burdens of collective security primarily upon a disadvantaged social group, and is likely, as well, to exacerbate unjustified prejudices and hostility. As this is not true either for random searches or for universal ones, racial profiling is much harder to justify than these other forms of security.[17]

Likewise, the differences between a uniformed police presence, CCTV, and a bus conductor or bathroom attendant are important to the justification of security in public places, and the justification of the one does not automatically mean that we should accept the others. The disadvantage of CCTV relative to a visible, uniformed police presence, for example, is that it provides no one who can come to our aid and, depending on how likely we are to forget that it is there, and how impetuous we are, it may do little to prevent crime. The prime uses of CCTV, therefore, are likely to be in the post-hoc identification of criminals, whereas deterrence as well as solidarity may be better fostered by the presence of identifiable people who are able to provide some oversight of public areas, even if they are also engaged in other tasks. [18]

People have privacy interests in public, then, which we can provisionally define as interests in anonymity, seclusion, confidentiality, and solitude. These are morally and politically important, even though it is unreasonable to demand the same degree of protection for our privacy in public places, to which all have access, as in areas where we are entitled to exclude others. [19] Privacy in public places, such as parks, streets, museums, cinemas, and pubs matters because many of us live in such crowded conditions that public space provides some of our best chances for peace and quiet, for a heart-to-heart with friends, or for relaxation and fun.

It is a mistake, therefore, to suppose that people lack legitimate interests in privacy once they leave their houses, or to suppose that privacy on public transport, at the park, or even at work is a contradiction in terms simply because these are all areas in which others may see us, overhear what we say, or bump into us without violating our moral or legal claims to privacy. After all, being snooped on and overheard by a passerby are not the same, nor does groping on the subway seem any more morally acceptable than at a cocktail party. It is therefore important, when thinking about security, to consider the differences between our privacy interests in public—our interests in anonymity, seclusion, confidentiality, and intimacy, for example—and their implications for the different forms of surveillance, if any, which may be justified.

A few years ago, for instance, some police forces in the United Kingdom attempted to force pubs to install CCTV on their premises as a condition for getting or retaining their entitlement to serve alcohol. [20] Now, alcohol clearly exacerbates tendencies to violence and aggression, and may make it easier for people to steal other people's property, and to deceive or coerce them. But to insist on treating all pubs as though they are the same is to ignore the differences for both privacy and security of small pubs, where people regularly meet and know each other, and the large, anonymous drinking places increasingly found in bigger cities. The threats to security posed by the former are very much smaller than the latter, and the intrusion on privacy created by CCTV may well be much greater, because of the greater degree of intimacy and informality characteristic of such settings. In short, the costs to privacy of surveillance are likely to vary even within spaces that are characteristically thought of as public.

We should, therefore, be wary of ignoring people's interests in privacy on the Internet, including in areas of the web open to all, rather than "closed" or part of recognizably private conversations. Clearly the web, like the street, the park, or the cinema, cannot be exempt from police scrutiny, nor can it be off-limits to social researchers. However, just as our privacy interests in parks, cinemas, streets, and pubs are more complex and diverse than is often assumed, so our privacy interests in public communications, including on the

Internet, cannot be simply divided into a public area—where police scrutiny or social research is assumed to pose no problems—and a private area, where complex legal safeguards are supposed to be required before we are subject to such scrutiny. If we would be troubled by the routine presence of unidentified police officers in health clinics or public libraries, we should be uncomfortable with the suggestion that no special justification or supervision is required for police scrutiny of, and participation in, debates on public websites.

A uniformed police presence, for example, might inhibit us from picking up the information pamphlets on sexually transmitted diseases discreetly available in the health clinic or seeking information about cancer or drug addiction in the library. But official surveillance that we do not know about leaves us vulnerable to misinterpretation of our thoughts and actions as well as to the misuse of state power. Once widespread, it creates a climate in which we are encouraged to see others as threatening, and ourselves as powerless and defenseless individuals. Surveillance can adversely affect the quality of our social relations and our subjective sense of ourselves, then, as well as our objective capacities to shape our own lives, whether we are concerned with places that are open to all, or those in which we are able to seclude ourselves.

## DEMOCRACY AS CONSTRAINT IN COUNTERTERRORISM

Democratic principles are a constraint on the ways we can respond to terrorism, just as they are to the ways we can fight crime, promote economic growth, or secure peace, love, and happiness at home and abroad. These constraints are partly institutional and partly created by the moral and political considerations that justify democratic institutions. There are two main ones I want to highlight here, in part because they tend to be shortchanged in the more familiar discussion of the ways liberty conflicts with security, or with efficiency. The first concerns the relationship among different liberties, rights and opportunities, and the second concerns the way we conceptualize and distribute the costs and benefits of security.

### Privacy vs. Security?

As we have seen, it is not possible to sharply differentiate political and nonpolitical rights, liberties, and opportunities—or constraints on religious freedom, sexual equality, or freedom from arbitrary arrest and imprisonment and rights to vote, stand for election to government, or to dissent from the political choices, associations, and actions of others. We cannot sharply differentiate political and nonpolitical liberties and rights partly because the political consequences of curtailing any particular liberty are hard to predict and because democratic politics cannot be neatly cabined in Parliament, or its regional equivalents, and limited to the choice of legislators every few years.

Constraints on privacy are necessary to protect "the rule of law," because we cannot form, pass, judge, and execute laws democratically without devices such as the secret ballot, or legal rights of confidential judgment, information, and association, which enable people carefully to explore alone, and with others they know and trust, what they should do as citizens.[21] Our legitimate interests in privacy are not negligible, or inherently of lesser importance than our interests in security. Nor are they always selfish or self-regarding. The latter assumption, I suspect, often underpins ideas about the lesser importance of privacy relative to other things. But a moment's reflection reminds us of the importance of confidentiality to our ability to keep *other people's* secrets, even when it might be in our personal interests to disclose them; and of the importance of anonymity, solitude, and confidentiality to our abilities to act with tact, discretion, and consideration for others, even when we do not share their particular sensibilities, interests, and commitments. Just as our willingness to grant privacy to others can reflect respect and trust—and be valued and desired for that reason—our willingness to act anonymously, confidentially, or discreetly can reflect a mature and considered decision to avoid burdening others with our problems, or to avoid forcing them to confront features of the world with which they may be unwilling or unable to cope.

Our interests in privacy, then, can be varied and inescapably tied to our sense of ourselves as moral agents. They are not, therefore, of obviously lesser importance than our interests in self-preservation—individual or collective.[22] This is partly because our interests in privacy are not purely instrumental but seem sometimes to be ways of affirming, even constituting, ourselves as people to be trusted, respected, and deserving of liberty, equality, and happiness.[23] Indeed, while privacy can be necessary to our security and be desired for that reason, people are sometimes willing to risk their lives and health in order to maintain anonymity, seclusion, and confidentiality. This would be unreasonable were privacy less important than security, but if, as I have suggested, it is inseparable from relationships and ideals that have ultimate value, then a willingness to risk physical security for privacy can be comprehensible, and even admirable.

Not all arguments for limiting privacy in the interests of security are consistent with democratic principles, or with the ways in which privacy can express our collective, as well as individual, interests in freedom, equality, and solidarity. We should therefore be wary of ethical guidelines, such as those propounded by Sir David Omand, which assume that whenever it is impossible to protect both privacy and security, the former should bow before the latter.[24] Omand's "ethical guidelines," which appear to be drawn from just war theory,[25] are meant to tell us when the state is entitled to limit people's privacy in the interests of security. They include "sufficient sustainable cause; integrity of motive; proportionate methods; proper authority; reasonable prospect of success; no reasonable alternative." Such guidelines ignore the ways in which privacy can be necessary to the security of at least some people, given prejudice, discrimination, and unfounded fear and hostility. In addition, they overlook the ways in which democratic government and principles depend on our willingness to constrain the quest for security in the interests of the privacy of members. In short, one worry about Sir Omand's pronouncements are their one-sided and unqualified character, which turn a problem in jointly protecting two values into a reason to sacrifice one to the other. This is unjustified, and has the predictable consequence that some people's security will be threatened because we are contemptuous of their privacy.

The U.S. Supreme Court decision in *NAACP v. Alabama* (357 U.S. 449 [1958]) is interesting in this context. The NAACP is the National Association for the Advancement of Colored People, and was originally founded as a nonprofit membership association. By 1957, the state government of Alabama was seriously concerned with its growing membership and use of civil disobedience against racial segregation. The state government therefore sought access to the membership list of the NAACP under an existing state statute aimed at ensuring that business associations be held responsible for any damage to life, liberty, or property that their activities cause. But while the court accepted that the government of Alabama had a legitimate interest in ensuring that associations, like individuals, can be held accountable for harm to others, it denied that this required them to have access to the full membership list of the NAACP, rather than to the names and contact information of its leaders. Freedom of association, the court argued, is a fundamental democratic right, and protections for anonymity can be essential to its exercise. So while the state has a duty to provide security for its citizens, the court maintained that people's interests in privacy and associative freedom legitimately constrain the ways that the state may fulfill that duty.

According to Sir Omand's guidelines, "integrity of motive" is essential to determine when our interests in security justify curtailing people's privacy by spying on them. But this appears to confuse the conditions necessary for the state to be justified in *exercising* its rights of surveillance with the question of *what rights*—whether moral or legal—the state is entitled to claim. At best, integrity of motive is relevant to the former; however, as the U.S. Supreme Court realized, in *NAACP v. Alabama,* it is irrelevant to the latter. For example, the purpose of requiring the NAACP to disclose its membership list was not fear for people's lives, liberty, or property so much as the desire to thwart the movement for civil rights. The motives for requiring the membership list in 1957, then, were not particularly reputable. They would surely have failed Omand's test of "integrity of motive." Nonetheless, as the court thought, democracy requires that governments be able to hold associations to account for their actions, and therefore to have some means of identifying their legal representatives, even if these do not require governments to record the names, addresses (or the license plates and photos) of ordinary people, even if they are engaged in social protest, or campaigning for radical change.[26] In short, Omand's six criteria—"sufficient sustainable cause; integrity of motive; proportionate methods; proper authority; reasonable prospect of success; no reasonable alternative"—provide guidance on the morally appropriate *claiming* and *exercise* of rights of surveillance. What they do not tell us is *which* moral or legal rights of surveillance follow from the state's duty to keep us all safe.

## Equality

Of course, we cannot always protect—let alone promote—the liberties and opportunities to which people are entitled. But if and when we can't, it matters *how the costs and benefits of any sacrifice are made* in counterterrorism, as in other aspects of public policy. In fact, I would suggest, it is necessary publicly to show that sacrifice *x* by group *y* is, indeed, necessary to prevent greater harms to some other group. Hence, it is necessary to discuss alternative ways of preventing harm, and how their respective costs and benefits are to be described and assessed.

An example may be helpful, and can illustrate why talk of "proportionate" sacrifices is often so empty and misleading. In 2009, the part of London in which I lived—Streatham—faced the loss of its local police station, in the interests of efficiency and cost effectiveness, to some "central" location somewhere else within the borough.[27] The move might have been justified, although given the appalling traffic in London, it is hard to be confident that shopkeepers, victims of domestic violence or young people would get the timely help that they needed if they had to depend on help from outside the area. But putting problems of response times aside, if we consider that it can take an ordinary person anywhere from half an hour to an hour or more to travel five to seven miles in that part of London, the consequences of such a move for democratic forms of policing and security become apparent. After all, the point of police stations, from a democratic perspective, is not simply that they enable police quickly to get to the scene of a crime/potential crime, but that they represent the local community, and are a focus for local hopes, complaints, knowledge, pride, and initiative. This is scarcely possible if people have to find anywhere from an hour to three hours, in already busy lives, for a round-trip visit to "their" police station.

Thus, whether we are concerned with powers to stop and search, wiretap, detain without trial, to limit choice of religious dress, expression, travel and employment, it matters how we describe and assess the costs and benefits of our actions. It matters, in order to avoid stigmatizing minorities and unpopular social groups for what is, typically, the behaviour of a very small percentage of their population. It is necessary to avoid cementing injustices and social problems—racial and sexual inequality, poverty, alienation, ignorance and hopelessness—that we already find hard enough to deal with. And it is necessary to avoid confusing democratic rights and liberties with alternatives, however efficient, familiar and seemingly attractive.

## Suicide Bombers

Before turning to democracy as a resource in the fight against terrorism, I would like briefly to suggest how the idea of democracy as a constraint on counterterrorism, and public policy more generally, may help us to handle the real and potential problems of *suicide bombers*.

I assume that an important goal of counterterrorism is to move suicide bombers away from suicide, even when we cannot yet stop them planting/ setting off bombs. The parallel here is to the IRA—and the importance of getting advance warning *that* a bomb is about to go off, even when it is impossible to prevent the bomb from being planted or triggered. In each case, what is at stake is saving lives but also—and importantly, from a long-term perspective—the ability to establish a relationship with bombers, however tenuous and difficult, in order to discuss alternative ways to achieve their ends, and different ways to think about those ends themselves.

To do this, it is essential that we can persuasively convey the message that the lives of suicide bombers are more valuable than they think; that they are valuable for reasons other than, or in addition to, those they believe; and that we recognize and care about their lives for reasons related to the reasons why we value our own, and those of our compatriots. Put simply, we need to convey the message that we want them to desist from *suicide*, not merely from *bombing*, and that our objections to the latter—that this is a dreadful way to die; that nobody deserves such a death; that nobody is entitled to inflict such a death on others—are connected to our objections to their suicide and to those who have encouraged/persuaded/ordered them to die in this way.

Of course, we are unlikely to be able to convey this message successfully in many cases, just as it is difficult to persuade some would-be bombers of the advantages of calling the police in order to avoid or, at any rate, to minimize death and injury. But there are some people who can be persuaded or are, at least, credible targets of persuasion. An important goal of counterterrorism is to work out how to reach and influence these people. However, the credibility and practical effectiveness of our claims of concern and care— or of the effort to turn potential suicide bombers into negotiating partners—is the way that our society treats its own members, as well as foreigners.[28]

While it is clear that foreign policy has made Britain a target of Muslim ire, I think we also need to consider the ways in which our *domestic* politics prevent an adequate response to suicide bombers at home and abroad, and may even foster the belief that killing oneself, along with others, is necessary to manifest the sincerity and strength of one's convictions, the urgency of one's cause, and one's claims to public attention.

## DEMOCRACY AS A RESOURCE IN COUNTERTERRORISM

It is important to the motivation and justification of democratic government that people have some hope of influencing the political agenda on things that they care about. Where people have this sort of influence, democracies can accommodate the classic "single-issue voter" described by political scientists, whose views are organized around one particular issue or set of issues—be they abortion, animal rights, global warming, self-rule for Ireland, Kashmir or Palestine. It is typically these people who are most readily alienated from democratic government, even though only a very small minority of those who are alienated will act out that alienation through politically motivated violence.

Democracy offers the promise that losing on the swings (for example, on economic policy) is compatible with gaining on the roundabouts (for example, civil liberties or foreign policy). So, while many people are not particularly enamoured of democratic government, let alone of their political leaders, they are unlikely to reject democracy as a means of handling political conflict. This is less likely to be true for those with single-issue, nonnegotiable causes, and this makes it a matter of some importance that people have multiple ways of competing for political power and positions of public responsibility, so that failure in any one of these is less likely to determine failure on all.

Making politics accessible to people in a variety of ways and through a variety of means encourages us to seek cooperative solutions to the realization of our cherished ends, even when these are eccentric or unpopular. Political participation can help us to see why compromise is a legitimate response to the demands of others, and how to structure compromises that respect the sincerity and importance of people's fundamental convictions, even when we cannot endorse them. Engagement with democratic politics is not guaranteed to produce satisfaction and can, sometimes, be alienating and dispiriting. But we are much less likely to be bitter and cynical about politicians as a class when we have tried our hand at politics; and we are more likely to accept the need to compromise in order to accommodate the interests of others when we have ourselves experienced the efforts of other people to accommodate our interests and concerns.

If these points are right, the centralized, hierarchical and hidebound character of British democracy—as of other well-established democracies—is a real obstacle to counterterrorism. Democratic entitlements to welfare, education, employment, and security imply rights to participate in determining what forms of these are desirable, how best to achieve these, and at what costs in terms of not just taxes raised and spent but also opportunities foregone and claims postponed or ignored. The real democratic agenda, therefore, is to improve people's abilities and opportunities to debate their rights and duties, their liberties and opportunities, and the proper distribution of resources in matters of security, as well as of education, employment and health, rather than to demand acceptance of a supposed code of "British values" or of their equivalents, such as "laicité."[29]

There are many ways in which we might try to do this, and there is research on democratic budget setting, prioritizing of health-care needs, and jury deliberation—as well as on democratic deliberation more generally—which can be examined and built upon.[30] How democratic deliberation is obviously depends on the way it is structured—what veto rights people have over discussion; what the terms of entry and exit are; what information is available to all, and what is secret; what sorts of coalitions are allowed and disallowed; who, if anyone, monitors or facilitates discussion. All these are important, because deliberation is not always free and equal, let alone capable of generating more light than heat.

Nor can all aspects of counterterrorism be openly debated—though this, it should be said, is as likely to be true of economic and foreign policy as of counterterrorism. Discussions may need to be confidential in order to facilitate the free and frank exchange of ideas—hence, in part, the ideal of cabinet secrecy. They may need to be limited in subject matter in order to avoid needless offense, or to enable people actually to sit down together. And, of course, public debate sometimes has to be limited to protect people, institutions, and facts of national interest.

But discussions of security can be useful even when they are based on historical cases, or on hypothetical ones. They can be comparative and quite general in focus—as when we compare attitudes to CCTV, ID cards and the storage and use of DNA samples in Britain and other countries. They can be useful when we consider how Britain differs from other democracies in its fairly extensive use of wiretapping for security and police purposes, but its unwillingness to allow that evidence in court.[31] We can compare the treatment of gang members and the incidence of gang crime amongst children in Boston and Chicago, compared to London or Liverpool, and its significance for racial profiling, for stop-and-search laws, and for the relationship between crime and terrorism.[32] Above all, it is possible to help people to think about, and confront, difficult questions of identity, value, and experience that are important to current efforts against terrorism, and that may be useful in considering what Donald Rumsfeld so memorably referred to as "unknown unknowns."

Take, for example, the role of Islam in Africa—in the conflicts in Sudan, Ethiopia, and Kenya. Why not encourage Muslims in Britain and elsewhere to discuss the role of race in Islam, just as it is appropriate to ask Christians or Jews to consider the way it has shaped, and continues to shape, their theology, culture and politics? Why not have television programs, newspaper and radio discussions on religion in contemporary Britain in which Asian Muslims and Christians from Africa and the Caribbean—two of the livelier religious groups in our country—discuss shared experiences of faith, racism, immigration, and international concerns, as well as their mutual suspicions?

These are merely examples—perhaps not good ones. But they illustrate how narrow in structure and subject matter most contemporary debates on religion and security really are; how much we have to learn about people's experiences of identity, religion and security; and how little we actually know about the sources of conflict and cooperation in our society.

In short, democratic debate and choice are important weapons in the fight against terrorism. Democratic education and deliberation are necessary to the justification of any public policy on surveillance, although they do not figure in Omand's "guidelines" for legitimate surveillance. Moreover, while governments and think tanks stress the importance of education in fighting extremism, and in justifying surveillance, most proposals in this area are astonishingly bland and vague. Above all, they seem utterly disconnected from the thought that, as citizens, we *need and are entitled* intelligently to discuss government policy on surveillance, just as we would employment policy, education, welfare, or policy on crime and punishment. We may differ in our desire and ability to master many of the relevant details or controversies—though this is unlikely to be any truer of surveillance than of employment or education policy, let alone pensions or the European Union constitution. And some things have to stay secret. We will therefore need to combine historical cases, the experience of other countries, and hypothetical examples in lay as well as expert discussions. But this is perfectly compatible with the assumption that ordinary citizens might be interested in, and should be able to discuss, the principles and basic practices of surveillance, as of counterterrorism more generally.

## CONCLUSION

I have argued that democracy is a resource, as well as a constraint, in the goals of counterterrorism and suggested that the two are intimately related. They are related in some of the same ways, and for the same reasons, that democratic government helps to prevent famine. As Amartya Sen showed, in some of the work for which he won the Nobel Prize in economics, democracies facilitate the effective use and sharing of information, as of other goods, because of the freedoms they secure.

Those freedoms come at a price and that price is not purely financial. It includes the death of people who would not have died, and might have had happier, more successful lives under other forms of government. In some cases, this is no cause for regret, because people are not entitled to secure their lives, liberty, and happiness by enslaving others. But matters are often more complicated, because people do not deserve to die or to be maimed because we may not inflict worse harms on others. To say that democracy is a resource, not merely a constraint, then, is not to underestimate the latter. Instead, it is to recognize that the dilemmas of counterterrorism, as of public policy more generally, arise because the constraints of democracy are our resources for securing voluntary cooperation, even in the face of involuntary conflict.

## NOTES

1. This chapter started life as a keynote address to the "Ethics and Counter-Terrorism workshops" organized by DEMOS at the Office of Security and Counter-Terrorism, The Home Office, United Kingdom, in January 2009. A revised form was presented to the Afternoon Discussion on "Terrorism, Democracy and The Rule of Law," sponsored by Baroness Nicholson of Winterbourne, memeber of the European Parliament (MEP), and the Indo-British Friendship Forum, The House of Lords, July 8, 2009, and published as a "Thinkpiece" for Compass, December 2009; available at www.compassonline.org.uk. Many thanks to Adam Moore for his invitation finally to present my ideas in a more scholarly form and for his help and advice in editing this chapter. Parts of this article draw on material previously published in *On Privacy* (New York: Routledge, 2011), and "Privacy, Democracy and Surveillance," the *Philosophers' Magazine* (2013). I am grateful for the permissions to republish parts of those texts here. I am very grateful to Henri Mottironi and Dan Grecu for help with this, my first work referenced using Zotero.

2. Unfortunately, this chapter was written before David Anderson's review of British terrorism legislation (especially the Regulation of Investigatory Powers Act), was made public. However, it can be accessed online at https://terrorismlegislationreviewer.independent.gov.uk. And for those who wish to follow some of the debate, which it has occasioned, see "'Undemocratic, Unnecessary, Intolerable' . . . The Official Verdict on Britain's State Snoopers," by John Naughton in the *Guardian*, June 13, 2015, http://www.theguardian.com/commentisfree/2015/jun/13/david-anderson-qc-investigatory-powers-report-gchq-undemocratic.

3. See, for example, Verena Erlenbusch, "How (Not) to Study Terrorism," *Critical Review of International Social and Political Philosophy* 17, no. 4 (2014): 470–91; and on p. 99 of *Securing the State*, David Omand refers to over 109 definitions of terrorism (David Omand, *Securing the State* [London: Hurst, 2010]).

4. Robert Goodin also focuses on the distinctively *political* aspects of the harms of terrorism in Robert E. Goodin, *What's Wrong with Terrorism?* (Cambridge, UK: Polity Press, 2006), and believes that the use of terror for political advantage is the "*distinctive* wrong that terrorists commit, making them terrorists and not mere murderers" (p. 49), although he repeatedly reiterates his point that the moral *badness* of terrorism comes from the violence used to create the terror (murder, mass murder, kidnapping, etc.), as distinct from the bare fact of trying to get one's political way through fear (though this, too, is presumptively bad). See, for example, pp. 184–85.

5. I discuss "outing" at more length in chap. 2 of *On Privacy*. See also Patricia Boling, *Privacy and the Politics of Intimate Life* (Ithaca, NY: Cornell University Press, 1996), 29–30.

6. Max Mosley, for example, was very clear that his effort to bring the *News of the World* to justice for invasions of privacy was something that few other people would be able to manage for financial, as well as personal, reasons. See *Mosley v. News Group Newspapers Ltd.* (2008) EWHC 687 (Q.B.).

7. I develop this argument in more detail in Annabelle Lever, "Privacy, Democracy, and Freedom of Expression," in *Social Dimensions of Privacy*, ed. Beate Roessler and Dorota Mokrosinska (Cambridge: Cambridge University Press, 2015).

8. I therefore disagree with the view of Jacqui Smith, then Home Secretary for the United Kingdom, who appears to suppose that the importance of prevention, rather than after the fact responsiveness, is more urgent in the case of terrorism than of murder, rape, domestic violence, robbery and corruption. The fact that most police investigations of the latter typically occur after the fact does not tell us about the relative urgency of prevention in these cases so much as the difficulty of prevention and, probably, the difficulty of using *law enforcement* rather than social policy, education, and the rest to influence people's behaviour. See Jacqui Smith, "In many respects, counter-terrorism work is distinctive in nature and not like other areas of law enforcement. The work of our security and intelligence agencies is, of necessity, covert. . . . We depend on the police and Security Service to identify these individuals before their plans come to fruition, to stop an attack from happening. This contrasts with the majority of police investigations, which happen after the crime has taken place." The Home Secretary was addressing the Smith Institute and the Centre for the Study of Terrorism at St. Andrews University on June 3, 2008 (www2.labour.org.uk/home_secretary_jacqui_smiths_speech_to_the_smith). The quotation comes from the section called "Our Objectives."

9. The fact that terrorist organizations are often engaged in racketeering, for example, underpins controversies about "collusion" in Northern Ireland and Massachusetts, where police and security agents often engaged in illegal activities that were hard to control. Sir David Omand raises this issue clearly at p. 10 in "The National Security Strategy: Implications for the UK Intelligence Community," a discussion paper commissioned and published by the Institute for Public Policy Research in the United Kingdom in February 2009; see www.ippr.org/publications/the-national-security-strategy-implications-for-the-uk-intelligence-community.

10. In *Securing the State*, David Omand refers to this as the "moral hazard" that comes with principal-agent actions. See pp. 285–86 and his discussion of the problem of shared intelligence and diplomatic collaboration with countries who use torture, pp. 271–77. However, as Omand notes, the shift in Britain in the 1980s from a situation where the existence of a secret organization was neither confirmed nor denied, to one in which it was openly acknowledged and given a legislative framework, has been generally welcomed because of its capacities to alleviate—though not remove—some of these problems. He quotes Sir Stephen Lander, a former director general of the Security Service: "We now had the assurance of statute law as opposed to the insecurity of royal prerogative, under which much agency activity hitherto notionally took place. That change played a key part in the 1990s and beyond in making the agencies more self-confident and thus more effective."

11. An interesting contrast comes from the practice of ostracism in ancient Greece. On this, see Sara Forsdyke, *Exile, Ostracism and Democracy: The Politics of Expulsion in Ancient Greece* (Princeton, NJ: Princeton University Press, 2005) and Judith N. Shklar, "Obligation, Loyalty and Exile," in *Political Thought and Political Thinkers*, ed. Stanley Hoffman (Chicago: Chicago University Press, 1998).

12. My conception of democracy has been shaped by Joshua Cohen's brilliant, if difficult, contribution, titled "Procedure and Substance in Deliberative Democracy," in *Philosophy and Democracy*, ed. Thomas Christiano (Oxford: Oxford University Press, 2003), 1–17, and by his work on democracy more generally. See Joshua Cohen, *Philosophy, Politics, Democracy: Selected Essays* (Cambridge, MA: Harvard University Press, 2009).

13. I have developed these ideas at length in Annabelle Lever, *A Democratic Conception of Privacy* (AuthorHouse, 2013) and Annabelle Lever, "Privacy and Democracy: What the Secret Ballot Reveals," *Law, Culture and Humanities* 11, no. 2 (2015): 164–83.

14. See, for example, Charles Fried, "Privacy," in *Philosophical Dimensions of Privacy: An Anthology*, ed. Ferdinand D. Schoeman (Cambridge: Cambridge University Press, 1984), 203–22, or Julie C. Inness, *Privacy, Intimacy and Isolation* (Oxford: Oxford University Press, 1992).

15. For a helpful discussion of the differences in legal notions of employee privacy in the United States and Europe, see Matthew W. Finkin, "Employee Privacy, American Values and the Law," *Chicago-Kent Law Review* 72, no. 1 (July 1996): 221–69.

16. Anita Allen has an interesting discussion of "catcalling" as an invasion of privacy and a marker of male space and dominance in Anita L. Allen, *Uneasy Access: Privacy for Women in a Free Society* (Totowa, NJ: Rowman & Littlefield, 1988). See chap. 5, "Privacy for Women in Public," especially pp. 128–40.

17. See Annabelle Lever, "Why Racial Profiling Is Hard to Justify," *Philosophy and Public Affairs* 33, no. 1 (2005): 94–110, and Annabelle Lever, "What's Wrong with Racial Profiling? Another Look at the Problem," *Criminal Justice Ethics* 26, no. 1 (Winter/Spring 2007): 20–28. For an excellent short book on the subject, see Naomi Zack, *White Privilege and Black Rights: The Injustice of U.S. Police Racial Profiling and Homicide* (Lanham, MD: Rowman & Littlefield, 2015).

18. Compare the views on CCTV of Jesper Ryberg, "Privacy Rights, Crime Prevention, CCTV and the Life of Mrs. Aremac," *Res Publica* 13, no. 2 (June 2007): 127–43, with those of Annabelle Lever, "Mrs. Aremac and the Camera," *Res Publica* 14, no. 1 (March 2008): 35–42, and Benjamin Goold, "The Difference between Lonely Old Ladies and CCTV Cameras: A Response to Ryberg," *Res Publica* 14, no. 1 (2008): 43–47.

19. This is a point well made by Helen Nissenbaum, although her ways of understanding the context-dependent aspects of privacy strike me as too uncritical of actual practices, and of elite theories about those practices, whereas I believe the starting point should be the weight and variety of the legitimate interests in doing various things, or in being in various places, rather than a theoretically pre-given definition of "context." See Helen Nissenbaum, "Protecting Privacy in an Information Age: The Problem of Privacy in Public," *Law and Philosophy* 17, no. 5 (1998): 559–96. As Jeremy Waldron persuasively argues, "The subway is a place where those who have some other place to sleep may do things besides sleeping." For those who lack anywhere of their own, public space provides their only chance of meeting their basic needs legally and with some modicum of privacy. See Jeremy Waldron, "Homelessness and the Issue of Freedom," in *Liberal Rights: Collected Papers, 1981–1991* (Cambridge: Cambridge University Press, 1993), 309–38.

20. Matthew Taylor, "Pub Landlord Wins Right Not to Fit CCTV Cameras," *Guardian*, March 11, 2009, http://www.theguardian.com/uk/2009/mar/12/cctv-pubs-privacy-ico; Matthew Taylor, "Pubs and Police Fall Out over CCTV in Bars," *Guardian*, March 15, 2009, http://www.theguardian.com/uk/2009/mar/16/pubs-police-cctv-in-bars.

21. Annabelle Lever, "Privacy Rights and Democracy: A Contradiction in Terms?," *Contemporary Political Theory* 5, no. 2 (2005): 142–62. And Lever, *A Democratic Conception of Privacy*, chap. 3 and on our political interests in privacy. See also Joshua Cohen, "Pluralism and Proceduralism," *Chicago-Kent Law Review* 69, no. 3 (1994): 569–618.

22. Hence I disagree fundamentally with Kenneth Einar Himma (see chapter 8 in this volume).

23. Benjamin Goold makes a similar point in his excellent "Privacy, Identity and Security," in *Security and Human Rights*, ed. Benjamin J. Goold and Liora Lazarus (Portland, OR: Hart, 2007), chap. 3, where he shows how the effects of automated surveillance in the wake of 9/11 have exacerbated the threats to "narrative" forms of identity, and their replacement by "categorical identities."

24. Alan Travis, "Fight against Terror 'Spells End of Privacy,'" *Guardian*, February 24, 2009, http://www.theguardian.com/uk/2009/feb/25/personal-data-terrorism-surveillance; David Omand, "NSA Leaks: How to Make Surveillance Both Ethical and Effective," *Guardian*, June 11, 2013, http://www.theguardian.com/commentisfree/2013/jun/11/make-surveillance-ethical-and-effective; Omand, "National Security Strategy." See also Omand's *Securing the State*, pp. 285–87 and pp. 324–35, for repetitions of these guidelines. However, in his discussion of privacy (pp. 110–11) he notes that "the total impact of individually justified measures

may add up to an unwelcome capability of the state to access information on its citizens for undefined purposes." It is not clear how his statement at p. 111 that trade-offs between personal privacy and security have "to be weighed for each technique" responds to that concern, even granted that "intrusions into personal privacy can and should be limited to the most serious challenges to security, from terrorism and serious crime and not from the multitude of minor misdemeanours that authority must therefore find less intrusive ways to prevent." Perhaps Omand's view is that we must just live with the collectively undesirable, even irrational, results of individually rational decisions—rather than straining to find ways to factor the risks of collectively irrational outcomes into our analysis of what it is rational to do in individual cases.

25. For reasons that will become apparent, I am skeptical about the appropriateness of using just war theories for thinking about the ethics of counterterrorism, or of security more generally, including the ethics of war. This is partly because just war theory is a tradition of ethical thought that still uses an ethical framework originally developed to determine when divinely ordained absolute monarchs might be justified in waging war on each other. It therefore treats the differences between democratic and undemocratic governments as irrelevant to what we are entitled to do. Its prescriptions and ways of thought therefore sit very uneasily with the perspectives on security which come out of democratic approaches to civil and criminal law, where the protection of civil liberties are of fundamental concern, irrespective of the intentions of our governments. Robert Goodin is similarly skeptical of the extension of just war theory to the analysis of terrorism and of security more generally—and implicitly, if not explicitly, skeptical about its use in thinking about the ethics of war. However, while his reasons are compatible with mine, they are more concerned with the implications of just war theory for our judgements about individual terrorist acts and people than are mine. See, in particular, Goodin, *What's Wrong with Terrorism?*, chap. 2.

26. See, for example, Rob Evans and Paul Lewis, "Police Forces Challenged over Files Held on Law-Abiding Protesters," *Guardian*, October 26, 2009, http://www.theguardian.com/uk/2009/oct/26/police-challenged-protest-files; and Rob Evans and Paul Lewis, "Kingsnorth: How Climate Protesters Were Treated as Threat to the Country," *Guardian*, October 26, 2009, www.theguardian.com/environment/2009/oct/26/kingsnorth-protests-climate-change-campaign.

27. The saga seems to have continued through 2014, with a new police station finally opening within Streatham. Streatham, at the time, had problems with gangs and drugs and contained a significant immigrant and refugee population with distinctive linguistic needs.

28. I am not thinking only of the treatment of interpreters in Afghanistan and Iraq, who have found it hard to obtain citizenship in Britain, but also of the treatment of the poor and disabled and of religious, racial and ethnic minorities in Britain. In a discussion on terrorism and democracy in the House of Lords in 2009, Steve Tsang referred to the work of Mike Aaronson on economic development and terrorism. While Western governments think of development as a sensible way to combat terrorism, the way in which such development is offered often serves to *discredit development*, not to inhibit terrorism. The reason is simple: recipients of aid are well aware that aid is self-interested, not altruistic, and that its benefits may fail to offset the risks of impoverishment, exploitation, and insecurity resulting from trade with the West. See Steve Tsang, *Combating Transnational Terrorism: Searching for a New Paradigm* (Santa Barbara, CA: Praeger Security International, 2009). The gist of this argument was presented at the House of Lords Debate on Terrorism, organized by Baroness Nicholson of Winterbourne, MEP, on February 23, 2009, apparently. I was not there.

29. On *laïcité*, see Cécile Laborde, *Critical Republicanism: The Hijab Controversy and Political Philosophy* (Oxford: Oxford University Press, 2008); Cécile Laborde, *Français, Encore Un Effort Pour Être Républicains!* (Paris: Seuil, 2013).

30. See, for example, Archon Fung, *Empowered Participation: Reinventing Urban Democracy* (Princeton, NJ: Princeton University Press, 2004); Albert Weale, "Democratic Values, Public Consultation and Health Priorities," in *Equity in Health and Health Care*, ed. Adam Oliver (London: Nuffield Trust, 2004), 41–51; and Annabelle Lever, "Democracy, Deliberation and Public Service Reform: The Case of NICE," in *Public Services: The New Reform Agenda*, ed. Henry Kippin, Gerry Stoker, and Simon Griffiths (London: Bloomsbury Academic Press, 2013), 91–106.

31. For American skepticism about the benefits of their use of warrantless wiretapping, see Eric Lichtblau and James Risen, "U.S. Wiretapping of Limited Value, Officials Report," *New York Times*, July 10, 2009, http://www.nytimes.com/2009/07/11/us/11nsa.html?th&emc=th. Apparently, the very secrecy of the covert-wiretapping program prevented the effective use and dissemination of any information that it provided.

32. See, for example, David A. Harris, *Good Cop: The Case for Preventive Policing*, (New York: New Press, 2005) and his earlier *Profiles in Injustice: Why Racial Profiling Cannot Work* (New York: New Press, 2003).

*Chapter Seven*

# Transparency for Democracy

## The Case of Open Government Data

### Kay Mathiesen

"Transparency" has become a buzzword in national and international discussions of good governance.[1] One prominent transparency strategy, open government data (OGD), envisions almost all data possessed by governments made freely available on the Internet.[2] Access to government information, such as that supplied by OGD, is said to be "essential to participation in the democratic process, trust in government, prevention of corruption, informed decision-making, the accuracy of government information, and provision of information to the public, companies, and journalists, among other essential functions in society."[3] Nevertheless, some scholars have questioned whether transparency in general, or OGD in particular, necessarily produces such benefits.[4] This chapter seeks to evaluate the merits of OGD, with particular focus on whether it has the potential to make political decision making more democratic. I will argue that there is a strong in-principle connection between public access to government information and democracy. There are, however, practical problems bridging the gap between making information publicly available and having an informed public. I will conclude by making some policy recommendations for how governments can make OGD more effective as a means for making our politics more democratic.

I begin by describing in more detail OGD as it has been developed in the United States, with particular attention to the policy guidelines adopted by the Obama administration. After considering a number of potential costs and benefits of OGD, I focus on the democracy argument as the strongest case for OGD. I then show how two prominent normative theories of democracy demonstrate a strong link between an informed public and democracy. I then note a potential objection to this defense—namely, both rational choice theory and empirical evidence suggest that the existence of available information will not necessarily translate to the public being more informed. After considering some possible responses to this objection, I make a few recommendations for how OGD can be implemented so as to facilitate access to information that will make decision making more democratic.

It should be stressed that this chapter does not ask what we should do about governments that are unwilling to make information available. Given the problem of over-classification and profligate labeling of information as "official use only," the reader may wonder whether the whole open government data discussion isn't a red herring. Indeed, one might see OGD initiatives as an effort to dump a lot of irrelevant information on the public in order to obscure the fact that the really important information is being suppressed. Luckily, there are plenty of other scholars hard at work on this issue.[5] I believe that there is a need to ask a slightly different question. This chapter asks what governments should do if they are willing to make information available to citizens. What policies and practices should they adopt? This question allows us to focus more precisely on what the goals of transparency initiatives should be and the difficulties in meeting those goals even when government officials are trying to be transparent.

Before proceeding, it will also be useful to have a more precise definition of transparency on hand. Transparency is most often discussed in the context of accountability. Andreas Schedler's well-known discussion of accountability describes transparency as one of two necessary conditions for accountability—the other being the ability or willingness to punish or reward those being held accountable.[6] He further distinguishes between two dimensions of transparency: (1) the informational dimension describing what was done and (2) the argumentative dimension explaining why it was done.[7] Since the focus here is on the value of OGD, which seeks to implement the informational, but not the argumentative, aspect of transparency, this chapter uses "transparency" only in its informational sense. Alon Peled defines informational transparency in relation to government as "openness to public scrutiny as defined by the rights and abilities of organizations and individuals to access government information and information about government."[8] In order to go from this descriptive definition to the normative claim that we ought to implement a transparency mechanism such as OGD, we need to know why such transparency is a *good* thing. The simple answer is that we want transparency so that people can be informed and acquire knowledge. But this answer itself raises a series of further questions:

- Will availability of government information actually lead to an informed public?
- What do we mean by an informed public? Does everyone have to be informed?

- What, precisely, are people being informed *about*? Is the information relevant and useable?

In order to answer these questions, we need to know what benefits we hope to achieve from transparency. I return to these questions in the final sections of the chapter. First, I describe OGD in more detail and consider the multiple benefits and costs of OGD that have been discussed in the literature.

## OPEN GOVERNMENT DATA

In 2008, a newly elected president Barack Obama pledged to work towards "an unprecedented level of openness in Government."[9] A key theme of this open government initiative was an increase in *transparency*, which the White House defined as "providing the public with information about their government's activities . . . disclosure about, for example, what federal agencies have done or will do. Transparency's premise is that citizens are entitled to know what, how, and why government does what it does."[10] One component of this initiative was to make government data accessible online. Such "open government data" has been defined as "non-privacy-restricted and non-confidential data, which is produced with public money and is made available without any restrictions on its usage or distribution."[11] Government data includes information about, produced by, and collected by government agencies, including "documents, databases of contracts, transcripts of hearings, and audio/visual recordings of events."[12] The Obama administration defines open data as "publicly available data structured in a way that enables the data to be fully discoverable and usable by end users."[13] Open government data platforms include http://www.data.gov, which provides access to data collected by government on topics ranging from climate to small business loans, and http://www.recovery.gov, which provides data on how the money dispersed as part of the 2009 Recovery Act was spent.

The Obama administration's open-government initiative is guided by principles set down in a memorandum from the Office of Management and Budget (OMB).[14] These principles express the common wisdom in open government circles about how transparency initiatives like OGD should be implemented. Indeed, the OMB guidelines largely mirror the recommendations in "Principles of Open Government Data" developed by a group of transparency scholars and openness advocates.[15] Thus, these principles will give the reader a good sense of the guiding ideas behind OGD proposals.

According to the OMB's principles, government information should be:

*Public.* There is to be "a presumption in favor of openness," consistent with valid reasons (e.g., privacy, security) for restricting access. The idea here is that all data should be shared unless there is a strong justification for *not* doing so.

*Accessible*. "Open data structures do not discriminate against any person or group of persons and should be made available to the widest range of users for the widest range of purposes, often by providing the data in multiple formats for consumption."

*Described*. "Open data are described fully so that consumers of the data have sufficient information to understand their strengths, weaknesses, analytical limitations, security requirements, as well as how to process them."

*Reusable*. "Open data are made available under an open license that places no restrictions on their use."

*Complete*. "Open data are published in primary forms (i.e., as collected at the source), with the finest possible level of granularity that is practicable and permitted by law and other requirements."

*Timely*. "Open data are made available as quickly as necessary to preserve the value of the data."

One presumption behind these requirements is that governments should not be in the job of picking and choosing which data to share. Not only that, the data should not be interpreted by the government, but should be made available as much as possible in raw form. The idea is that then there is less room for governments to massage the data in ways which may obscure any information that might make government officials look bad. Also, governments should not be in charge of picking what information is relevant, who should have access to it or how it should be interpreted. Even if government officials have the best intentions, it is difficult to predict ahead of time what information someone may find useful and for what purposes. Thus, it is better to put out all the information and let the public decide what is valuable.

## BENEFITS AND COSTS OF OPEN GOVERNMENT DATA

Numerous benefits of OGD have been suggested in the literature; these include citizen empowerment, economic stimulus, improvement of government services, harnessing the wisdom of the crowd, and avoiding unnecessary duplication of information gathering.[16] According to one study,[17] there are four main reasons governments give for why they adopt OGD initiatives: (1) to improve the functioning of government, (2) to promote economic development, (3) to raise the well-being of citizens through the provision of actionable information, and (4) to enhance democratic accountability and participation.[18] I will consider the potential impact of OGD on democracy in some detail later in this chapter. At this point I want to briefly consider the first three reasons. Some of these reasons are less compelling than others.

The hope that OGD can improve the functioning of government by better enabling government agencies to share information provides a rather weak reason. To facilitate sharing information between agencies, all that is necessary is to make the information available via a single shared platform; it does not require making the information public. At best we might see this as a side benefit to making the information public, rather than a reason to do so.

A more direct benefit of OGD is its potential to stimulate the economy by providing business and nonprofit organizations with information that they can use to develop and improve products and services. In so doing OGD is expected to improve the well-being of citizens. According to Open Data 500 (http://www.opendata500.com), an organization that tracks the uses and impact of OGD, businesses and nonprofits have used data provided by OGD to help consumers do such things as identify available grants and loans, track school performance, and access cutting-edge research in a variety of fields, including information about legislation and spending. If it were costless to provide OGD, then there would seem ample reason based on the second two benefits alone to make the information publicly available. If something costs nothing, but will produce a benefit, then, of course, we ought to do it. Indeed, this view of the matter is frequently expressed in popular media outlets. However, as a number of authors have pointed out, there are costs and risks to releasing government data.[19]

First, there is the actual monetary cost of making the information accessible in terms of the costs of hardware, software, and personnel. Often the information is not already in formats that can easily be shared; thus, there is cost in transforming the formats so that the data are machine readable and shareable across multiple platforms. If we add the fact that this data must be refined in various ways (e.g., private or secret information must be redacted, metadata must be added to make it searchable), the costs increase. The potential costs of OGD extend beyond the monetary, however. Even when agencies make an effort to redact or anonymize private information, the inadvertent release of confidential or sensitive information is still a real possibility. Indeed, work in data science demonstrates that it is much easier to reidentify people from supposedly anonymized data than was previously thought.[20] Furthermore, to put a modern-day spin on the old adage, "data is power" and this power can be used for good or ill. For example, public records may be used in ways that end up discriminating against certain categories of people in access to housing, health insurance, etc. The data may also be misused unintentionally. Many who praise OGD do it on the basis of the potential to use Big Data analysis on the data provided, but the legitimacy of Big Data methods for scientific discovery has been called into question.[21] Additionally, with greater openness may also come greater caution and conformity within bureaucracies, leading to *less* information being shared.[22] Finally, even when the data is released, accessed and used in ways intended by the government, there may be unintended consequences. Michael Gurstein, for example, worries that "'open data' empowers those with access to the basic infrastructure and the background knowledge and skills to make use of the data for specific ends."[23] The consequence is that OGD is "empowering the empowered" by creating a "data divide."

It would be a good thing for the government, economy, and people's lives to be improved by the provision of information. But, in pursuing such goals, it is important to pay attention to the above costs and potential negative consequences of transparency. If opening up government data is primarily a matter of producing good consequences, then it is an open question whether the putative benefits of open data outweigh the costs. In the following section I consider arguments for OGD that are not a matter of costs and benefits, but are instead linked to deontological considerations of various sorts that create an obligation on the part of government to provide access to government data.

## BEYOND BENEFITS AND COSTS

### Property

It is sometimes argued that the state is obligated to make government data openly available on property-rights grounds. Government information is the property of the public, it is argued, because the information was produced or gathered using public funds. According to the eminent economist Joseph Stiglitz, for instance, "Information gathered by public officials at public expense is owned by the public—just as the chairs and buildings and other physical assets used by government belong to the public."[24] He concludes that the public has a right to have access to this information based on this property right.

Stiglitz's position is flawed, however. While the public may, in principle, own government buildings, computers, and so on, it does not follow that the public has a right to unrestricted access to these things. Such unfettered access would seriously interfere with the government's ability to carry out its functions. Of course, there is a difference between such physical objects and information; information is nonrivalrous—both the government and the public can use the same piece of information at the very same time. However, while it does not *exclude* government officials from using the information, as noted above, providing information to the public is not costless.

It is true that, if I have a right to some piece of property, I should be able to access and use it. But I do not have a right that others provide me with the means of accessing that property. If my property is in another country, no one owes me a plane ticket to get there. Similarly, the public may "own" the information, but it does not follow that the government is obligated to spend funds on making it easily accessible. Of course, the funds that are used to implement OGD are themselves public, but the question is whether OGD is the best use of those funds, and that is a political decision not predetermined by the property rights of the citizens. Furthermore, there already exist freedom of information laws that allow individuals to ask for specific information from the government—this may be sufficient to fulfill the information property rights of the public. Moreover, it is hard to reconcile the inference that we should have access because we own the information with the existence of reasonable restrictions (such as privacy and secrecy) on what information is released. Thus, while the argument from property provides a *prima facie* case for release of government information, by itself it does not establish the obligation of the government to institute OGD policies.

## Publicity

Philosophers typically discuss the idea of transparency under the label "publicity." By publicity they mean the condition wherein government policies and laws are publicly known. The *principle* of publicity, what Immanuel Kant calls "the transcendental principle of the public law," holds that "all actions relating to the right of other human beings are wrong if their maxims are incompatible with publicity."[25] A law is incompatible with publicity if its being known would undermine the purpose of enacting the law. Notice that this "transcendental formula of public law" is purely hypothetical, however. It only requires that the law *could be made public*, not that it actually be made public. Kant's principle of publicity itself is compatible with a lack of transparency, as long as the government's practices, policies, laws and their justifications do not *require* secrecy. However, as David Luban argues, the best way to ensure that a law *could* be made public is to *make* it public.[26] In practice, it is unlikely that government policies and practices would pass the publicity requirement unless there is actually a requirement that they be made public. Otherwise, there is too much room for self-deception on the part of government officials. Thus, we can make an argument from Kant's principle of publicity to the requirement for transparency.[27]

Kant's principle of publicity specifically focuses on law; similarly, John Rawls is concerned with the publicity of *rules*.[28] Thus, any justification of transparency based on their conceptions of publicity will not extend to the broad range of information made available via OGD. Jeremy Bentham's notion of publicity, however, provides a justification for the accessibility of a wider range of information, including the discussions and actions of legislators. Bentham gave two arguments for the publicity of the activities of legislators. First, Bentham held that making information public was the best way to create trust in government. This is a claim also often put forward by open-government advocates.[29] It is not obvious that this is true, however. Onora

O'Neill points out that the implementation of stricter transparency legislation in the United Kingdom coincided with a *decrease* in trust of the public in government.[30] Of course, it may be that the governments are not trustworthy and with more information the public simply becomes aware of this fact. Nevertheless, the claim that transparency creates trust is an empirical one, which needs further evidence to support it. Second, Bentham believed that publicity of the activities of the legislature was the best way to prevent corruption. According to Bentham, "the eye of the public makes the statesman virtuous."[31] This justification will be considered in more detail in the section on accountability below.

## Accountability

As noted at the beginning of this chapter, transparency is most often valued as a means to, or an aspect of, accountability. In a democracy the government is accountable to the citizens, paradigmatically through the mechanism of elections. As Hanna Pitkin puts it, the representative (and by extension other government officials) "must eventually be held to account so that he will be responsive to the needs and claims of his constituents, to the obligations implicit in his position."[32] We can only call someone to account if we know what he or she has done, and transparency mechanisms are intended to provide us with this needed information. As Bentham noted, an important element of accountability is surely the regulating effect that it has on the actions of government officials, who know that they will be held to account. Thus, the value of accountability is not merely that we can get rid of government officials who fail to act as we want them to, but that we can affect their decision making in the first place.

While its necessity for accountability is an important ground for valuing transparency, the value of transparency goes beyond its role in accountability. Even if it were not possible to hold government officials accountable for anything (suppose, for example, that we could elect, but not reelect or remove politicians from office), it would still be valuable for citizens to have information about the activities of government and the condition of society as a whole. As I argue in more detail below, such information can shape our understanding of the nature and role of government, the value of regulation, and the possibilities for improving things through government action. Much more promising is the claim that the right to government information, and, thus, to transparency mechanisms like OGD, is tied to basic rights of citizens to self-government, which include but are not limited to holding public officials accountable. The next section focuses on this "democracy argument" for transparency.

# THE DEMOCRACY ARGUMENT FOR TRANSPARENCY

"Democracy" has been described as an "essentially contested" concept;[33] that is, any particular definition will refer to a particular set of political values and understandings that are themselves a matter of debate. In other words, any theory of democracy will have to take a position on fundamental normative questions, such as the goal or value of democracy. Thus, rather than providing a single definition of democracy, I consider the value of informational transparency from the perspective of two prominent normative theories of democracy: public choice and deliberative democracy. I argue that no matter which normative theory of democracy we choose, an informed public is essential to the functioning of democracy as described by the theory. Admittedly, there is a limitation to this sort of argument. The argument here is intended to show that, on two prominent theories of democracy, citizens must be informed, but it does not show that in principle all reasonable normative conceptions of democracy require an informed public. There may be other theories of democracy under which an informed public is not necessary. Nevertheless, the argument here should provide strong, though not decisive, support for the claim that an informed public is necessary.

Under the widely held "public choice" model of democracy, people express their preferences for government policies through their votes;[34] the resulting decision is a result of the aggregation of these votes. While public choice theorists often adopt the economic model of choice without providing any reason why government should be determined by the preferences of the public, there is a normative justification for this conception of democracy. The view that leaders ought to govern for the common good goes all the way back to Aristotle. More modern understandings substitute the interests of the people for the idea of a common good. John Stuart Mill argued that democracy is the best strategy for ensuring that governments actually act in the interests of the public.[35] As Mill puts it, "the rights and interests of every or any person are only secure from being disregarded when the person interested is himself able, and habitually disposed to stand up for them."[36] Thus, on Mill's conception, a democratic government is one where each person is "able and habitually disposed" to stand up for her interests. Democracy, then, is valuable as a means for ensuring that the government rules in the interests of the people. From this view of the value of democracy, it becomes clear why democracy requires an informed public. If democracy is about ensuring that government policies actually serve the interests of the citizens, then the citizens have to be in an epistemic position such that they can choose policies and candidates who are likely to best satisfy those interests. Furthermore, one cannot know what one actually prefers if one is lacking information about the world (for example, about such things as the past track records of policies and government officials). An ignorant vote may express what the voter believes to be her preferences, but not what she would actually prefer.

While the public choice approach to democracy is still the most widely used—particularly in social science—some of its assumptions have been called into question. One influential critique argues that the public choice model is overly individualistic, failing to recognize that democracy is fundamentally a matter of deliberating about our common good.[37] Democracy is not just about voting; it is also about how we interact with each other in the public sphere. "Deliberative democracy" has sought to correct for this problem in the public choice aggregative conceptions of democracy.[38] For deliberative democrats, the goal of deliberation on political choices is the development of a shared view of the public good or, if such is not available, by reasoning together among citizens and representatives, we express respect for each other and keep open the possibility of future agreement.

There are two aspects to deliberative democracy: the expressive and the epistemic. The expressive aspect emphasizes the role of deliberation in manifesting equal respect amongst citizens.[39] This expressive aspect is not merely a matter of feeling, but is required by the fundamental interest each person has "in being treated as a person with equal moral standing among his fellow citizens."[40] If only some have essential information about the choices available, then there is an important inequality among the participants. In short, equal participation requires individuals to have the information necessary for genuine decision making. However, if deliberation allows us to show respect for each other as equals, but is terrible at settling on a choice that is actually good, then the case for deliberative democracy would be very weak.[41] Thus, it is central to the deliberative democracy argument that deliberation has epistemic worth, generally resulting in decisions that actually promote the public good (or, in any case, do better on this score than do other approaches).

Mill suggested that democracy provides a superior practical and epistemic strategy for choosing policy.[42] As Thomas Christiano puts Mill's point, "Since democracy brings a lot of people into the process of decision making, it can take advantage of many sources of information and critical assessment of laws and policies."[43] For the deliberative democrat, it is important that this information processing does not just occur at the time of voting. Discussion in the public sphere, when supported by democratic norms of freedom of expression and association, provides more sources of information for decision making and a public forum for sorting through that information. There is also a benefit in the information being shareable, creating common knowledge; information that is open between us provides a common epistemic resource, which can be the basis of collective political action. However, if the activities of the government are not known, then this epistemic virtue of democracy cannot function. We cannot collectively critically assess policies and practices of which we are ignorant.

## DOES ACCESSIBLE INFORMATION LEAD TO AN INFORMED PUBLIC?

I argued above that both the public choice and the deliberative democracy conceptions of democracy require that citizens be informed about the activities of government. Thus, insofar as OGD enables citizens to be more informed, it makes society more democratic on both these theories. There is, however, a serious objection looming here. As it has been said, "open data has no value in itself; it only becomes valuable when used."[44] But will it be used? There are two reasons to worry that it won't. First, people may not have a reason to take the trouble to look up the information and, second, even if they do, they may not end up informed by it.

Famously, Anthony Downs argued that citizens have very little incentive to gather information about political matters.[45] According to Downs's rational-choice approach, the costs of being informed are high relative to the impact of a single individual's vote, because one individual's vote has little chance of making a definitive difference in the outcome of an election.[46] Empirical evidence appears to bear out Downs's theoretical argument; it has been said that "the political ignorance of the American voter is one of the best-documented features of contemporary politics."[47] If voters generally do not gather information relevant to the political decisions they are called on to make, then making more information available will have little value. Indeed, politicians and government officials could make government information public, secure in the knowledge that there will be no consequence to it being known. We may build it, but they won't come, and, thus, we should have saved ourselves the time and expense.

Those writing on democratic decision making are, of course, aware of the worry raised by Downs. Some seek to avoid the complications posed by Downs's theory by narrowing the conception of transparency to mere availability of information. For instance, Frederick Schauer says that "transparency is about availability and accessibility, but these attributes of transparency are agnostic on the question of who might take advantage of that availability or accessibility and at what cost."[48] As long as the information is available, people may choose to access and use the information. If some people do not wish to spend their time learning about what the government is doing and has done, then they should be free to choose not to do so. A system that required otherwise would impinge on people's freedom to develop and pursue their own conceptions of the good. As Christiano points out, citizens should not be required to spend all of their free time informing themselves about all the issues.[49]

The problem with this response, however, is that both conceptions of democracy discussed above rely on the public being informed—not just on their being free to inform themselves if they so choose. Furthermore, the justification for OGD given by policy makers relies on the fact that it will inform the public, not just that it will allow the public to be informed if they wish (and all the evidence shows they mostly don't wish). Given the costs and risks of OGD, as discussed early in this chapter, it is not clear that the good of the mere freedom to access information can justify the implementation of a program like OGD.

Things are even worse for OGD if we consider the fact that those few regular citizens who seek information from sources like http://www.data.gov and http://www.recovery.gov are unlikely to come away informed. We must be careful not to confuse the availability of information with the accessibility of information. Information may be there and we may take the time to try to access it, but it may be so hard to find, time consuming to process, difficult to comprehend and irrelevant to our concerns so that it has little or no impact on our actual knowledge. As I have argued elsewhere, genuine access to information requires that the information seeker is enabled to reason and act based on the information—this means that the information must be findable, reachable, comprehensible and useable.[50] But, some of the OGD policies I described in the first section of the chapter actually impede the accessibility of the information. If information is given at the "finest level of granularity" as required by the OMB principles, then it is unlikely to be accessible to the average citizen. A simple search of http://www.data.gov finds a huge array of data sets on a vast variety of topics. Finding data relevant to an average citizen's question about government policies and activities requires a high degree of sophistication in the use of these data sets. Thus, even if voters were motivated to seek information relevant to the political decisions they are called upon to make, OGD by itself does not greatly increase the likelihood that they will find it.

In his work, Christiano has endeavoured to deal with these sorts of problems by specifying what citizens need to know about in order to participate in democratic decision making.[51] Christiano argues that the role of citizens is to "think about what ends the society ought to aim at and leave the question of how to achieve those aims to experts."[52] Citizens cannot be expected to know all the details that would be necessary to choose particular policies that would pursue the ends they find valuable and appropriate for government. But, according to Christiano, this is not a problem; the public determines the ends and goals of government—voting for candidates who they believe will pursue these ends and goals. The politicians and other government officials then use their resources to determine which policies would best achieve these ends and goals. This focus on ends, rather than means, lessens the information burden on citizens. People may not be motivated to become experts on the best specific policy choices, but they are experts on their own values, and thus, on the goals that government should be pursuing as guided by those values.

Christiano's view allows us to avoid the Downs problem, but at the cost of making projects like OGD pointless from the perspective of democracy. If it is not even the proper role for citizens to determine policy, then why would they need access to the sorts of detailed information provided by OGD? There are reasons, however, to doubt whether Christiano can so easily draw the distinction between the sorts of information needed by citizens and the sorts of information needed by policy makers. First, as Christiano points out, even if focusing on goals is sufficient for the purpose of democratically authorizing representatives, it is not sufficient for the purpose of holding representatives accountable for their policy choices. In order for me to hold someone accountable, I need to know about the means that she has chosen in pursuing the goals she had committed to. As Christiano himself admits, "there is a huge principal/agent problem here."[53]

Second, it is not as easy to separate ends from means. Suppose my conception of the good includes a government which ensures everyone has access to health care. Of course, that is not the only thing I think government should be doing. I may have other ends that I think government should be pursuing which are as important or even more important to me. In order to know whether my goal of universal access to health care is consistent with the fulfillment of my other, more important, goals, I need to know something about the details of the possible policies. I need to know what sorts of policies have been tried and how they have fared. If under the best policy we can currently come up with, universal access will require the sacrifice of one of these other, more important, goals, I will no longer think that my representatives should take universal access to health care as a goal. Thus, it isn't really possible to separate out my choice of goals for government from the details of policy.

A number of authors, most notably Samuel Popkin,[54] have pointed out that there are ways that citizens can gain the benefits of being informed about politics that do not place as big of a burden on them, thus avoiding the Downs problem that there is insufficient incentive to spend the time to be informed. Popkin's suggestions also help address the problem of how we move from the mere availability of information to accessible information. Popkin notes two methods: "everyday information"[55] and what he calls "information shortcuts."[56] Everyday information is the sort of information that one gathers in one's ordinary activities. Since accessing OGD is unlikely to be an "ordinary activity" for most of us, this method has limited applicability here. Information shortcuts are more applicable—it may be that most of us don't need to bother going to OGD websites. We can rely on others who have a strong interest or who are paid to gather and interpret such information for us, what Popkin calls "interpersonal influence."[57] We can gain knowledge from others, including those close to us, such as friends, family, colleagues, and even acquaintances, and from "information intermediaries"[58] such as the media and public intellectuals.

By relying on other people, I may be able to leverage their knowledge and information in my own political decision making. It is likely that persons will tend to know about those areas that most directly affect them or in which they have a strong interest. So, my environmentalist friends know the details of government policy related to global warming, while I know the details of law and policy related to intellectual property. Indeed, we may know a lot collectively, even though each of us individually has large holes in his or her knowledge. Our friends who are experts in a particular area may serve as "designated knowers" for the rest of us. We can rely on their informed opinions of the situation without having to go through the basic data ourselves. Compare a paper written by a group of scientists who work in different sub-specialties: none of the scientists knows all the information necessary to establish the claims in the paper, but taken collectively, they do.

There are a couple of potential problems with this solution, however. First, not only do there need to be people who know things, but there also need to be people willing to listen; thus, it assumes a more deliberative form of democracy where people engage in open discussion on political issues. This might not be a problem; it just depends on how optimistic you are about the prospects for deliberative democracy. The second (and more worrying) problem is those who are the most motivated to become informed on a topic are often those who have a special concern about a topic. We might think that their being better informed would mean that their views on the topic would be closer to the truth, but their very interest in the topic may mean that they have a preexisting bias in favour of a particular position. Since research indicates that getting contrary evidence tends to solidify people in their preexisting beliefs,[59] the fact that they have accessed the information does not necessarily mean that their beliefs are in accordance with it.

Information intermediaries—such as news agencies and political parties—can also provide information shortcuts by gathering information and delivering it in predigested and easy-to-understand communications. These intermediaries now include such things as social media (e.g., Facebook, Twitter, Reddit), blogs, information aggregation systems (e.g., Tumblr), and even apps. When supported by the analyses and interpretations by a variety of academics and other experts, the media in all its forms can provide information that is easy to find, reach, comprehend, and use. Indeed, it has been argued that the government ought to leave such interpretive work solely to such nongovernmental intermediaries. According to an influential paper by

David G. Robinson, Harlan Yu, William P. Zeller, and Edward W. Felten, "Private actors, either nonprofit or commercial, are better suited to provide government information to citizens and can constantly create and reshape tools that individuals use to find and leverage public data."[60]

One problem with reliance on information intermediaries, however, is that persons tend to select which channels they will listen to. Thus, they are less likely to get a broad range of points of view or information on a wide range of issues and they are more likely to get information that confirms what they already believe. Furthermore, we may worry that "the public does not have the cognitive capacities to determine which intermediary provides information that is better processed than another."[61] Nevertheless, while relying on our friends and information intermediaries is not unproblematic, it does provide us with an argument that citizens can and do get information about the activities of government from various sources. However, there is still much that government can do to make it easier for these information shortcuts to work for us.

## RECOMMENDATIONS

The main moral to derive from the above is that it is not enough to simply make all the data that the government has available. More needs to be done both at the level of the information provision itself and at the broader societal level. The following recommendations go from a focus on OGD itself to broader conditions that are necessary in order for OGD to have the hoped-for impact on democracy. While these recommendations focus on OGD, they apply more generally to many transparency initiatives. It should be noted that the recommendations I make below will likely increase the cost of OGD, but the increased costs can be justified by the fact that they are more likely to give people real access to information. Even if governments take these recommendations to heart, however, there are questions of how the benefits gained from greater access to government information should be balanced against the costs ands risks discussed earlier in this chapter.

### Prioritize and Interpret

The effort to provide access to information should seek a balance between providing as much data as possible and providing the most relevant data with useful interpretations. While all information may be useful to citizens in making choices, information about the activities of government is particularly important. This is not just in terms of what information is prioritized for release but also in terms of how much description and other enriching of the data is needed. In many cases there may be information intermediaries who are willing and able to do the interpretive work, but this may not always be the case. In those situations where intermediaries are not doing the job, government has to play a part in making information more accessible to the public. And there is nothing that prevents governments from providing both raw, uninterpreted data and information from these data sets interpreted in ways likely to be of use to citizens. It may be objected that one reason to avoid prioritizing and interpreting data in the way that I have suggested is that it gives the government more leeway to massage the data in ways that benefit the government. This concern is legitimate. However, if the alternative is that the data is won't be accessed or is not relevant or useful to the public, then the actual situation is that the information is unknown to the vast majority of the public. So, it is not a choice between accessible raw and complete data and accessible interpreted data, but between data inaccessible to the average citizen (because it is difficult to find and difficult to comprehend) or interpreted data accessible to the average citizen.

## Fill Gaps

Even when the OGD is genuinely accessible to the public, it may still be the case that there is important information that the public does not have. OGD only requires that governments share the data they have; it says nothing about what sorts of information the government *should be* collecting. There are, of course, questions about whether the government is currently collecting *more* than is consistent with individual privacy. Here, however, we are concerned with cases where governments do not collect enough information or do not collect information on topics of importance to citizens' lives. An OGD initiative that was truly oriented towards supporting democracy with information would attend to what sorts of questions are most important to democratic decision making and that would be best gathered by governments. One way that gaps can be discovered is by creating venues for citizens, civil society organizations, media, and academics to point out what sorts of information may be missing. [62]

## Support Intermediaries

As discussed above, information intermediaries have an important role to play in analyzing and presenting information from OGD. We would expect that OGD initiatives will not be as successful in actually informing the public in societies lacking strong civil-society institutions such as a free press, public interest groups and educational institutions such as libraries and universities. The government can, however, do things to support these intermediaries in analyzing, interpreting, and disseminating information. In addition to strengthening laws and policies that fund and protect such institutions, the government can offer monetary and other support tor academics and public-interest intermediaries to engage in the work of analysis and interpretation. While the uses of the information provided by OGD may far outstrip what government officials could predict, it may also be true that there are areas where the government could encourage the work of intermediaries, by, for example, conducting periodic reviews of OGD so as to find holes where information important to voters is not being distributed through intermediaries.

## Educate

While information intermediaries are important, citizens should be empowered with the skills to analyze and evaluate information themselves. Even when intermediaries take on the burden of analysis and interpretation, citizens should be able to evaluate the credibility of intermediaries and to effectively reason from the information provided. Thus, one important way to increase the epistemic value of OGD is to educate citizens in critical thinking and reasoning skills as well as technological skills that allow them to understand how data can be analyzed to extract useable information.

## CONCLUSION

Digital technologies, such as the Internet, allow us to share data and information quickly and easily with anyone with Internet access, which in the United States is currently over 86 percent of the population.[63] Thus, such technologies have the potential to democratize information and knowledge. When applied to government data, they also have the potential to make politics more democratic. This potential is genuine, but it is unlikely to be adequately realized without careful consideration of how the data provided via the Internet can actually *inform* the public. Attention must also be paid to the costs and risks associated with making government data widely available. In this chapter, I have attempted to articulate the various costs and benefits of open government data initiatives, such as that implemented by the Obama administration, and I have sought to more clearly articulate the connection between democracy and an informed public. I have argued that, while in principle OGD should make political decision making more democratic, it will not automatically do so. If, however, in designing OGD programs, governments attend to the need to prioritize and interpret data, fill in the gaps where information is lacking, support intermediaries who make government information more accessible, and support educational institutions that give citizens the tools to understand and evaluate that information, then OGD may indeed reach its potential to make our politics more democratic.

# NOTES

1. I want to thank the members of the University of Utah Philosophy Department and the attendees of the 2015 Information Ethics Roundtable for useful comments on an earlier version of this chapter. I would also like to thank Don Fallis, Susan Dovi, Laura Lenhart, and Chad Schoenveldt for their helpful conversations on the ideas in this chapter.

2. White House, *The Obama Administration's Commitment to Open Government: A Status Report* (2011), http://www.whitehouse.gov/sites/Default/files/opengov_report.pdf.

3. Paul T. Jaeger and John Carlo Bertot, "Transparency and Technological Change: Ensuring Equal and Sustained Public Access to Government Information," *Government Information Quarterly* 27, no. 4 (2010): 371.

4. See, e.g., Amitai Etzioni, "Is Transparency the Best Disinfectant?" *Journal of Political Philosophy* 18, no. 4 (2010): 389–404; Michael B. Gurstein, "Open Data: Empowering the Empowered or Effective Data Use for Everyone?," *First Monday* 16, no. 2 (February 2011): doi: 10.5210/fm.v16i2.3316; Onora O'Neill, "Transparency and the Ethics of Communication," in *Transparency: The Key to Better Governance?,* ed. Christopher Hood and David Heald (Oxford: Oxford University Press, 2006), 75–90; Harlan Yu and David G. Robinson, "The New Ambiguity of Open Government," *UCLA Law Review Discourse,* 59 (2012): 178–230.

5. See, e.g., Michael P. Colaresi, *Democracy Declassified: The Secrecy Dilemma in National Security* (Oxford: Oxford University Press, 2014); David Pozen, "Deep Secrecy," *Stanford Law Review* 62, no. 2 (2010): 257–339; Alasdair Roberts, *Blacked Out: Government Secrecy in the Information Age* (Cambridge: Cambridge University Press, 2006); Geoffrey R. Stone, "Secrecy and Self-Governance," *New York Law School Law Review* 56, no. 1 (2011): 81–101.

6. Andreas Schedler, Larry Jay, and Marc F. Plattner, *The Self-Restraining State: Power and Accountability in New Democracies* (Boulder, CO: Lynne Rienner, 1999).

7. Ibid., 14–15.

8. Alon Peled, "Re-Designing Open Data 2.0," in *CeDEM13: Conference for e-Democracy and Open Government,* ed. Peter Parycek and Noella Edelmann, 2nd ed. (Krems: Edition Donau-Universität Krems, 2013), 244.

9. White House, *Open Government,* 4.

10. Ibid., 5.

11. Marijn Janssen, Yannis Charalabidis, and Anneke Zuiderwijk, "Benefits, Adoption Barriers and Myths of Open Data and Open Government," *Information Systems Management* 29, no. 4 (2012): 258; see also Peled, "Open Data," 244.

12. "The 8 Principles of Open Government Data," 2007, http://opengovdata.org.

13. White House, Office of Management and Budget, "Open Data Policy—Managing Information as an Asset," memorandum for the heads of executive departments and agencies, May 9, 2013, 5, https://www.whitehouse.gov/sites/default/files/omb/memoranda/2013/m-13-13.pdf.

14. Ibid., 2.

15. "The 8 Principles of Open Government Data," 2007, http://opengovdata.org.

16. Janssen, Charalabidis, and Zuiderwijk, "Open Data and Open Government"; Peled, "Open Data," 244.

17. N. M. Huijboom and T. A. Van den Broek, "Open Data: An International Comparison of Strategies," *European Journal of ePractice* (March/April 2011).

18. See also White House, *Open Government,* 16–17.

19. Frank Bannister and Regina Connolly, "The Trouble with Transparency: A Critical Review of Openness in e-Government," *Policy & Internet* 3, no. 1 (2011): 10–21.

20. Arvind Narayanan and Vitaly Shmatikov, "Myths and Fallacies of 'Personally Identifiable Information,'" *Communications of the ACM* 53, no. 6 (2010): 24–26.

21. Martin Frické, "Big Data and Its Epistemology," *Journal of the Association for Information Science and Technology* 66, no. 4 (2015): 651–61.

22. Peled, "Open Data," 246.

23. Gurstein, "Open Data"; also see O'Neill, "Transparency," 87–89.

24. Joseph E. Stiglitz, "On Liberty, the Right to Know, and Public Discourse: The Role of Transparency in Public Life," 7 at https://www0.gsb.columbia.edu/faculty/jstiglitz/download/2001_On_Liberty_the_Right_to_Know_and_Public.pdf.

25. As translated by David Luban in "The Principle of Publicity," in *The Theory of Institutional Design*, ed. Robert E. Goodin (Cambridge: Cambridge University Press, 1996), 155.

26. Ibid.

27. It is actually a bit more difficult to derive actual publicity from Kant's principle than this implies. It has been argued that Kant's principle applies not to the actual public, but to an ideal and rational public (Kevin Davis, "Kant's Different 'Publics' in the Justice of Publicity,' *Kant-Studien* 83, no. 2 [1992]: 170–84, as cited by Axel Gosseries, "Publicity," in *The Stanford Encyclopedia of Philosophy*, ed. Edward N. Zalta, Fall 2010 edition, http://plato.stanford.edu/archives/fall2010/entries/publicity/). Thus, it is conceivable that a law that passes the principle of publicity at the same time should not be made known to a non-ideal and frequently irrational public.

28. John Rawls, *A Theory of Justice* (Cambridge, MA: Belknap Press of Harvard University Press, 1971).

29. See, e.g., Jaeger and Bertot, "Transparency."

30. O'Neill, "Transparency," 76.

31. Jeremy Bentham, *The Works of Jeremy Bentham*, published under the Superintendence of his Executor, John Bowring (Edinburgh: William Tait, 1838–43), vol. 10.

32. Hanna Fenichel Pitkin, *The Concept of Representation* (Berkeley: University of California Press, 1967), 57.

33. Frank Cunningham. *Theories of Democracy: A Critical Introduction* (New York: Routledge, 2002), 3.

34. Dennis C. Mueller, "Public Choice: An Introduction," in *The Encyclopedia of Public Choice*, ed. Charles K. Rowley and Friedrich Schneider, vol. 1 (New York: Kluwer Academic, 2004).

35. John Stuart Mill, *The Collected Works of John Stuart Mill*, vol. XVII: *Essays on Politics and Society Part I*, ed. John M. Robson (Toronto: University of Toronto Press, 1977).

36. John Stuart Mill, *The Collected Works of John Stuart Mill*, vol. XIX: *Essays on Politics and Society Part II*, ed. John M. Robson (Toronto: University of Toronto Press 1977).

37. Joshua Cohen, "Deliberation and Democratic Legitimacy," in *Deliberative Democracy: Essays on Reason and Politics*, ed. James Bohman and William Rehg (Boston: MIT Press, 1997).

38. Amy Gutmann and Dennis Thompson, *Why Deliberative Democracy?* (Princeton, NJ: Princeton University Press, 2009), 13–21.

39. Gutmann and Thompson, *Deliberative Democracy*, 21.

40. Thomas Christiano, "The Authority of Democracy," *Journal of Political Philosophy* 12, no. 3 (2004): 273.

41. Gutmann and Thompson, *Deliberative Democracy*, 22.

42. Mill, *On Liberty*.

43. Thomas Christiano, "Democracy," in *The Stanford Encyclopedia of Philosophy*, ed. Edward N. Zalta, Spring 2015 edition, http://plato.stanford.edu/archives/spr2015/entries/democracy/.

44. Janssen, Charalabidis, and Zuiderwijk, "Open Data and Open Government," 260.

45. Anthony Downs, *An Economic Theory of Democracy* (New York: Harper, 1957).

46. Downs, *Economic Theory*.

47. Larry M. Bartels, "Uninformed Votes: Information Effects in Presidential Elections," *American Journal of Political Science* 40, no. 1 (1996): 194.

48. Frederick Schauer, "Transparency in Three Dimensions," *University of Illinois Law Review* (2011): 1344.

49. Thomas Christiano, *The Rule of the Many: Fundamental Issues in Democratic Theory* (Boulder, CO: Westview Press, 1996).

50. Kay Mathiesen, "Facets of Access: A Conceptual and Standard Threats Analysis," in iConference 2014 Proceedings, 2014, doi: 10.9776/14265.

51. Christiano, *Rule of the Many*; "Authority of Democracy"; "Democracy."

52. Christiano, "Democracy."

53. Ibid.

54. Samuel L. Popkin, "Information Shortcuts and the Reasoning Voter," in *Information, Participation, and Choice: An Economic Theory of Democracy in Perspective,* ed. Bernard Grofman (Ann Arbor: University of Michigan Press, 1993).

55. Popkin, "Information Shortcuts," 17–18.

56. Ibid., 18–33.

57. Ibid., 19.

58. Paul M. Healy and Krishna G. Palepu, "Information Asymmetry, Corporate Disclosure, and the Capital Markets: A Review of the Empirical Disclosure Literature," *Journal of Accounting and Economics* 31, no. 1 (2001): 406.

59. Brendan Nyhan and Jason Reifler, "When Corrections Fail: The Persistence of Political Misperceptions, *Political Behavior* 32, no. 2 (2010).

60. David G. Robinson et al., "Government Data and the Invisible Hand," *Yale Journal of Law & Technology* 11 (2008): 161.

61. Etzioni, "Transparency," 13.

62. It should be noted that powerful social actors may want more information gathered so they can use it in ways that are to their benefit (empowering the empowered). Thus, governments will have to carefully weigh the possible misuses of this information before they begin collecting it.

63. Internet Live Stats, "Internet Users by Country (2014)," http://www.internetlivestats.com/internet-users-by-country/.

*Chapter Eight*

# Why Security Trumps Privacy

## Kenneth Einar Himma

In this chapter, I consider the scope of informational privacy relative to our interests in security and argue, in particular, that the right to privacy must yield to these interests in the case of a direct conflict.[1] I begin with a case directly rooted in what I take to be ordinary intuitions and then continue with an argument grounded in the distinction between intrinsic and instrumental value. While I offer arguments from a number of different perspectives, I will be largely concerned with showing that the mainstream approaches to justifying state authority presuppose or imply that security interests can justify infringements of privacy rights. For example, I argue that utilitarian and contractarian justifications of state authority entail that when privacy conflicts with the most important security interests, those security interests trump the privacy interests. The claim that security trumps privacy is meant to express the more intuitive, but admittedly vague, idea that security and privacy are commensurable values and that, as a general matter, security is a more important value from the standpoint of morality than privacy.

## THE CONCEPT OF SECURITY

I take the concept of physical security to refer to a variety of interests a person has in the healthy continuation of his or her life and the life of his or her community. By "healthy," I mean a continuation of his or her life and community that is free of certain kinds of encumbrances characteristic of diseases and serious injuries in the case of a person's life and characteristic of certain kinds of crises in the life of a community.

At the outset, it is important to stress that security interests do not embrace interests not immediately related to the survival and minimal physiological well-being of the individual. My interest in security encompasses my interest in continuing life, my interest in being free from the kind of physical injury that threatens my ability to provide for myself, my interest in being free from the kind of financial injury that puts me in conditions of health- or life-threatening poverty, and my interest in being free from psychological trauma inflicted by others that renders me unable to care for myself.

It should be abundantly clear that morality protects these interests in the strongest terms available to it. Unless one is a complete skeptic about morality and moral objectivity, little argument is needed to show that we have a moral right to be free from acts that pose a high risk of causing either our death or grievous injuries to our bodies. Moreover, I would hazard that nonskeptics about morality would also accept that the moral right to physical security is sufficiently important that a state is, as a matter of political morality, obligated to protect it by criminalizing attacks on it, as a condition of its legitimacy. No state authority that failed to protect this right could be morally legitimate; at the very least, no state authority that failed to do so could be justified in claiming a legitimate monopoly over the use of force.

Security interests are not, however, just about our own well-being; they encompass the well-being of other persons whose activities conduce to our own physical security. We are social beings who live in societies in which there is a pronounced division of labour that makes the security of one person dependent upon the security of other persons in a variety of ways—some more abstract, some less abstract.

In part, what explains the moral importance of security interests is not just the content of certain interests they include, such as life, but also the range of interests and range of threats encompassed by this notion. As is true of the concept of privacy, an analysis of the concept of security entails nothing about whether our interests are protected by morality; substantive argument is needed to do this work. But understanding the concept of privacy helps us to see that the idea that such interests are of moral significance is both intelligible and plausible; the same is true of an analysis of the concept of security, conceived of as including serious threats to economic interests. Even at this preliminary point, one would expect security interests to be, at the very least, deserving, as a matter of political morality, of legal protection.

## Interests in Personal versus Collective Security

As it turns out, the concept of security is ambiguous as between two interpretations. My interest in personal security extends no further than my having an interest in my own security. Accordingly, my interest in personal security is concerned with my being protected from violent acts of assault and theft, but is indifferent with respect to other people being protected from such acts. My interest in collective security is an interest I have in the continuing existence of the social group I inhabit as providing an environment in which I and other people are free from the threats of violence and theft, and hence, which provides necessary, though not sufficient, prerequisites for the possibility of leading a meaningful human life. My interest in "national security," of course, is an interest in collective security—in particular, an interest in the continuing existence of the national group to which I belong.

There is, of course, an obvious relation between the two: if I live in a society that lacks collective security, then it is highly probable that I will also lack personal security. If people everywhere are rioting, then my individual, or personal, well-being is threatened—to some extent—even if I am sitting at home with all the doors bolted shut. If I feel I have to sit in a "safe room" to escape the direct threat to my security, then I am no longer leading a meaningful, flourishing life. For all practical purposes, my life is organized around defending myself from attacks on my life—surely not a desirable state of affairs for any practically rational being.

It might be that some persons are so selfish that they care about collective security only insofar as it impacts their own security, but I would be surprised—at the risk of overestimating the capacity for human empathy—if this were generally true. There is no doubt that there are many people with pathological psychological conditions who care only about their own interests and would hence care about collective security only because it bears on their personal security; for these people, the interests of other people count for nothing. But most people who share a communal life with us in society form social bonds—bonds that extend to people we have never met in virtue of their being a member of the same tribe or community. Although the empathetic bonds extended to those solely in virtue of tribe membership will be considerably weaker than those extended in virtue of the development of mutually satisfying personal relationships, they are significant bonds. Most of us who watched the floodwaters rise on people clinging for life to their roofs in New Orleans in the aftermath of Hurricane Katrina cared very deeply about what was happening to them. We care, of course, about our own security, but we also care a great deal about the security of our community—and not just because it bears on our safety and security.

I believe that morality protects some of these interests in collective and personal security to such an extent that they rise to the level of a right. Nevertheless, it is not at all clear how to draw the line between those interests not covered by a right to security and those interests covered by a right to security—and I cannot attempt to do so here.

The point I want to make here is that I am perfectly comfortable assuming our moral interests in privacy rise to the level of a right that a legitimate state is obligated to protect as a precondition of its legitimacy, and that, as I will show from a number of vantage points, the same is true of the right to security. In addition, I will provide a number of arguments—some of them grounded in individual morality and some grounded in major approaches to theorizing about the conditions a state must satisfy to be morally legiti-mate—that the right to security trumps the right to privacy when the two come into conflict.

## WHAT EXACTLY DOES "SECURITY TRUMPS PRIVACY" MEAN?

The meaning of the claim that security trumps privacy is not immediately obvious. At the outset, this much has been clear: if it is true that security trumps privacy, then it is also true that privacy is not an absolute right. Since the slogan "security trumps privacy" entails that when security and privacy are in some sort of direct conflict, security defeats privacy, it follows that privacy is not absolute.

But, quite frankly, this does not tell us much; the claim that privacy is nonabsolute does not tell us anything about how it should be weighed against other nonabsolute rights, and I do not wish to claim that security is an absolute right because I think this thesis is as counterintuitive as the thesis that privacy is an absolute right. If it were true, for example, that security was an absolute right, and privacy necessarily yields in the event of any conflict at all, then it would follow that it is morally justifiable for the state to sacrifice all interests in privacy if necessary to achieve just the slightest gain in security. I take this to be so obviously false as to constitute a counterexam-ple to the claim that security is absolute, at least relative to privacy.

The claim that security trumps privacy is meant to express the more intuitive, but admittedly vague, idea that security and privacy are commen-surable values and that, as a general matter, security is a more important value from the standpoint of morality than privacy. This does not commit me to the claim that all values are commensurable; perhaps there are two values that simply cannot be weighed against one another. But it does commit me to the claim that there is a hierarchy of commensurable morally protected inter-ests and rights, which include security, privacy, and perhaps others, and that security has a higher position in the hierarchy than privacy. Indeed, I am tempted to think that security interests—construed to include freedom from grievous threats to well-being, which include death, grievous bodily injury, and financial damage sufficiently extensive to threaten the satisfaction of basic needs, and hence survival, of a person—are at the top of the moral hierarchy, encompassing as they do the rights to life and physical preserva-tion.

The epistemology of resolving conflicts among rights is somewhat easier in the case of other interests that are not quite as broad as the security interest, as defined here. To say that the right to life trumps the right to property seems to entail that if one is confronted with a choice in which one has to damage one person's property or end the life of another person, it will always be the case that the right thing to do is to damage the property.

The epistemological problem of articulating a methodology for balancing competing security and privacy claims is quite difficult, and I cannot claim to be able to do that here because security might, in general, be more important than privacy, but privacy interests sometimes win in a conflict with security interests. It would not, for example, be permissible to disclose the most private information of one thousand people to save one person from being bruised severely on her leg. The relevant elements of the respective interests fall well short of being of comparable importance relevant to the privacy and security of affected persons.

Given the difficulties associated with working out a detailed epistemology of weighing competing privacy and security claims, I will have to content myself here with resting on another less than fully perspicuous formula to express my view. Other things being equal, a security interest defeats a privacy interest that has the same level of moral importance to privacy that the first element has to security.

Here is an example of what I have in mind, but it will fall far short of providing the sort of epistemic principle that would enable us to sort these issues out. If the life of one innocent person is at stake and can be saved only by disclosing the most private information of another innocent person, it is morally permissible, though obviously regrettable, to disclose that information in order to save the life. Here the most important value protected by security comes into conflict with the most important value protected by information privacy; the result in this case is that the security interest is more important.

Of course, this case—as well as the case in which we can save someone from a bruised leg only by disclosing the most private information of one thousand people—is theoretically uninteresting because it is so easily resolved. The cases of real interest are those posed by various provisions of the USA PATRIOT Act where there is no consensus among theorists and laypersons about how to balance the competing interests—even where it is clear that there is a genuine conflict that a particular provision is intended to resolve.

One conspicuous class of issues involves how to compare a case in which some more important element of security that involves a small class of persons, possibly consisting of one, is weighed against some less important element that involves a much larger class of persons. There are two dimensions to balancing these interests: (1) the importance of the interest relative to the type of interest involved, and (2) the number of people whose interests in security are implicated compared to the number of people whose interests in privacy are implicated. Both factors count for something in the weighing process, but I have disappointingly little to say by way of clarifying how the latter issue should be worked out. Again, the epistemological challenges are so difficult, multifaceted, and nuanced that I could not even begin to take a stab at them here.

How to resolve either issue in a principled way is not something I can admit to having even the beginnings of a theoretical account for; I merely want to make a multifaceted case that security interests are, as a general matter, ranked more highly on the hierarchy of commensurable moral values than privacy interests. This would entail that the class of all security interests possessed in whatever form by every person is more important, from the standpoint of morality, than the class of all privacy interests possessed in whatever form by the same individual. This, as we have seen, is compatible with situations in which someone's privacy interests defeat someone else's security interests.

But something like a detailed epistemology would be needed to make out a rigorous theoretical explanation of the idea that, other things being equal, security interests trump privacy interests that are as important to privacy as the security interests are to security. First, one would need some sort of vertical ranking of both security and privacy interests, which includes some mechanism for deciding where along the spectrum of privacy and security interests competing interests are of comparable internal importance. Thus, for example, it is easy to see that life trumps the most private facts about oneself, but not so easy to see where the interest in financial security lines up with other information about oneself that is private. Second, one would have to come up with a calculus for aggregating security and privacy interests across persons so that they can be properly weighed against one another. Is one life more valuable than the most private information of ten people? One hundred? One thousand? The problem here arises because the number of persons whose security interests are implicated might not be the same as the number whose privacy interests are implicated. Finally, one has to have some sort of reasonably accurate probability calculus for determining the likelihood that a measure proposing a trade of privacy for security will result in securing the appropriate increase in security without causing a greater diminishment in privacy than can be justified by that increase. As is readily evident, these are three quite difficult problems to work out.

I should point out that privacy interests and security interests are commensurable in the sense that they can at least sometimes be compared and weighed accurately in the case of conflict. This is surely so some of the time; as noted above, the interest someone has in the privacy of information about someone being homosexual cannot outweigh the interests of three hundred thousand people whose lives depend on the disclosure of that information. This, of course, is a far-fetched case, but it demonstrates beyond doubt that privacy and security interests will frequently be commensurable along both dimensions—the dimension of importance and the dimension of assessing that importance across different size classes of individuals—a prerequisite for being able to claim that, as a general matter, security interests, properly defined, are more important, other things being equal, than informational privacy interests.

This, however, should not be taken to imply that security and privacy interests are always commensurable. It might be that sometimes conflicts arise between security interests and privacy interests that cannot accurately be weighed because they are simply incommensurable values. For example, some property interests might not be commensurable with some privacy interests; sentimental attachments that are vital to a person's sense of well-being might, or might not be, commensurable with informational privacy interests. Nothing in the thesis of this chapter should be construed to imply that we can always resolve conflicts—or even that an omniscient God can always do so—because nothing in this chapter should be construed as implying or presupposing that it is a necessary truth that the relevant values are commensurable. I would surmise that in the vast majority of cases they surely are, but there might be some small class of cases in which they are not. I am not entirely sure of whether this latter claim is true, but the issue is much too complicated to take on here. I simply want to gesture in the direction of the potential concerns here.

## THE ARGUMENT FROM INTUITIVE CASE JUDGEMENTS

From an intuitive standpoint, the idea that the right to privacy is an absolute right seems utterly implausible. Intuitively, it seems clear that there are other rights that are so much more important that they easily trump privacy rights in the event of a conflict. For example, if a psychologist knows that a patient is highly likely to commit a murder, then it is, at the very least, morally permissible to disclose that information about the patient in order to prevent the crime—regardless of whether such information would otherwise be protected by privacy rights. Intuitively, it seems clear that life is more important from the standpoint of morality than any of the interests protected by a moral right to privacy.

Still, one often hears—primarily from academics in information schools and library schools, especially in connection with the controversy regarding the USA PATRIOT Act—the claim that privacy should never be sacrificed for security, implicitly denying what I take to be the underlying rationale for the PATRIOT Act. This also seems counterintuitive because it does not seem unreasonable to believe we have a moral right to security that includes the right to life. Although this right to security is broader than the right to life, the fact that security interests include our interests in our lives implies that the right to privacy trumps even the right to life—something that seems quite implausible from an intuitive point of view. If I have to give up the most private piece of information about myself to save my life or protect myself from either grievous bodily injury or financial ruin, I would gladly do so without hesitation. There are many things I do not want you to know about me, but should you make a credible threat to my life, bodily integrity, financial security, or health, and then hook me up to a lie detector machine, I will truthfully answer any question you ask about me. I value my privacy a lot, but I value my life, bodily integrity, and financial security much more than any of the interests protected by the right to privacy.

It is true, of course, that the hierarchy defined by my personal attributions of value may not reflect the hierarchy implied by the moral values themselves, but I would be surprised if there are any rational persons who would react differently to the choice presented above. Personal valuations can be idiosyncratic and for this reason not tell us anything about the corresponding moral values. But if it is true, as I would hypothesize, that very few, if any, people would choose to withhold some piece of private information about themselves if needed to save their lives or protect them from serious physical injury or financial ruin, that is a pretty good reason to think that these valuations do tell us something about morality. It would be very odd if, on the one hand, all, or nearly all, rational persons assign greater value to what I have described as the most important of security interests than to the most important of privacy interests where there is a genuine conflict between the two, but, on the other hand, morality assigned more value to privacy than to security. It is fairly easy to see, however, that my intuitions are widely shared in the United States. As an empirical matter, citizens in the United States frequently indicate a willingness to trade privacy for enhanced security. For example, a Harris poll conducted on October 4, 2004, three years after the attacks of 9/11, supports this claim.[2]

## CONSIDERATIONS OF INTRINSIC AND INSTRUMENTAL VALUE

In determining what morally protected interests people might have, philosophers frequently distinguish two kinds of value. An entity has instrumental value if, and only if, it has value as a means to some other valuable end. By contrast, an entity has intrinsic value if, and only if, it has value as an end in itself. Money is an example of something with only instrumental value; while money clearly has value as a means to other ends, such as nutrition and recreation, it does not seem to have any value as an end in itself. By contrast, one's own happiness is an example of something with intrinsic value. While it might make sense to value some other person's happiness as a means to some other end, it makes little sense to think of one's own happiness as primarily a means to some other end.

There are two concepts of intrinsic value that make use of this distinction—one primarily normative, and the other primarily descriptive. The normative concept is concerned with what rational moral agents ought to value as deserving of respect as ends in themselves. An entity intrinsically valuable in this sense has value as an end in itself, regardless of whether any rational agents actually value it this way. Thus, attributions of this kind of value are normative in the sense they are independent of the actual valuations of rational agents: if every rational agent failed to value an entity E with intrinsic value in this sense, each would be making a moral mistake. Attributions of intrinsic value in this normative sense are disconnected from what we actually value as an empirical matter.

Entities with intrinsic value in this sense are moral patients entitled to moral respect. Unlike something with only instrumental value, something with intrinsic value may not be used by an agent without some thought to its interests. Whereas the appropriate manner for thinking about things with only instrumental value is cost-benefit analysis, intrinsically valuable things have a right to some consideration in a moral agent's deliberations. For example, if nonhuman animals have intrinsic value in this sense, moral agents have an obligation to consider their interests in deliberations about acts that may affect those interests.

By contrast, the descriptive concept is concerned with identifying the sort of ends we characteristically pursue; the issue here is what, as an empirical matter, we typically regard worth pursuing for its own sake. An entity has intrinsic value in this sense if, and only if, as an empirical matter, most of us actually value it as an end in itself; a thing has instrumental value if, and only if, most of us value it as a means.

The moral significance of being regarded as an end in itself by moral persons—that is, of having intrinsic value in the descriptive sense—is different from that of being owed an obligation of respect—that is, of having intrinsic value in the normative sense. As persons, we have a morally protected interest in what we typically intrinsically value that is fundamental in not deriving from some other more basic interest. Persons have a special moral status in the world in virtue of being, or potentially being, both moral agents with obligations and moral patients with rights. Respect for beings with this status entails some measure of respect for their characteristic ultimate ends.

This helps to explain why we have fundamental moral rights to life and liberty. It is surely true that we view our lives and our liberty as instrumentally valuable; being free and alive are necessary conditions for pursuing a life that is happy. But it is also clearly true, I think, that we typically view continued conscious existence and liberty as vitally important ends in themselves; we care passionately about these things for their own sakes—and not merely because they are useful for other purposes. Given the vital intrinsic importance of these ends, it is not surprising that they are the objects of fundamental rights.

In any event, the following can safely be said about the significance of rights that protect what is intrinsically valuable relative to rights that protect what is instrumentally valuable. If X is a right that protects something that is instrumentally valuable as a means to Y, something that is intrinsically valuable and protected by a right, Y is the more important value of the two from the standpoint of morality because the value of X derives from the value of Y in the following sense: but for the intrinsic value of Y, X would not be instrumentally important, and hence, would receive no moral protection.

It seems to follow that rights where the value is purely instrumental are not as important as rights providing the ends to which the former rights are intended to secure. If our interest in X is purely instrumental as a means to securing Y, and both X and Y are morally protected in virtue of our interests in them, it seems clear that what is of ultimate importance from the standpoint of morality is Y. X is protected only because it facilitates the achievement of Y. If X did not conduce to Y in the appropriate way, X would not be protected, but Y would be, other things being equal. Since Y is the interest of ultimate value that is not contingent upon securing something else of moral importance, and X lacks this property, it seems reasonable to conclude that, from the standpoint of morality, Y is more important an interest than X.

This is surely true of property. As John Locke points out, we need to be able to consume material things to survive and to flourish in all the ways that human beings ought, as a moral matter, to flourish.[3] Property is ultimately protected then because of its crucial instrumentality to the achievement of these ends: without property, neither brute survival nor a morally meaningful life is possible. But clearly property is less important than brute survival, and property is also less important than whatever aspects of human flourishing to which property is essential are deemed significant enough to be ultimate ends protected by morality. This explains why property rights are less important than rights to life and liberty—though neither of the latter need necessarily be construed as being absolute.

The same also seems to be true of the right to informational privacy and the right to, or interest in, security. Informational privacy is valuable only as a means to an end. If certain pieces of information about me were not likely to be used in ways that have damaging consequences to my well-being, I would not care one bit whether they were widely known. My hair is dirty blond, something I take no pains to hide because the risk that someone will use this information to discriminate against me in some way that significantly diminishes my well-being is virtually nil. By contrast, I care about personal information about my health because my being at high genetic risk for a particular disease, if this turns out to be true, might lead a potential employer not to hire me. There is no piece of personal information about myself that

I value keeping private as an end in itself; privacy is all about avoiding embarrassing and otherwise damaging social consequences.

Security, on the other hand, is something I value instrumentally because it is a precondition for living a meaningful, enjoyable human life, but it is also something I value intrinsically. Continued sentient existence, bodily integrity—for example, having four limbs that I can move by volition—and financial security are ends in themselves and hence intrinsically valuable. Indeed, in many cases, I value privacy of information as a means to protecting security interests that I value intrinsically. Insofar as this is true, it seems reasonable to conclude that security is a more important value than privacy from the vantage point of individual and political morality.

Moreover, it is noteworthy that theorists who attempt to justify privacy protection in virtue of its value converge on characterizing its value, though not necessarily explicitly, as wholly instrumental. Charles Fried characterizes the value of privacy in terms of its value in facilitating intimate relationships; the value of privacy is a means to the intrinsic goods of personal intimacy.[4] Edward Bloustein argues that informational privacy is valuable as a means of protecting autonomy and one's sense of self as deserving of respect.[5] James Rachels argues that informational privacy protects against a number of harms and discriminatory behaviours as well as helps us control our social relationships with others.[6]

To my knowledge, no author has made a plausible case that any element of informational privacy is intrinsically valuable or counts as a basic constituent of human well-being or flourishing. If privacy is purely instrumentally valuable as a means of securing other goods, including security, that are intrinsically valuable and are constitutive of human well-being and flourishing, then it is reasonable to conclude that privacy is less important, from the standpoint of morality, than security.

## SECURITY VERSUS PRIVACY FOR THOMAS HOBBES AND JOHN LOCKE

A "classical" social contract theory is one that grounds the beginnings of an account of coercive state authority in an agreement that is actual in the sense that every party to the agreement has either expressly promised to be bound by the authority or done something that justifies attributing a promise to that party; in the latter case, the promise is said to be "tacit" or "implied."[7] Social contract theories that take this approach tend to be "classical" in the more intuitive sense that they are, as a historical matter, the earliest versions of the theories, which also correctly suggests that the approach of social contract theories has changed over time. I take the social contract theories of Hobbes and Locke, while differing in many respects, to be paradigmatic examples of classical social contract theories.

Classical social contract theories begin with the postulation of a mythical presocial state, called the state of nature, in which the goods that are needed to satisfy basic needs are insufficient to satisfy the needs of persons in that state. In the state of nature, there are none of the benefits associated with our living together cooperatively in a society of even the smallest scale.

To begin, there is no central authority of any kind, such as a state, to coercively enforce rules that limit behaviour in the state of nature. There is hence nothing in the state of nature, other than a person's own efforts, to protect him or her from being victimized by other people. The only limits on the behaviour of other persons towards any particular citizen are that citizen's ability to fend off physical attacks and other sorts of assaults on other interests he or she might have—such as an interest in food he or she has gathered.

Hobbes and Locke, the first classical social contract theorists, differed on whether morality governs life in the state of nature—Hobbes taking the counterintuitive position that everything is permissible there—but they clearly agreed that life in a state of nature is sufficiently unpleasant that any practically rational person will want out and be willing to sacrifice some measure of autonomy to a state in exchange for a similar sacrifice on the part of all others. While Hobbes believed this meant that people voluntarily submit to the authority of a sovereign whose authority is unlimited in the sense that the sovereign can commit no moral wrong against its subjects, Locke believed that people voluntarily submit to a state authority that enacts laws through democratic procedures while simultaneously respecting the natural moral rights to life, liberty, and property that persons have even in the state of nature. Either way, people are plausibly presumed to actually agree to be bound by the common authority as a way of escaping the state of nature, which both theorists believe is the only alternative to life in a society governed by a sovereign entity of some kind with coercive authority.

It is clear that the primary motivation in the state of nature for submitting to a coercive state authority is to escape the extreme unpleasantness associated with life in that state. One's physical security is always in danger in the state of nature; one's life is always in danger—whether directly or indirectly. One must, most obviously, be on guard against threats of deadly physical violence; the price of failure to be sufficiently vigilant will frequently be grievous bodily injury or death. Less obviously, one must guard against having one's few possessions taken by other persons.

Indeed, while Hobbes was pretty explicit that the very point of submitting to the sovereign was to gain some measure of physical security by giving up the unlimited freedom one has in the state of nature, Locke believed that the very point of the state authority is to protect property. Although it may therefore seem that Locke and Hobbes disagree about the basic value that people submit to authority to achieve, the appearance is misleading. Locke presumably believes that in the state of nature the principal threat to security consists in the threat of having one's few possessions taken, assuming that the extreme scarcity of the state of nature presents the primary threat to security against which people have to guard.

This is, in part, what explains a number of features of Locke's famous argument for natural property rights. First, Locke argues, in effect, that people need to consume material objects in the commons to survive and that the moral right of self-preservation ensures that there must be some morally justified way to take things out of the state of nature and appropriate them. Locke argued that we can acquire a property right in an unowned object by mixing something to which we have a property right—our labour—with that object in a way that creates new value. But that is simply the mechanism Locke identifies as acquiring a moral property right in something, which he has antecedently concluded must exist as a consequence of our right to preserve our lives—and the reasoning is compelling: if we have a moral right to Y, and X is a necessary means to Y, then we have a moral right to X.[8] The very foundation of Locke's argument for natural property rights is grounded in an interest in the preservation of one's life that is central to the notion of security.

Second, the compelling importance of the interest in security explains one of the limitations on the natural property rights that the state is morally obligated to protect. Locke famously limited the capacity to acquire property rights in the state of nature to objects that belong to no one—"original acquisition"—by two provisos, one more telling than the other, for our purposes. The less relevant proviso is that one can never acquire an object for the purpose of destroying or wasting it, which is intended to try to preserve the stock of scarce resources as much as possible. The more relevant proviso is that one can acquire a property right in an otherwise unowned material object only if there is enough of that object of similar quality left for everyone else. The idea here is that original acquisition in these circumstances does not exacerbate the conditions of scarcity that are likely to promote violent conflict among persons; as Locke puts the point, "No Body could think himself injur'd by the drinking of another Man, though he took a good Draught, who had a whole River of the same Water left him to quench his thirst. And the Case of Land and Water, where there is enough of both, is perfectly the same."[9] Accordingly, the state's most important obligation is to protect property, in Locke's view, precisely because the protection of property will ensure the public peace and minimize threats to physical security. Protection of property, though first among the state's priorities, is a means to the ultimate end of protecting security by ending the war of all against all that occurs in the state of nature. For classical social contract theorists, then, the most important value that submission to state authority is intended to pursue is security.

It follows, of course, that whatever the rest of the hierarchy of values might look like, the value of privacy is less, according to classical social contract theories, than the value of security. The rights to life and freedom from intentionally inflicted grievous physical injury trump the right to privacy, if there is such, when the latter comes into direct conflict with the former. Of course, Locke would rank the right of property alongside the other rights or interests mentioned above as constituting the right or interest in security because he believes protection of property is so important to protection of security. But classical social contract theories all converge in implying (1) that the right or interest in privacy is not absolute, and (2) that the right or interest in security trumps the right or interest in privacy when the two come into direct conflict—though neither theory tells us much about how or when these interests might directly conflict.

## SECURITY VERSUS PRIVACY FOR JOHN RAWLS AND ROBERT NOZICK

Perhaps the most fundamental idea in John Rawls's famous theory of justice as fairness is "the idea of a society as a fair system of social cooperation over time from one generation to the next."[10] Implicit in the claim that society is a fair system of cooperation, as Rawls understands that claim, are two further claims: (1) the terms that govern societal cooperation ought to be reasonably acceptable to each participant, and (2) those terms ought to be reasonable from the standpoint of the participant's own prudential interests.[11] Accordingly, Rawls attempts to identify the fair terms of cooperation by means of a hypothetical agreement among rational participants: the principles of justice constraining the state's lawmaking activities are, in his view, those that would be chosen by rational persons in an "original position."[12]

The crucial idea of the original position is defined by three elements of normative theoretical importance. First, persons in the original position must be free and equal to preclude any unfair bargaining advantages among the parties. Second, persons in the original position are assumed to be concerned only to maximize their own interests, and are not assumed to take an interest in the welfare of other persons.[13] The reason for this is that the most that can be assumed about the motivations of any human being is that she is motivated by her own prudential interests. While many human beings are motivated by altruistic considerations, not everyone is. To ensure that the principles chosen by persons in the original position are universally acceptable, Rawls defines the original position in such a way that the only psychological assumptions on which it depends are true of every human being. Third, and most important, persons in the original position are shielded from information about their own contingent abilities and circumstances by the so-called veil of ignorance.[14] Persons behind the veil of ignorance do not know, for example, how smart, athletic, physically attractive, socially adept, wealthy, or healthy they are.

A person in the original position, then, knows nothing about the abilities and properties that distinguish her from other people. In effect, such a person knows no more about herself than she does about any other person; what knowledge she has about herself is limited to knowledge of those properties that she shares with every other person.

There are two points worth making about the original position. First, it should be clear that the original position in Rawls's theory does the work of the state of nature in the classical social contract theories. The veil of ignorance forces a person to make a choice, and it should be clear that one of the relevant factors in making the choice will be to avoid some of the extreme unpleasantness associated with the state of nature. Second, the point of the veil of ignorance is to seal off information that is irrelevant as far as justice is concerned. Although the principles of justice are chosen by rational agents concerned only in advancing their own interests, they must make their choices only on the basis of information that is morally relevant. Information about a person's intellectual abilities is morally irrelevant because those abilities depend largely on circumstances over which she has little control: who her parents are, where she was born, and how much education she has are largely matters of luck. While such fortuitous circumstances are, of course, relevant with respect to one's prudential deliberations, they are irrelevant with respect to one's moral deliberations—and the choice of principles of justice is ultimately a moral choice. Accordingly, persons in the original position must choose principles that will advance their interests no matter what abilities and propensities they turn out to have.

The imposition of the veil of ignorance prevents persons in the original position from adopting an interest-maximizing principle for pursuing their prudential interests. In conditions of full information, a rationally self-interested agent can pursue a strategy that aims at maximizing her own utility. In particular, such an agent can assess the expected value of each act A by calculating the differential between the expected benefit of A—that is, the magnitude of the benefit associated with A multiplied by its probability—and the expected cost of A—that is, the magnitude of the cost associated with A multiplied by its probability—and select the act with the highest expected value. By selecting the act with the highest expected value, the agent optimizes her prospects for maximizing her own utility.

In conditions of highly restricted information, however, rationally self-interested agents must adopt a more conservative "maximin" strategy and choose behaviours that are minimally necessary to protect themselves against highly undesirable outcomes. As Rawls describes it, the maximin strategy "tells us to identify the worst outcome of each available alternative and then to adopt the alternative whose worst outcome is better than the worst outcomes of all the other alternatives."[15] The maximin rule, unlike the ordinary prudential strategy of maximizing expected value, takes into account only the relative magnitude of the worst possible outcomes; it does not take into account any information that assesses the comparative probabilities of the various options because such information is not available. In effect, then, rationally self-interested agents deploy the maximin strategy as a means for avoiding the most unacceptable of undesirable outcomes.

While some authors argue that the maximin strategy is not the only rational strategy applicable in situations of high risk and uncertainty,[16] it should be clear that something very like the maximin strategy is rationally deployed in such situations. A somewhat perverse example is helpful in illustrating the point. From the standpoint of prudential rationality alone, it is rational for someone with full information to play the most dangerous games if the prize is large enough and the odds of losing are remote enough. Whether it is prudentially rational, for example, to play a game of Russian roulette with one bullet depends on the amount of the prize and on the number of empty chambers in the gun. While it would clearly be irrational to play if I know the prize is one dollar and there is only one empty chamber in the gun, it is clearly rational to play if I know the prize is $100 million and there are six billion empty chambers; one incurs a substantially greater risk of death every time one gets into an automobile. In these cases, there is sufficient information to adopt an interest-maximizing strategy that will sometimes dictate playing the game. However, a more conservative maximin strategy is appropriate from the standpoint of prudential rationality if I lack information about some of the salient probabilities. For example, if I am not told how many empty chambers there are in the gun, it is clearly rational to adopt a maximin strategy that requires me to decline the game as a means of avoiding the worst of undesirable outcomes.

Although the motivation for the veil of ignorance is largely moral, its effect on the deliberations of agents in the original position is prudential in character. Since the veil of ignorance denies people any information about themselves that would tell them how likely they are to win or lose in society, they must adopt a more conservative prudential strategy for selecting the principles of justice than the interest-maximizing strategy that is available in conditions of full information. They must, as a matter of prudential rationality, choose those principles that are minimally necessary to enable them to avoid the very worst outcomes. Since a maximin strategy will enable them to do this, it is rationally deployed by agents in the original position.

Rawls believes that a person in the original position will avoid the very worst outcomes by choosing a principle that affords her maximum liberty compatible with everyone else's having comparable liberty and a principle that assures that economic inequalities will conduce to her benefit no matter where she winds up in society. According to the Liberty Principle, "Each person is to have an equal right to the most extensive scheme of basic liberty compatible with a similar scheme of liberty for others."[17] According to the Difference Principle, "Social and economic inequalities are to be arranged so that they are both (a) reasonably expected to be to everyone's advantage, and (b) attached to positions and offices open to all."[18] The person in the original position thus uses a maximin strategy to enable her to avoid catastrophic situations in which her freedom is denied or in which economic inequalities are permitted at her expense.

Here it is essential to consider some of the catastrophic situations that the two principles of justice are chosen to avoid. The Liberty Principle, which allows the maximum freedom to each compatible with similar freedom for all, takes directly into account the consequences to physical security of allowing people to do whatever they feel like doing. Utterly unrestricted freedom is likely to lead people to resolve conflicts of interests by violent behaviours—violence being an obvious threat to physical security. The Difference Principle seeks to protect people from the effects of life-threatening poverty when there are more than enough resources to satisfy everyone's basic needs, which is likely to result in violent conflicts. The concern here is to avoid the catastrophic consequences associated with debilitating illness, injury, or disability that prevent a person from providing for her own needs. These are clearly provisions and concerns that are intended to protect people from threats to life and from threats of grievous bodily injury or debilitating disease and disability, which fall within, if not the province of, physical security—something closely related.

It should be noted that nothing in these principles necessarily protects any of the privacy interests that are typically protected by privacy rights. Of course, in some cases, one might argue that protection of privacy is necessary to ensure the full exercise of liberty rights, but these are two different issues that are only contingently related; after all, the value of privacy is not one accepted universally among cultures, and what is considered private varies from culture to culture depending on other contingent features that vary with culture. As was the case with the classical theories, the right to, or moral interest in, privacy is not absolute and must clearly sometimes yield to protection of physical security.

Rawls's theory is sometimes treated as though one must test the legitimacy of every proposed law by subjecting it to analysis from the original position—something I doubt to be correct. But if this is the correct interpretation, no practically rational self-interested agent would choose a principle making the interest in privacy absolute.

The following is an easy way to see this: suppose we were considering a law that made it possible for the state to combat terrorism by obtaining the library records of patrons meeting a certain description without disclosing to patrons that their records have been disclosed. What would someone in the original position say about this? It depends on how much more we assume about its efficacy. If, for example, the law would save one hundred thousand lives while slightly changing the reading habits of just one person, it would be irrational not to accept the act. However, if the act would prevent just one broken arm while severely changing the reading habits of millions of people, then it would probably be irrational to accept the act. From the original position, the act's legitimacy turns largely on the effects it will have on both security and speech—issues that are empirical in character. Because we do not know from the original position exactly what the facts are with respect to the relevant numbers, we will, in adopting the maximin perspective, seek to choose the rule with the most acceptable of the worst outcomes. In other words, we will choose to allow the state to combat terrorism this way be-cause, from a position of highly limited information, the worst possible out-come of adopting the rule is better than the worst possible outcome of not adopting the rule: changing the reading habits of millions without saving any lives is preferable to the number of lives that might be lost in a worst-case scenario if the rule is not adopted.

From our current vantage point in combating terrorism, of course, this sort of provision, which mirrors one in the USA PATRIOT Act,[19] is clearly not justifiably adopted. The problem is that, given our particular experience with terrorists, we have enough information to be justified in believing that a rule like this is not likely to achieve its purposes since we have good reason to believe terrorists are not likely to seek out information in a way easily traced to them. The issue, however, is what would we say when we lack sufficient information to estimate the expected costs and benefits of such a provision. Because we have adopted something like a maximin perspective from this position, we would adopt a presumption in favour of what we rationally take to be the most important value from a self-interested perspec-tive. From the standpoint of self-interest, most people will share the intuition that security is more important than privacy and make a presumption in favour of the act given its purpose.

Accordingly, in the absence of any information which would enable us to predict the efficacy of such a restriction on privacy, the worst-case scenario that the maximin strategy forces us to reject is being killed by terrorists. The worst-case scenario with respect to privacy is that the state learns we are reading something that is really embarrassing. On the assumption that we cannot estimate the probabilities from the original position, we choose what seems to us from a position of much greater information one of the most knuckleheaded provisions of the PATRIOT Act.

In closing this section, it is worth noting one conspicuous difference between classical social contract theories and Rawls's contract theory. The former relies on the idea that people actually consent to the social contract that establishes the state authority, whereas the latter relies on the weaker idea that people in the original position would consent to the two principles of justice if they were in a position that they are clearly not in. Otherwise put, the classical theories rely on actual consent, whereas Rawls relies on hypothetical consent. Something like this, as we will see, will turn out to be true of Robert Nozick's version of contract theory.

Classical social contract theories of legitimacy begin with the mythical state of nature—a presocietal state that is the alternative to life in society under a central lawmaking authority. The state of nature, as we have seen, offers none of the benefits of society: no technology, no art, no communion with other people, and no family. Because life in the state of nature is a "warre of everyone against everyone" and is "nasty, brutish, and short,"[20] classical social contract theories infer that people either explicitly or implicitly consent to the authority of the state as a means of avoiding such a bad life. Since any social arrangement, and hence any state, is preferable to the state of nature, the state can be presumed legitimate as something to which citizens actually or impliedly promise obedience.

Nozick believes there are at least two problems with this strategy. First, it assumes that people would always behave very badly towards one another. Indeed, this comes close to assuming that people are inherently violent and bad. If the intrinsic goodness of people cannot confidently be assumed, neither can the intrinsic badness of people. Second, it assumes that there could not be a state that is worse than the state of nature. As Nozick points out, there are some possible states so bad, so oppressive, that even the state of nature would win. I would rather live in the state of nature than be subject to state-sponsored torture.

Accordingly, Nozick begins from a more modest assumption. He focuses on what he thinks is the best anarchic alternative to the state. In particular, he focuses upon a presocial situation in which people generally, though not always, satisfy moral constraints, and generally, though not always, act as they ought. In such an anarchic situation, people do not always behave well, but they usually do. According to Nozick, "If one could show that the state would be superior even to this most favored situation of anarchy, the best that realistically can be hoped for, or would arise by a process involving no morally impermissible steps, or would be an improvement if it arose, this would provide a rationale for the state's existence; it would justify the state."[21]

In arguing for his libertarian theory of legitimacy, Nozick starts from certain Lockean assumptions about the state of nature and natural rights and by a series of steps that he takes to be inevitable, each one permissible under morality, shows that every rational person starting from the best possible anarchic situation would move to a situation with a minimal state—a minimal state being one that limits its coercive functions to protection of the moral rights to life, liberty, and property.

It is important to realize that there are two major streams to the analysis—and both play a crucial role in justifying the general conclusion that the minimal state is morally legitimate. The first is, of course, that each transition from anarchic existence to the minimal state is morally permissible. The second is that each transition is inevitable given certain basic facts about human well-being and psychology. Although it may appear less important, the second step is vital to the success of the argument. Nozick's argument will justify only those states that arise out of such a series of transitions. Nozick takes care of this problem by arguing that each step in the series is inevitable, given certain basic facts about human beings. Because there is, in effect, no other way to get from the anarchic state of nature to the minimal state, the minimal state can be presumed legitimate no matter where it occurs. For this reason, Nozick can validly draw the general conclusion that every minimal state is morally legitimate.

Although Nozick regards the state of nature as more pleasant than Hobbes and Locke did, he also realizes that life in the state of nature remains both unpleasant and unstable; people may not always behave badly, but they frequently do enough to make the state of nature a condition people want to escape—and this, as a matter of practical rationality, requires some sort of response. Initially, people deal with this difficulty by forming groups devoted to the mutual protection of all their members, a response that is morally permissible under the natural law, since people have a right to form consensual associations, and also have the right to defend themselves and other persons.

This will alleviate some of the difficulties associated with defending oneself, but Nozick argues such associations will have to be refined in certain ways. First, everyone will always be "on call," which involves tremendous inconvenience. Second, it is not clear how protective associations will resolve conflicts between their members. Third, it is not clear how to resolve disputes between members and nonmembers.

Most important, problems are likely to arise as a number of protective associations arise in the same region and members of different protective associations begin to have conflicts. While such problems are not likely to become serious when both associations agree on the disposition of the case, they can become serious when they disagree. If one association wants to punish the member of another association that wants to protect its member, the two associations are likely to wage battles. The eventual result of such battles will be that one protective association—a dominant protective association that will become a justified minimal state—will achieve ascendancy in the region, because opponents either are absorbed after defeat or move away.

Whether the minimal state is morally legitimate, in Nozick's view, will depend in part on whether it attempts in good faith to stay within the limits of the Lockean laws of nature. If it systematically and intentionally aggresses against the natural rights of others, then it will not be legitimate; it will be an "outlaw" association. If, however, it makes a point of respecting the natural rights of persons and minimizes violations, it will be legitimate to that extent.

As is true of classical social contract theory, the primary motivation for every rational being to move from a presocial state of nature to a society with a central authority is to achieve more security than is otherwise possible—even though Nozick's conception of the state of nature is somewhat more benign than that of the classical theories. Moreover, the minimal state is subject to the constraints of the Lockean conception of morality, which takes the primary purpose of the state to be protection of property—presumably because property is necessary to the survival of each person and is hence the most likely motivation for persons to threaten the security, and therefore rights to life, of others. To prevent such conflicts, the state must be especially concerned with protecting the right to property, and hence, derivatively, the right to life.

Although it is true that some privacy interests either fall within the ambit of liberty interests or are prerequisites for the meaningful exercise of liberty requirements—I am less likely to freely express my right to speech on the Internet if I feel that my movements and anonymity are tracked and compromised—it is crucial to note that Nozick's theory of the legitimate minimal state, as is true of every other theory we have considered, does not expressly name privacy as an interest or right that the minimal state is morally required to protect as a precondition of its legitimacy.

This suggests that, for Nozick's theory as for each other theory we have considered, security is the most important value. Although there is no talk of a "right" to security, security provides the morally legitimate motive for making the various transitions that move each rational person from a presocial state of nature to life under a society with a coercive and centralized state authority. This entails that security is the ultimate value that the state is morally obligated to protect and that when legitimate security interests directly conflict with legitimate privacy interests of comparable importance, the former trump the latter. Thus, for Nozick, as with every other theorist we have considered, if there is a privacy right, it is far from being absolute.

## SECURITY VERSUS PRIVACY FOR UTILITARIAN
## THEORIES OF STATE LEGITIMACY

According to utilitarianism, the moral value of any act is fully determined by its effect on net aggregate utility among members of the community. Utilitarian moral theories posit a particular state of affairs as objectively good—the maximization of aggregate utility—and define an act as morally right to the extent that it promotes this favoured state of affairs and morally wrong to the extent that it fails to promote this favoured state of affairs. Since an act's effect on utility is an extrinsic feature of the act, utilitarian theories presuppose that the moral quality of an act does not depend on its intrinsic, or inherent, features, and hence that no act is inherently good or inherently bad. Acts are good or bad only insofar as they conduce or fail to conduce to the utility of members in the community.

As a general moral theory, utilitarianism applies both to acts of individuals and to acts of the state. Applied to the state, it implies that the state's lawmaking authority is constrained by a duty to enact laws that maximally promote aggregate community utility.[22] Utilitarian theories of legitimacy, then, assess acts of the state entirely in terms of whether they sufficiently conduce to the favoured state of affairs—maximal promotion of utility among the citizenry. The state's sole obligation, according to this view, is to act in ways that have the effect of maximally promoting net utility among its citizens.[23]

It is commonly thought that utilitarian theories that evaluate acts in terms of total utility are inconsistent with the idea that individuals have any moral rights of the sort we commonly take for granted. There are two related reasons for this. First, it is easy to come up with counterexamples that seem to show that utilitarianism requires what we take to be the violation of any right. For example, a doctor would be morally obligated under utilitarianism to painlessly kill a healthy but otherwise irreversibly depressed homeless person with no friends or family in order to harvest his organs and save the lives of persons who contribute greatly to maximizing utility. Second, as we saw earlier, the infringement of a right, as a conceptual matter and a matter of substantive morality, cannot be justified by the consequences to public utility of doing so; similarly, Nozick speaks of side constraints as doing the same work. Rights, on this common conception, "trump" consequences. The problem with utilitarian "rights" is that, as the counterexamples show, any interest we take to be covered by a right can be justifiably infringed if the consequences of doing so are favourable enough. As far as moral rights are concerned, utilitarianism seems inconsistent with there being any.

It is crucial to note, however, that the issue of whether the state should recognize and protect legal rights is an analytically distinct issue from the issue of whether there are any moral rights. It might be that any failure on the part of the state to protect what we (mis)take—if act utilitarianism is true—to be foundational moral rights would result in the kind of social instability that is inconsistent with maximally promoting social utility. If this turns out to be true, then the state will be obligated, under a utilitarian theory of legitimacy, to provide legal protection of rights to life, liberty, property, and presumably privacy—although these, strictly speaking, will not qualify as "moral" rights.

Even so, it seems clear that privacy interests will generally receive lesser protection than security interests under such a theory. If utility is defined subjectively, then it seems clear that this will be the case; many people in the former Soviet Union who are better off in terms of liberty, and possibly even income, have expressed preferences to return to the totalitarian regime precisely because they felt more secure under the protection of a police force that seemed to be everywhere. This, of course, is not an obviously irrational preference. I would prefer physical security over just about any other right—with the possible exception of a certain affluent standard of living. Indeed, despite all the hysteria in the United States about the violation of privacy rights by laws such as the USA PATRIOT Act, most people seem to be as happy, on any subjective measure, as always.

If, on the other hand, utility is defined objectively in terms of well-being, it seems clear that security is more important than privacy. It seems very difficult to make the case that, as an objective matter, people are better off in terms of well-being if they sacrifice security, other things being equal, for privacy. While privacy interests seem important in cultures like ours with well-being as an objective matter, it seems absolutely clear that security from death or grievous bodily injury is more important than privacy interests and will trump those interests in the event of a direct conflict, as I have defined that idea. According to utilitarian theories of state legitimacy, then, it is reasonable to conclude that privacy interests or rights are not absolute.

Again, the claim is not that any increase in security, no matter how small, is likely to offset any sacrifice in privacy, no matter how extensive. Doubts about the efficacy of a law in protecting security at the expense of privacy might have the effect of making people very unhappy even when these doubts are incorrect. But, other things being equal, people will regard the most important security interests they have as being morally more important than the most important privacy interests they have, suggesting that security is more important than privacy on a subjective conception of utility; and, on an objective conception of flourishing and well-being, that seems straightforwardly correct. Whether the utilitarian standard is defined in terms of subjective conceptions of happiness or pleasure, or whether it is defined in terms of objective conceptions of well-being and flourishing, a utilitarian theory of legitimacy seems clearly to afford more protection, other things being equal, to security interests than to privacy interests. As I have put this idea elsewhere, security trumps privacy.

## CONCLUSION

In this chapter, I have argued that the moral interest in or right to privacy is not absolute and is sometimes outweighed by the moral interest in or right to security. I have argued that many of the mainstream approaches to normative theories of state legitimacy presuppose, assert, or imply that privacy is less important from the standpoint of political morality than security. Accordingly, under ordinary intuitions and each of these theories, security interests trump, or outweigh, privacy interests when the two come into conflict.

## NOTES

1. This chapter draws from previously published material. See Kenneth Einar Himma, "Privacy Versus Security: Why Privacy is Not an Absolute Value or Right," *San Diego Law Review* 44, no. 4 (2007): 857.

2. Harris Interactive, "The Harris Poll #73: Public Perceptions of Likelihood of Future Terrorist Attack Leads to Continuing Support for Tough Surveillance Measures to Prevent Terrorism" (2004), www.prnewswire.com/news-releases/public-perceptions-of-likelihood-of-future-terrorist-attack-leads-to-continuing-support-for-tough-surveillance-measures-to-prevent-terrorism-according-to-harris-interactive-74024172.html?$G1Ref.

3. John Locke, *The Second Treatise of Government*, ed. C. B. Macpherson (Indianapolis, IN: Hackett, 1980).

4. Charles Fried, *An Anatomy of Values* (Cambridge, MA: Harvard University Press, 1970), 140–44.

5. Edward J. Bloustein, "Privacy as an Aspect of Human Dignity: An Answer to Dean Prosser," *New York University Law Review* 39 (1964): 962, 973–74, 1002–1003.

6. James Rachels, "Why Privacy Is Important," *Philosophy & Public Affairs* 4, no. 4 (1975): 323, 325–30.

7. Thomas Hobbes, *Leviathan*, ed. Richard Tuck (Cambridge: Cambridge University Press, 1991), 88–89. See also Locke, *The Second Treatise*, 18–39.

8. It seems clear that people have a moral right to consume what they need to survive if it does not belong to anyone else. But this gets us, at most, the existence of moral property rights in objects needed to survive; it would not justify a moral right to accumulate the amounts of property currently held by the world's richest persons.

9. Locke, *Second Treatise*, 291.

10. John Rawls and Erin Kelly, *Justice as Fairness: A Restatement* (Cambridge, MA: Harvard University Press, 2001), 5.

11. Ibid., 6.

12. John Rawls, *A Theory of Justice*, rev. ed. (Cambridge, MA: Belknap Press of Harvard University Press, 1999), 15–19.

13. Ibid., 10.

14. Ibid., 11.

15. Rawls and Kelly, *Justice as Fairness*, 97.

16. See, e.g., John C. Harsanyi, "Can the Maximin Principle Serve as a Basis for Morality? A Critique of John Rawls's Theory," *American Political Science Review* 69, no. 2 (1975): 594, 598.

17. Rawls, *Theory of Justice*, 53.

18. Ibid.

19. See 50 U.S.C. § 1861 (Supp. IV 2004).

20. Hobbes, *Leviathan*, 88–89.

21. Robert Nozick, *Anarchy, State, and Utopia* (New York: Basic Books, 1974), 5.

22. Henry Sidgwick, "Utility and Government," in *Social and Political Philosophy: Contemporary Readings*, ed. George Sher and Baruch A. Brody (Fort Worth, TX: Harcourt Brace College Publishers, 1999), 35.

23. John Stuart Mill argued that considerations of utility justified the general principle that the state can legitimately prohibit only those acts that are harmful to others. According to Mill's view, utility is most likely to be maximized in a society where people are free to develop and act on their own conceptions of the good; people who are allowed to pursue their own values and plans are more likely to develop the sorts of skills and abilities that will make them useful to other people. John Stuart Mill, *On Liberty*, ed. David Bromwich and George Kateb (New Haven, CT: Yale University Press, 2003), 86–138.

*Chapter Nine*

# Why Privacy and Accountability Trump Security

## Adam D. Moore

Imagine you live in a world where each individual is responsible for his or her own security. This world is full of risks, from thieves, thugs, and extortionists to grifters, Ponzi-scheme artists, and hustlers. Also, imagine that you are not very good at providing security for yourself and decide to outsource this important task. Surveying the possibilities, you find that by moving to different areas, there are several distinct options.

In the Thomas Hobbes security zone, individuals are monitored around the clock without regard to privacy, liberty, or property. Total transparency and access yield nearly complete security. Using facial-recognition technology, virtual frisking, big data and predictive analytics, and video recorders, along with a host of other known and secret technologies, each individual is monitored and recorded around the clock. The chief security officer, known as Mr. Leviathan, is virtually unaccountable for how he conducts his business and is not subject to the sorts of intrusions common to typical Thomas Hobbes policy holders. Moreover, Mr. Leviathan is more or less free to pick fights with other security providers in other zones, upgrade surveillance equipment, and militarize his security forces at the expense of policy holders.

John Locke Inc., the primary competitor to Thomas Hobbes, falls at the other extreme. In the John Locke zone, security is promoted by protecting individual rights to life, liberty, property, and privacy. With a known and written law, recourse to impartial judges, and robust accountability provisions, basic rights are set aside only in rare cases. When rights are set aside, automatic and public review processes inform everyone of the reasons for some action or policy. Moreover, security officers are not free to start fights with other security agencies and are subject to the same sorts of rights and penalties as other John Locke policy holders.

While fictional, there are some interesting lessons to be learned by engaging in this sort of thought experiment. If you had to pick between these security agencies, which one would you choose and why? Arguably, if these were the only two choices, the obvious winner is the John Locke agency. There are lots of reasons. The most compelling, in my view, is that the Thomas Hobbes agency itself becomes a security threat. Without robust accountability, it would be hard to maintain that giving this sort of power to some company or government promotes, rather than undermines, individual security. Criminals, terrorists, or grifters are nowhere near as dangerous as Thomas Hobbes style governments. There are too many examples for us to deny Lord Acton's dictum that "power tends to corrupt, and absolute power corrupts absolutely."[1] If information control yields power and total information awareness radically expands that power, then we have good reason to pause before trading privacy for security.

Also note how security is tied to accountability and to the overall legitimate functions of an agency or state. Simply put, the more a state does for us, the more power it will likely need to complete its tasks. Standing against this increase in power will be the accountability provisions necessary to protect security. Giving a security provider a big gun with no or few accountability protections will debase security.

But this is exactly what we have been doing in the United States for decades. Consider the National Security Agency's current bulk collection of data under the Planning Tool for Resource Integration, Synchronization and Management (PRISM), which would have remained secret had it not been for the whistle-blowing of Edward Snowden.[2] Or consider abandoned programs such as the Terrorist Information and Prevention System (TIPS) and Total Information Awareness (TIA), which were attempts by the U.S. government to circumvent Fourth Amendment privacy protections.[3] Proposed new legislation, such as the Cyber Information Sharing and Protection Act (CISPA), would expand both surveillance authority and secrecy for our government agencies.[4]

In response to these concerns, security officials typically offer one of four different arguments. According to the "just trust us" argument, we should let those in power decide the correct balance between privacy, accountability, and security. A second view minimizes privacy interests by calling into doubt the activities privacy may shield. This view, called "nothing to hide," maintains that individuals should not worry about being monitored. Only those who are engaged in immoral and illegal activity should worry about government surveillance. A third strand, similar to the "nothing to hide" argument, is the view that "security trumps." This latter account holds that security interests are, by their nature, weightier than privacy claims. Security is about life, limb, and property, and these interests will nearly always trump privacy or accountability concerns. Ken Himma, in this volume, defends a "security trumps" position. The final argument centers on consent. Many individuals voluntarily offer information, even private information, on social media sites, email, web pages, blogs, smartphones, and the like. By engaging in these activities, we are consenting that others may watch. The "consent" argument maintains that citizens have agreed to be monitored.

After presenting each of these arguments in more detail, an analysis and critique will be offered. While perhaps compelling at first glance, each of these arguments has serious flaws and should be rejected. The reason privacy and accountability trump security is because without the appropriate balance between these three important values, there can be no robust security. [5]

## "JUST TRUST US" — TRADING CIVIL RIGHTS FOR SECURITY

According the "just trust" account, we should give the benefit of the doubt to those in power and assume that officials will not override individual rights without just cause. While moral saints are rare, the individuals who pursue public office generally do so for noble and moral purposes. Public officials typically seek office to promote the public good and are generally well-meaning and sincere people. Applying community norms, these individuals typically create policy with the best of intentions. Because of their position, public officials and government agents are more knowledgeable about the risks and threats that we face. Moreover, this process for balancing privacy and security is efficient in that those with the relevant information can make timely decisions to maximize security protections in an ever-changing world. Finally, accountability is ensured because if citizens don't agree with the way security is provided, they can always elect new leaders.

Arguably, there are good reasons to distrust this method of establishing an appropriate balance between privacy and security. Justice Brandeis, dissenting in *Olmstead v. United States*, wrote, "Experience should teach us to be most on our guard to protect liberty when the government's purposes are beneficent. Men born to freedom are naturally alert to repel invasion of their liberty by evil-minded rulers. The greatest dangers to liberty lurk in insidious encroachment by men of zeal, well-meaning but without understanding."[6] Brandeis, like Lord Acton quoted in the opening, worries about human corruptibility and the incremental debasing of liberty and privacy. In a crisis, even the most noble among us are susceptible to favouritism, stubbornness, and suspect reasoning. While the cases noted below are based in U.S. history and law, the point being made is more general.

Consider President Abraham Lincoln's situation at the start of the Civil War. Lincoln declared a state of emergency and suspended the legal rights of citizens in the border states of Maryland, Kentucky, Missouri, and Tennessee. In addition to arresting nineteen members of the Maryland state legislature, Lincoln imprisoned over thirteen thousand civilians and suspended the writ of *habeas corpus*.[7] While Lincoln was not an "unthinking" man of zeal, the notion of a president exercising "emergency powers" in a time of crisis based on his own subjective assessment of the issues at stake sets a bad precedent.

Several other cases also deserve mention. The internment of Japanese-Americans during World War II, the McCarthyism of the1950s, the COINTELPRO operations and the Church Committee findings of the 1970s, and the numerous abuses connected to the USA PATRIOT Act each point towards reasons why "just trust us" is a bad idea.[8] In this volume, Nadine Strossen highlights numerous further abuses in her chapter "Post-9/11 Government Surveillance, Suppression & Secrecy." For each of these cases, in hindsight and after cool reflection, few would maintain that the balance between security, accountability, and privacy was appropriately struck.

To understand how weak the "just trust us" argument really is, imagine if we turn the tables, so to speak. Imagine that we gave power and authority to a secretive group of tenured and untouchable university professors to oversee the operations of the National Security Agency (NSA), Central Intelligence Agency (CIA), and Federal Bureau of Investigation (FBI). Agents who are found to be "questionable" by these professors are monitored, sanctioned, seized, and held without bail. Tenured university professors are well-meaning and good people. If the rationale for "just trust us" is compelling, then the NSA, CIA, FBI, and other law-enforcement groups should be fine with this process of trading their privacy and liberty for our security. My guess is that these groups would object precisely because the process is secretive and those in control are unaccountable.

## THE "NOTHING TO HIDE" ARGUMENT

A counterpart to the "just trust us" view is the "nothing to hide" argument.[9] According to this argument, we shouldn't care if our security providers are watching because we have nothing to hide. Only criminals would care and we should not let them determine surveillance policy. The basic rationale of the "nothing to hide" view is that objecting to surveillance is admitting some sort of guilt. Eric Schmidt of Google sums this up nicely: "If you have something that you don't want anyone to know, maybe you shouldn't be doing it in the first place."[10]

As with "just trust us," this argument is rather weak. There is sensitive personal information that we each justifiably withhold from others, not because it points towards criminal activity, but because others simply have no right to access this information. Imagine that upon exiting your house one day, you find a person searching through your trash, painstakingly putting the shredded notes and documents back together. In response to your stunned silence, this person proclaims, "You don't have anything to worry about—there is no reason to hide, is there?" Consider someone's sexual or medical history. Imagine someone visiting a library to learn about alternative life-styles not accepted by the majority. Hiding one's curiosity about, for example, a gay lifestyle may be important in certain contexts. This is true of all sorts of personal information, such as religious preferences or political party affiliations. If we understand privacy as the right to control access to and uses of bodies, locations, and certain sorts of information, then the fact that someone has "nothing to hide" is simply irrelevant in most cases.

Finally, as with "just trust us," it is easy to turn the "nothing to hide" argument on its head. Certainly the politician, police chief, and NSA agent have nothing to hide. They should embrace total transparency like the rest of us. Resistance to this sort of monitoring indicates guilt on their part. Again, imagine our group of secretive, powerful, and unaccountable university professors watching over the NSA, CIA and FBI. Suppose these professors have the power and means to deploy secretive surveillance technologies against security agents who are deemed suspicious or threatening. As with "just trust us," this case highlights a hidden assumption—that we owe each other transparency and there is no difference between "can" and "should." In our imaginary case, just because this group of secretive professors can unilaterally deploy surveillance technologies to watch NSA, CIA and FBI agents does not mean that this level of access is owed or appropriate.

## THE "SECURITY TRUMPS" VIEW

According to what might be called the "security trumps" view, whenever privacy and security conflict, security wins—that is, security is more important than privacy. In the typical case, security protects fundamental rights like the right to life or property. Privacy may protect important interests, but these interests will never be as important as the security of life and limb. Ken Himma defends a version of this position in the preceding chapter.

First, it is not clear why a "security trumps" view should be adopted over a "privacy trumps" view. Bodily privacy—the right to control access to and uses of one's body—seems at least as fundamental or intuitively weighty as security. In fact, one could argue that security only gets its value derivatively based on what it is protecting. According to this view, security would be an instrumental value, something used to promote intrinsic values, while privacy would be understood as an intrinsic value.

Second, given that we generally promote individual security by authorizing others, it would be advantageous to maintain certain checks against those who provide security. Privacy is one of these checks. The point is not that privacy is absolute. Rather, the point is that before we set aside privacy for security, it would be prudent to put certain accountability safeguards in place. Giving governments too much power undermines the mission of providing for security—the government itself becomes a threat. This point was put nicely by John Locke: "This is to think, that Men are so foolish, that they take care to avoid what Mischiefs may be done them by *Pole-Cats*, or *Foxes*, but are content, nay think it Safety, to be devoured by *Lions*."[11] It is also important to note the risk of mischief associated with criminals and terrorists compared to the kinds of mischief perpetrated by governments—even our government. In cases where accountability provisions and independent oversight are lacking, governments pose the greater security risk.

Here we are rejecting the rule that security trumps in every case, independent of process or procedure. In fact, it seems odd to maintain that any increase in security should be preferred to any decrease in privacy—note that Himma does not make this mistake. Such a view would sanction massive violations of privacy for mere incremental and perhaps momentary gains in security. Also, given that others will provide security and power is likely a necessary part of providing security, we have strong prudential reasons to reject the "security trumps" view.

It is false to claim that in every case more privacy means less security or more security entails less privacy. Security arguments actually cut the other direction in some cases—it is only through enhanced privacy protections that we can obtain appropriate levels of security against industrial espionage, unwarranted invasions into private domains, and information warfare or terrorism. Consider how privacy protections enhance security when considering encryption standards for electronic communications and computer networks. Although the NSA's position is that the widespread use of encryption software will allow criminals a sanctuary to exchange information necessary for the completion of illegal activities, consider how this security argument actually cuts the other direction. National security for government agencies, companies, and individuals actually *requires* strong encryption. Industrial espionage and cyber crime costs over $400 billion annually.[12] In 2007, a cyber attack took down government communications and banks in Estonia.[13] A report from the CSIS Task Force on Information Warfare and Security notes that "cyber terrorists could overload phone lines . . . disrupt air traffic control . . . scramble software used by major financial institutions, hospitals, and other emergency services . . . or sabotage the New York Stock Exchange."[14] Related to information war, it would seem that national security requires strong encryption and more privacy.

Finally, those who defend the "security trumps" view rarely discuss the consequences of the surveillance policy they are promoting or whether an alternative might exist that better protects both privacy and security. Consider, just for example, almost any predominantly developed "isolationist" country—perhaps Switzerland. My guess is that these sorts of countries do not have much terrorist activity and likely do not have higher crime rates than the United States.[15] One way to obtain more security would be to change our selectively interventionist policies and in this way protect both security and privacy.

## THE CONSENT ARGUMENT

According to the consent argument, by voluntarily offering information, even private information, on social media sites, email, web pages, blogs, smartphones, and the like, we are agreeing that others may watch. In living our lives, we each cast off vast amounts of data that others may notice. Given that all this information is freely shared, it would seem odd to complain that others are watching.

But this view is just as weak as the others. Consider how difficult it would be to opt out of the vast array of information-gathering systems that surround us. Wearing a disguise and paying in cash will not defeat facial-recognition technology, video surveillance, or predictive analytics. In many U.S. states and various European Union countries it is illegal to wear a mask or disguise to conceal one's identity.[16] Also, many of the surveillance systems used by our security providers are unknown to us data targets. Obviously, we can't consent to covert surveillance. Note as well the ability to evade the watchers may depend on deploying antimonitoring technologies beyond the financial means of most individuals. Independent of financial capacity, it would seem that few of us actually have a robust choice to opt out of our surveillance society.

Consider the now infamous case where, after data mining, Target figured out that one of its patrons was pregnant. After purchasing items such as vitamins and lotion, she received coupons for baby-related products. Her father was somewhat shocked that Target was seemingly pushing a "get pregnant" agenda on his teenage daughter, only to find out that she was indeed pregnant.

There are two important points highlighted by this case. First, the daughter's consent to let Target track her purchasing habits is not also consent for any and all downstream uses of that information. Second, Target's actions violated her right to privacy by figuring out and exposing sensitive personal information to others.

Consider big-data analytics that can analyze a small set of disparate data points, containing no personal identifying information, and then reidentify some particular individual.[17] Take three or four seemingly innocuous data points: a forty-something-year-old male, with a PhD, who once lived in Michigan, plays recreational ice hockey, and owns a 1976 Cadillac Eldorado. Crunch the numbers, and poof—yours truly is pulled like a rabbit from a hat. In sharing these sorts of facts about ourselves, we do not also consent to reidentification.

## CONCLUSION: WHY PRIVACY AND ACCOUNTABILITY TRUMP SECURITY

If I am correct, the views captured by "just trust us," "nothing to hide," "security trumps," and the "consent" argument fail to establish defensible reasons for the sort of surveillance society that has been pushed upon us. One marker of power is the ability to demand information disclosures from others while keeping one's own information secret. As data mining and profiling have become the norm, many have become frustrated with and alarmed at a perceived loss of power. Governments and corporations control vast amounts of information, including sensitive personal information about citizens, and use this information for their own ends. The average information target or citizen has little power to demand disclosures from governments and corporations, and even less power to control the vast amounts of information being collected and stored. To directly answer a question raised in the introduction to his anthology—was the whistleblower Edward Snowden a hero or villain? I say he was a hero. By giving us a glimpse at the vast array of secret surveillance capabilities being used, Snowden offers us a chance at resetting the balance of power.

Consider the following case. Suppose that Fred gives Ginger, a mere acquaintance, his gun in order to provide security—perhaps Ginger is a much better shot. Assuming that Ginger is like the rest of us, it would be irrational of Fred to agree to a situation where Ginger could decide the best course of action independent of input, constraint, or consequences—it would be hard to believe that in this case Fred has *promoted* his security interests. Ginger, in this case, would be too much like Mr. Leviathan of the Thomas Hobbes security agency. This, in part, captures my argument against "just trust us," "nothing to hide," and "security trumps." In furthering his own security interests, Fred would likely insist on several rules before employing Ginger as his protector. In general, there would be rules that provide a check on those with the power to provide security, rules that require a rational basis for overriding rights, and rules that allow for review of the adopted processes, as well as different protection policies that may provide better protection of rights.

Rules that provide a check on the power of security providers are necessary so that security is not also debased. These sorts of rules could include judicial review and public oversight of laws that promote some interests at the expense of others. By insisting on an objective, independent authority, bias, prejudice, and clouded reasoning can be minimized. Oversight also ensures the accountability of the actors involved. Subjects could vote their protectors out of power or institute criminal sanctions against those who overstep the law. Public oversight, and the accountability it may promote, would require transparency.

As with rules that provide a check on power, there would also be rules that require a rational basis for rights balancing or trading. In cases where security is promoted at the expense of privacy, property, or liberty, we would require a rational basis for the rule. Probable cause is an example. If an agent of the government can demonstrate that a target committed, is committing, or will commit a crime, then an independent authority, like a judge, can issue a warrant or subpoena. Unlike the reading of tea leaves or the emotional judgments of a politician in a moment of crisis, a process like demonstrating probable cause before an impartial authority has a rational basis. There may be other sets of rules that achieve the same results; the point is not about this specific set. Rather, the point is about what would be rational to endorse as a security enhancement.

Unless our security providers are saints (and we know that they are not) it would be irrational to give power without fairly precise accountability rules in place. This is just to say that a necessary condition for robust security is accountability. Also note that those we hire to provide security have privacy rights as well. It is not as if becoming an NSA agent, for example, entails total transparency for these workers. NSA agents don't owe us total transparency any more than we owe them this sort of access.

Another way to put this argument is that without establishing vigorous practices that promote privacy and accountability, we cannot attain robust security. I do not deny that in specific instances the physical security of life and limb are more important than informational privacy. But as soon as we glance upward to the level of practices, things become complex. It is simply not true that practices promoting security always trump practices that promote privacy and accountability. This is one of the great fictions of our time.

Echoing a point made in the introduction to this volume, I simply don't think that we owe each other the sorts of information access championed by security advocates. In a world where we don't owe each other much—where our government is not licensed to play big mommy, big daddy, and big brother—*privacy* for citizens and *accountability* for those wielding governmental power are more important than most of the security "enhancing" practices deployed or desired by governments. Liberals who support a larger role for government—where the government is required to provide or mandate health care, food, jobs, education, leisure time, social justice, and so on—also seemingly advocate for a world where we owe each other a lot. In this world, as the domain of how we can be held to account grows, it seems that the domain of privacy must shrink. Conservatives have a similar problem. Those who think that part of a government's purpose is to police the world—to adopt an overly broad notion of "national interest" and send troops, money, or diplomats to proselytize around the globe—will also concur that we owe each other a lot. Again, accountability grows as privacy shrinks. In a world where the moral landscape is thick—on liberal or conservative grounds—it is difficult to find a place for privacy.

We have become a nation of the watchers and the watched. Why do we allow US politicians, in response to freedom of information requests, to black out or redact large portions of documents twenty, thirty, or fifty years old, yet at the same time the average citizen is subject to unparalleled levels of intrusion? Administrative subpoenas in the United States, for example, allow government officials to search without a court order. Arguably, politicians, police chiefs, or NSA data analysts are more accountable to us than we are to them. It is alarming that they can know so much about us while we know so little about them.

It seems like we have fallen under the spell of a very dubious principle where "can" implies "should." We *can* monitor, track, hoard, aggregate, and search ever-increasing amounts of data. We *can* use big-data analytics and predictive software to determine what someone might do or where they might be at some future time. We *can* use GPS trackers, walking or gate technology, spy cameras, facial recognition tools, and email scanning software to monitor virtually every aspect of our lives.

We *can* march unthinkingly towards a watcher-based society where most of us are information targets—data points to be watched and, yes, controlled. But *can* does not imply *should*. Think about what would follow if it did. We need to stop all of this, take a step back, and ask if this is the sort of world we want to promote. Moving towards a society of the watchers and the watched is not inevitable.

## NOTES

1. Lord Acton to Bishop Mandell Creighton, April 3, 1887, in *The Life and Letters of Mandell Creighton* (New York: Longmans, Green, 1904).

2. See Alan Rusbridger and Ewen MacAskill, "Edward Snowden Interview—The Edited Transcript," *Guardian*, July 18, 2014, http://www.theguardian.com/world/2014/jul/18/-sp-edward-snowden-nsa-whistleblower-interview-transcript.

3. See Electronic Privacy Information Center, "EPIC Alert 9.23," newsletter, November 19, 2002, https://epic.org/alert/EPIC_Alert_9.23.html.

4. See Mark Jaycox, "Congress Should Say No to 'Cybersecurity' Information Sharing Bills," *Deeplinks* (blog), Electronic Frontier Foundation, January 8, 2015, https://www.eff.org/deeplinks/2015/01/congress-should-say-no-cybersecurity-information-sharing-bills.

5. Several of the arguments to come draw from previously published material. See Adam D. Moore, *Privacy Rights: Moral and Legal Foundations* (University Park: Pennsylvania State University Press, 2010), chap. 10, and "Privacy, Security, and Government Surveillance: Wiki-Leaks and the New Accountability," *Public Affairs Quarterly* 25, no. 2 (April 2011): 141–56.

6. *Olmstead v. United States*, 277 U.S. 438, 479 (1928).

7. Jacob Lilly, "National Security at What Price?: A Look into Civil Liberty Concerns in the Information Age Under the USA Patriot Act of 2001 and a Proposed Constitutional Test for Future Legislation," *Cornell Journal of Law and Public Policy* 12, no. 2 (2003): 451.

8. See Moore, "Privacy, Security, and Government Surveillance," and *Privacy Rights*, chap. 10, for numerous other cases.

9. For a lengthy analysis of this argument, see Daniel Solove's "I've Got Nothing to Hide and Other Misunderstandings of Privacy," *San Diego Law Review* 44, no. 4 (Fall 2007): 745–72.

10. CNBC broadcast, cited at http://www.huffingtonpost.com/2009/12/07/google-ceo-on-privacy-if-n-383105.html, December 4, 2009.

11. John Locke, *The Second Treatise of Government,* ed. C. B. Macpherson (Indianapolis, IN: Hackett, 1980), chap. 5, sec. 93.

12. Ellen Nakashima and Andrea Peterson, "Report: Cybercrime and Espionage Costs $445 Billion Annually," *Washington Post*, June 9, 2014, http://www.washingtonpost.com/world/national-security/report-cybercrime-and-espionage-costs-445-billion-annually/2014/06/08/8995291c-ecce-11e3-9f5c-9075d5508f0a_story.html.

13. Joshua Davis, "Hackers Take Down the Most Wired Country in Europe," *Wired Magazine*, August 21, 2007, http://archive.wired.com/politics/security/magazine/15-09/ff_estonia?currentPage=all.

14. Cited in Christopher Jones, "Averting an Electronic Waterloo," *Wired Magazine* Online News Flash, February 1999.

15. See "Switzerland Terrorism Stats," http://www.nationmaster.com/country/sz-switzerland/ter-terrorism.

16. See, for example, Stephen J. Simoni, "'Who Goes There?'—Proposing a Model Anti-Mask Act," *Fordham Law Review* 61, no. 1 (1992): 241–74.

17. See Paul Ohm, "Broken Promises of Privacy: Responding to the Surprising Failure of Anonymization," *UCLA Law Review* 57, no. 6 (2009): 1701.

*Chapter Ten*

# Privacy, Transparency and Accountability in the NSA's Bulk Metadata Program

## Alan Rubel

Disputes at the intersection of national security, surveillance, civil liberties, and transparency are nothing new, but they have become a particularly prominent part of public discourse in the years since the attacks on the World Trade Center on September 11, 2001. This is in part due to the dramatic nature of those attacks, in part based on significant legal developments after the attacks (classifying persons as "enemy combatants" outside the scope of traditional Geneva protections, legal memos by White House counsel providing rationale for torture, the USA PATRIOT Act), and in part because of the rapid development of communications and computing technologies that enable both greater connectivity among people and the greater ability to collect information about those connections.

One important way in which these questions intersect is in the controversy surrounding bulk collection of telephone metadata by the US National Security Agency (NSA). The bulk metadata program (the "metadata program" or "program") involved court orders under Section 215 of the USA PATRIOT Act requiring telecommunications companies to provide records about all calls the companies handled and the creation of a database that the NSA could search. The program was revealed to the general public in June 2013 as part of the large document leak by Edward Snowden, a former contractor for the NSA.[1]

A fair amount has been written about Section 215 and the bulk metadata program. Much of the commentary has focused on three discrete issues. First is whether the program is *legal*; that is, does the program comport with the language of the statute and is it consistent with Fourth Amendment protections against unreasonable searches and seizures? Second is whether the program infringes privacy rights; that is, does bulk metadata collection diminish individual privacy in a way that rises to the level that it infringes persons' rights to privacy? Third is whether the secrecy of the program is inconsistent with democratic accountability. After all, people in the general public only became aware of the metadata program via the Snowden leaks; absent those leaks, it is unlikely there would have been the sort of political backlash and investigation necessary to provide some kind of accountability.

In this chapter I argue that we need to look at these not as discrete questions, but as intersecting ones. The metadata program is not simply a legal problem (though it is one); it is not simply a privacy problem (though it is one); and it is not simply a secrecy problem (though it is one). Instead, the importance of the metadata program is the way in which these problems intersect and reinforce one another. Specifically, I will argue that the intersection of the questions undermines the value of rights, and that this is a deeper and more far-reaching moral problem than each of the component questions.

The chapter is organized as follows. First, I explain Section 215 and its legal basis; I argue that the section is plausibly legal, but that it is based on a very permissive interpretation of the law. Next, I argue that although the program affects privacy rights, it is at least plausible that those rights are not unjustifiably infringed. I then address the question of the program's transparency, and argue that it is indeed a problem (though largely because of the legal and privacy questions). Finally, I argue that the deeper and more far-reaching worry is that because of the mix of legal, privacy, and transparency problems, the metadata program undermines the *value of whatever privacy rights we have*.

## THE PROGRAM AND ITS LEGAL BASIS

### Section 215 Record Collection

Section 215 of the USA PATRIOT Act (the "business records" provision),[2] allows the Federal Bureau of Investigation to obtain a court order requiring other entities to produce "any tangible thing"—including any records—in order to protect against international terrorism. Specifically, it provides that

> the Director of the Federal Bureau of Investigation or a designee of the Director . . . may make an application for an order requiring the production of any tangible things (including books, records, papers, documents, and other items for an investigation to obtain foreign intelligence information) . . . to protect against international terrorism or clandestine intelligence activities.

There are several limitations to the FBI's ability to collect information under Section 215. Most important, there must be some grounds for believing that the items and records sought are "relevant to an authorized investigation."[3] The FBI may not conduct an investigation based "solely" on activities protected by the First Amendment of the US Constitution, and the FBI must follow "minimization procedures" that limit the extent to which tangible things can be retained, disseminated, and used.[4]

## Tangible Things

The design of the bulk telephone metadata program tracks Section 215's basic features. To begin, the program collects records about telephone calls, and not the contents of calls. When one makes or receives a telephone call, one's phone company automatically creates a record of certain call details, including for example the number dialed/received, the call's time, date, and duration, trunk identifier, and calling card numbers used. Because the information is merely "about" the call, and not the contents of the call itself, it is called "metadata"—a term long familiar in information studies fields, but becoming popularized in the wake of the Snowden leaks. The records that phone companies keep of call metadata are "tangible things" and hence eligible for production under Section 215.

Based on Section 215, the Foreign Intelligence Surveillance (FISA) Court approved the NSA's request for an order to obtain "all call detail records" from certain phone companies in the United States.[5] In practice, this means that phone companies subject to the order must provide the NSA with all records pertaining to phone calls to and from its customers, and most of the data provided comes from calls between persons in the United States.[6] Although phone companies collect information about the locations of mobile phones when calls are made (based on the locations of cellular towers used in sending and receiving signals), phone companies do not currently provide that information to the NSA.[7] However, the NSA has collected such information in the past in order to test whether it would be feasible to incorporate into the bulk metadata program, and some location information may be inferred from other metadata collected (e.g., area codes for landline phones and trunk identifiers). The order requires phone companies to produce the relevant records on a daily basis, and the NSA must request the FISA Court to renew the order every ninety days.

## Relevant To

Even though metadata records are clearly "tangible things" under Section 215, that is not a sufficient legal basis to receive a court order. Rather, the request for an order must be based on "reasonable grounds to believe that the [records] are *relevant to*" a foreign intelligence or terrorism investigation.[8]

The FISA Court has determined that the relevance standard is a low hurdle. Specifically, it has determined that relevance depends on whether information sought is "necessary for NSA to employ tools that are likely to generate useful investigative leads to help identify and track terrorist operatives."[9] The court accepts the premises that bulk data collection is necessary to identify the much smaller subset of terrorist communications and that making connections among communications is likely to generate useful investigative leads that help identify and track terrorist operatives. Hence, the court concludes that the bulk metadata program meets the Section 215 relevance requirement.[10] That is, in order to ensure that the metadata for terrorist communications is included in its data, the NSA must collect all the metadata. Moreover, because the value of metadata may be apparent only after connections have been established, the FISA Court has determined that the information must be collected on an ongoing basis to ensure that historic information is not lost.[11]

## Minimization Procedures

Although the relevance standard under Section 215 is broad, the retention and use of the bulk metadata is limited by minimization requirements, which are a required component of the FBI's application for a court order under Section 215.[12] The government is prohibited from accessing the data for any other intelligence or investigative purpose.[13] Hence, the data may not be used for general law enforcement purposes. Only certain trained, authorized persons have access to the data; access is afforded only via a query process, which in turn must be based on reasonable, articulable suspicion (RAS).[14] Information is kept for years. The government must notify the FISA Court immediately of any cases of noncompliance.

The bulk metadata is consolidated, and analysts may only use the consolidated data by making queries. The records are searched based on a telephone number or some other selection term, which is used as a seed. In order to perform such a search, one of a small number of NSA officials must determine that there is "reasonable, articulable suspicion that the selection term is associated with terrorism."[15] It is unclear what it means for a phone number to be "associated with terrorism."

The result of these minimization procedures is that "[t]he vast majority of the records the NSA collects are never seen by any person."[16] Additionally, "[O]nly the tiny fraction of the telephony metadata records that are responsive to queries authorized under the RAS standard are extracted, reviewed, or disseminated by NSA intelligence analysts, and only under carefully controlled circumstances."[17]

So, because the metadata is based on business records, which are "tangible things" under Section 215, because they are in some sense relevant to ongoing investigations, and because the NSA has minimization procedures in place, the program appears at least facially consistent with the Foreign Intelligence Surveillance Act statute.

## Constitutional Basis

Regardless of whether the bulk metadata program is consistent with the FBI's and NSA's statutory authority under Section 215, there is a question as to whether it is consistent with the government constitutional limits under the Fourth Amendment of the U.S. Constitution. The Fourth Amendment provides that

> the right of the people to be secure in their persons, houses, papers, and effects, against unreasonable searches and seizures, shall not be violated, and no Warrants shall issue, but upon probable cause, supported by Oath or affirmation, and particularly describing the place to be searched, and the persons or things to be seized.

In order to determine whether government information collection violates the Fourth Amendment it is first necessary to determine whether the government's actions constitutes a *search* (seizures are not at issue here). The amendment prohibits unreasonable searches and seizures; hence, if information collection does not constitute a search, then (*a fortiori*) it cannot constitute an *unreasonable* search. There is a two-part test for determining whether an activity constitutes a search, which was established in *Katz v. United States*.[18] First, a person must have exhibited a subjective expectation of privacy, and second, that expectation must "be one that society is prepared to recognize as 'reasonable.'"[19] Often the two parts are shortened into the pithier question of whether a person "has a reasonable expectation of privacy."

Two cases are crucial in explaining the applicability of the *Katz* test to telephone metadata. The first is *United States v. Miller*.[20] In that case federal agents sought Miller's bank records via subpoena, having neither the probable cause nor the warrant required for searches under the Fourth Amendment. The Supreme Court determined, however, that business records held by third parties (here, banks) are not protected by the Fourth Amendment, as one does not have a reasonable expectation of privacy in those records. A person engaging in business with a bank voluntarily discloses financial information to the bank; she thereby "takes the risk . . . that the information will be conveyed by that person to the Government."[21]

The second case, *Smith v. Maryland*, is even more on point. Smith robbed a woman's home. After doing so, he began making threatening phone calls to her and drove past her house. The woman collected Smith's license plate information, and police were able learn his address and phone number. They then got the phone company to install, without a warrant, a device (a "pen register") that could record the numbers dialed from Smith's home. They used information gleaned from the device to obtain a warrant, searched Smith's home, and found evidence of the robbery. The Supreme Court determined that neither part of the *Katz* test was met. That is, people do not have an actual expectation of privacy in numbers dialed, nor would such an expectation be one that society would recognize as reasonable. The court reasoned that persons voluntarily reveal numbers dialed and received from their phones, and hence (as in *Miller*) they take the risk that such information will be revealed by third parties to the government. [22]

A significant proportion of commentators on the program have concluded that it is consistent with statutory and constitutional law. In *ACLU v. Clapper*, a federal court dismissed an action seeking an injunction against the NSA's metadata collection, determining that the plaintiffs were unlikely to prevail on their claims that the program violates FISA and the Fourth Amendment. [23]

## Legal Criticisms

Despite the decision in the *Clapper* case, the academic support for the government's interpretation of Section 215, and the Supreme Court's decisions rejecting the idea that gathering of third-party and transactional information constitutes a search under the Fourth Amendment, there is significant support for the view that the program is not consistent with the law.

One federal court has arrived at a different conclusion than the *Clapper* court. In *Klayman v. Obama*, the District Court for the District of Columbia granted (and subsequently stayed) a preliminary injunction against the NSA's collection of telephone metadata on Fourth Amendment grounds. [24] Specifically, it determined that the bulk collection of metadata is sufficiently different from the pen register collection of numbers dialed by one phone; *Smith v. Maryland* isn't applicable. Rather, the DC court found more relevant the recent case of *United States v. Jones*, in which the U.S. Supreme Court determined that placing a GPS device on a car and following it for several weeks constituted a search under the Fourth Amendment. [25] In this case, a concurring opinion distinguished between long-term monitoring and more isolated information gathering, allowing that constant following via GPS could constitute a search, even where discrete elements of that following would not. Following *Jones*, the DC court determined that bulk metadata collection could constitute a search even where discrete collection of metadata would not.

In addition to the constitutional claims, there are several criticisms based on Section 215. The Privacy and Civil Liberties Oversight Board (PCLOB), an independent executive agency formed in response to recommendations made by the 9/11 Commission, issued a report on the bulk metadata program in January 2014. It found several flaws in the NSA's (and, hence, the FISA Court's) interpretation of Section 215, each of which casts some doubt on whether the program is legal.

First, the PCLOB questions the entity collecting the information. Section 215 authorizes the FBI to make business-records requests. However, the bulk telephony metadata program is conducted by the NSA—an organization with a wholly separate mandate, statutory authorization, and leadership. Nothing in Section 215 suggests that the FBI can transfer its authority or routinely share information gleaned pursuant to business records requests with other entities. Second, the PCLOB questions whether the metadata program collects information "relevant to" any ongoing investigation. While there are always some terrorism-related investigations occurring, and, hence, the information is relevant to investigations in some sense, there is no particular investigation to which the program is relevant. Third, the board questions the practice of collecting records on a daily basis. Typically records requests are made retrospectively—there is an investigation, and preexisting records are collected as part of that investigation. Here, though, there is a prospective order that requires collections of whatever records are produced each day. Finally, the PCLOB questions whether *Miller* and *Smith* are adequate to deal with contemporary capacities to gather information.

## Legal Conclusions

In the end, it seems that the metadata program is plausibly legal, but it pushes against even very expansive interpretations of Section 215 and Fourth Amendment law. The agency conducting the program (the NSA) is different than the agency authorized to make the requests under Section 215 (the FBI). The interpretation of "relevance" under Section 215 is so broad that it would render almost any vast collection of persons' information legal, and the "relevance" of most information gathered depends on the information collected being exhaustive. There is no connection to any specific investigation, and new records are produced daily rather than in response to new requests. Moreover, although collection of metadata is not a Fourth Amendment search under *Smith v. Maryland*, that case is four decades old, and the technological change may have rendered it obsolete, especially in consideration of the "mosaic theory" advanced under a concurrence in *United States v. Jones*.

### PRIVACY RIGHTS

In the previous section I argued that the primary concern with the bulk metadata program cannot be its legality. The program rests on a permissive, aggressive, and envelope-pushing legal interpretations, but is nonetheless at least plausibly legal. The program is also problematic on the grounds of privacy, regardless of the program's legality. However, criticizing the program on straightforward privacy grounds also has some important limitations.

People have at least some moral rights to privacy. By this I just mean that there are some cases in which individuals have valid claims that others not surveil, collect information about, monitor, or distribute information about them, and those claims are the individuals' moral due.[26] It is this right that allows one to justifiably assert that, for example, one has been wronged by others listening in on one's phone calls without permission, or that one has been wronged by an insurance company publishing one's health information for the world to see. I won't spend much time arguing for this right, for a couple of reasons. First, there is substantial literature on privacy and privacy rights already. Accounts of the basis for privacy rights include those focused the importance of privacy in human well-being and flourishing, privacy being the object of persons' autonomous choices, privacy being at times a *condition* of autonomous choice, privacy as an important condition for liberal democracy, and privacy as a condition for many and varied social relationships.[27] More important, though, is that absent valid claims to privacy (which is to say, privacy rights), arguments about whether bulk metadata collection (or any other surveillance program) is justified can't get off the ground. This is not to say that, all things considered, the metadata program is unjustified. Rather, it is to say that *if* the metadata program is justified, either it does not infringe whatever privacy rights we have or, if it does infringe privacy rights, other considerations are sufficient to override privacy rights.

That the metadata program affects privacy should be uncontroversial. The Section 215 orders require that telecommunications providers provide the NSA with metadata from all cell phone calls using their networks. As a result, information about individual cell phone users and their calls end up in a database that can be easily queried by federal agents. And even though that metadata is collected in the course of telecommunications business, the orders expanded the range of persons able to access and make use of that information. Hence, individuals' privacy regarding their cell phone communications decreased with respect to the federal government. Given the minimal account of privacy rights I suggest above, it follows fairly easily that the program infringes privacy rights. We have some moral claim that government actors not collect information about the people with whom we communicate, and the metadata program does just this. Now, because that is a fairly austere account of privacy rights, it remains an open question whether the infringement here is substantial, and whether benefits of the program suffice to override those rights. There are some reasons to think the infringement is not substantial and that the benefits may outweigh it.[28]

First, the information collected in the context of the metadata program is limited. Specifically, the Section 215 court orders request numbers dialed, numbers of calls received, call durations, trunk identifier information, and similar transactional information. The NSA does not collect information about the content of phone calls, and it does not collect phone locations (at least not in this particular program). Certainly, who one communicates with and for how long is information in which one may have a privacy right. But it is arguably less intrusive than lots of other types of information: GPS location information, eavesdropping on call content, computer searches. Of course, the fact that there are more intrusive means of surveillance does not entail that lesser intrusions are permissible.

Second, the information collected as part of the program is already systematically collected by telecommunications companies. The metadata at the heart of the program (numbers called, call durations, and so forth) is information that telecommunications companies must collect simply in order to provide services. Hence, independently of whether the metadata program existed, any user of those services would not have privacy regarding his or her telephone metadata with respect to his or her telecommunications provider. The metadata program simply extends the group of entities having access to that information to include the NSA. While this decreases people's privacy, the moral weight of the decrease would seem to be less than if the information were not already collected for reasons unrelated to the metadata program. Third, the program includes minimization procedures. Specifically, the database created from the records could be searched only by querying the database based on a "seed" number, for which agents had reasonable suspicion of a connection to a foreign intelligence. It was not subject to browsing, or to querying based on other numbers.

The last consideration is that, even if we suppose that the program affects privacy rights, do we have good reason to think that the program is effective enough to justify any infringement? Perhaps so. There is significant controversy as to whether the program leads to gains in security.[29] The PCLOB has concluded that there is at least *some* benefit to the program, if limited.[30] And in a separate statement, one member of the PCLOB stressed that the *future potential* benefits of the program provide justification for its existence.[31] Of course such an argument has important gaps. It rests on a substantial and speculative empirical claim. Moreover, even if there is some benefit, it cannot tell us whether that benefit is great enough to subsume the privacy rights at issue. Nonetheless, whatever the benefits of the program are, they mitigate the degree to which privacy rights are themselves dispositive.

So, there is no question that our privacy diminishes based on the metadata program, and it plausibly infringes privacy rights. But there are important limitations on the degree to which it infringes privacy rights: the type of information collected, the fact that telecommunications companies collect the information in any case, the limitations on use, and the fact that many of us will feel no ill effects. And while we should be skeptical of claims about the efficacy of the program, the possibility of its efficacy may serve to justify the rights infringement. Here I want to be clear that I am not arguing that the program is, all things considered, a justifiable infringement of privacy. Rather, I am arguing that the discrete privacy concerns cannot really explain the depth of worry about the program.

## TRANSPARENCY

A third question surrounding the metadata program centers on its secrecy. Requests for Section 215 court orders are issued to the FISA Court. That court meets in secret, and hence the orders are themselves secret. Moreover, the existence of the program was unknown until (and would likely never have been revealed but for) the Edward Snowden revelations in 2013.

The mere fact that some court orders are secret is a criticism of the existence of the FISA Court in the first instance, rather than a criticism of the metadata program overall. But the existence of a secret, widespread, and longstanding surveillance program is more problematic, such as when the phone data of every person in the United States was potentially collected and stored, and yet no one in the general public was aware of the program. There is no question that some facets of government require at least a degree of secrecy in order to be effective, and the precise contours of a surveillance program are plausibly such a case.

However, as Dennis Thompson has argued, lest we abandon the possibility of democratic accountability for security programs altogether, there must at least be a kind of "second order" transparency. That is, we must have an idea about the kind of policy or practice that is largely carried out in secret.[32] It would appear, though, that there is no second-order transparency in the case of the metadata program. That is because the legal interpretation on which the program is based pushed so forcefully against the plausible bounds of statutory law. Not only was the program itself secret, but the legal interpretation of Section 215 on which it is based was secret. More importantly still, that interpretation was one that no person could reasonably have anticipated to have been operating within the FBI and NSA. Although the program is plausibly legal, it is so only when we read the statute with the specifics of the metadata program in mind. The government's interpretation of "relevance" is envelope-pushing, and the metadata collected is relevant to "an authorized investigation" only insofar as there are continuously *some* authorized investigations occurring. No one interpreting the statute without already knowing of the metadata program could reasonably anticipate that Section

215 could support such widespread information collection. Hence, there is a failure of even second-order transparency.

## UNDERMINING THE VALUE OF RIGHTS

In the previous sections, I have argued that (1) the metadata program is plausibly legal, though based on an envelope-pushing statutory interpretation; (2) the metadata program infringes privacy rights, but those infringements are limited and possibly justified by benefits; and (3) there are important transparency problems both in the secrecy of the program and in the obscurity of the legal interpretation on which it is based. But the deeper problem with the program is the way the legal issue, the privacy issue, and transparency issue intersect. Specifically, that intersection undermines the value of rights to right-holders.

Elsewhere, I have argued that there is an important distinction to be made between rights themselves and the value of rights to right-holders, and that under certain conditions there is an obligation to ensure the full value of rights to right-holders.[33] That obligation is independent of whether the original right is itself infringed, and it is independent of whether the right itself is justifiably infringed.

To illustrate the distinction I have in mind, consider the right to access government records. In the United States, the Freedom of Information Act (FOIA) provides people the right to access documents created by the federal government; all fifty US states have similar laws that pertain to state and local government information. These are legal rights, but they are justified by a moral right to have important information about a government acting on one's behalf, a right to be governed only under conditions to which reasonable persons could consent, and the instrumental values of making easy use of information and helping to ensure reasonably good governance. The right to access government records includes the ability to receive information upon request, the assurance that the government actually will retain important records, and that any costs to access be reasonable. Now compare the governments of two similar states: Cheese State and Beer State. The government of Cheese State keeps its records in electronic format, and can provide for, example, property records, budgets, meeting minutes, reports and so forth via the Internet in machine-readable form. This allows people making records requests to get information quickly and to easily search, extract and compile information in the records. By contrast, the government of Beer State keeps its records on paper only. Responding to information requests in Beer State requires that files be copied or scanned (which takes longer), and it is much more difficult to search, extract and compile data from Beer State records. In both Cheese State and Beer State, people have fully intact rights to access government records. However, the *value* of the right to people in Cheese State is greater because they are better able to make use of the right.[34]

What matters here is the *objective* value of the right, or the ability of the right-holder to make use of the right or to benefit from the right should the right-holder need to. This contrasts with the subjective value of a right, or the degree to which right-holders subjectively value a right. So, in the open-records case, Attie might not care much about the form in which her state will provide access to records as a general matter; indeed, she might not even be aware of her access rights. Suppose, though, that she wishes to invest in property, and would like to search the property records of dozens of parcels in a short period of time. It would be much easier for her to conduct that search if the records are kept in electronic form. Hence, the value of the right is greater to her objectively, even if she doesn't realize it.

Now, under some circumstances, states have an obligation to ensure the full value of rights to right-holders, though not always. Consider the right to vote. That right is more valuable to an individual right-holder where she can sell her votes to the highest bidder,[35] but surely the state has no obligation to permit such sales, even though the objective value of the right to the right-holder is diminished where selling votes is prohibited. Compare, though, the case in which a person has a right to vote, but lacks sufficient information about candidates or issues to make a reasonable decision in an election. There, it is at least plausible that the state has failed in a responsibility to ensure that the right to vote is valuable to right-holders. The difference in the two cases is that in the vote-selling case, the value of the right to the right-holder conflicts with the justification for the existence of the right in the first place, whereas in the low-information case, the value of the right *aligns* with underlying justification. The right to vote is justified in order to ensure that government reflects (at least to some degree) the will of its people, as a means for people to exercise political self-direction, and to encourage demo-cratic accountability. Each of those depends on, among other things, voters having adequate information; each is thwarted to the extent that people can sell their votes.[36]

There are other criteria to determine whether states have an obligation to secure the full value of rights. One is that state action precipitates a right's diminished value. Consider again the open records example. A state's failure to digitize records is plausibly a failure of its duty to secure the value of the right to access information. By contrast, if Attie does not have the financial resources to invest in property, her right of access to property records is less valuable to her (objectively), but it would not seem that the state has an obligation to secure the value in that case. Another criterion is that states only have obligations to secure the full value of rights where they can actually do so; after all, one cannot have an obligation to do something that one is unable to do.

## Privacy

How, then, does the value of rights bear upon the metadata program? Consider first the right to privacy. As noted earlier, there are a number of different justifications for privacy rights. Instrumental accounts base privacy's value on what it does: providing space for individuals to function and flourish, establishing a condition in which many and varied social relationships can exist and thrive, and preventing others from treating individuals unfairly on the basis of personal information. According to other views, privacy is important based on persons' autonomy, or the ability to determine for oneself what one values, and to act according to those values as one sees fit. Privacy can be the *object* of autonomous action, as when one determines that it is important to act and make decisions without the scrutiny of others. And as Stanley Benn has argued, the nature of and meaning of persons' actions may change depending on whether others observe those actions; an action done for its own sake is distinguishable, on this view, from an action done partly for the sake of an observer.[37] Privacy may also be a *condition* of autonomous choice; where one is closely surveilled, the degree to which their views, projects, and actions are the result of their own deliberation rather than others' diminishes.[38]

Earlier I claimed that the metadata program infringes privacy rights (though perhaps justifiably). More problematic is the way that the program undermines the value of privacy rights to right-holders. It does this in several ways. First, the fact that the program was secret made it impossible for people to *tell* whether their privacy was diminished by the federal government. Of course, whether one can tell that his or her rights have been infringed is a different matter from whether those right have actually been infringed, and hence the secrecy of the program cannot be an infringement of the privacy right itself. Why, though, does the inability to tell whether one's privacy has been infringed diminish the value of the privacy right? Among the justifications for rights to privacy is that they are instrumentally important (for the salubrious effects of having distance from scrutiny, for opportunities to flourish, for political processes, for varied relationships). Strictly speaking, these depend on *beliefs* about privacy. The secrecy of the program prevents people from knowing the status of their privacy; preventing people from being able to interpret their circumstances, in particular their circumstances with respect to an important right, is an affront to their autonomy,[39] and that affront to autonomy is independent of whether people would change their actions based on knowledge of surveillance, and independent of whether the surveillance is (considered by itself) a justified infringement of privacy rights.

The secrecy of the metadata program itself is only part of the way it diminishes the value of rights. At least as important is the aggressive legal interpretation on which the program is based, which is an interpretation that no one could reasonably anticipate without some prior knowledge of the program. The inability to interpret statutes and constitutional provisions that protect rights means that a person cannot reasonably anticipate the *types* of rights infringements that one is likely to endure. So, while the secrecy of the program conflicts with autonomy interests by precluding one from understanding just how she is being treated ("Am I being surveilled?"), the aggressiveness and secrecy of the legal interpretations conflict with an autonomy interest in anticipating the *rules governing* how one is treated ("Could I be legally surveilled?").

A third, and related, way in which the program undermines the value of privacy rights is that it forestalls persons' opportunities to *assert* or *claim* their moral due. While rights protect interests (in well-being, in autonomy, in political processes), as Joel Feinberg has argued, the importance of rights includes the fact that right-holders can assert them. [40] Persons' interests may be harmed in myriad ways. Sometimes it is based on broad phenomena to which a person may object, but with respect to which she has no right. So, a policy decision to, for example, build a metro line in location A rather than location B might harm Lucille in that she stood to benefit from having it in location B, and perhaps even invested in property on the hope that the line would be in location B. But that would not infringe a right, and she cannot assert some individual claim to have the line where she wishes. By contrast, rights warrant individuals to make claims. Privacy rights allow one to say that "*I* have a claim that others not collect my information." But where rights infringements are secret, as in the case of the metadata program, it is impossible to assert such a claim.

So, the metadata program does more than infringe privacy rights. The lack of transparency surrounding the program (including both the existence of such a program and the obscurity of the legal interpretation underwriting it) make whatever privacy rights we actually have less valuable. The value that is diminished is in each case part of the value that justifies the right in the first place (autonomy, the ability to make use of rights, the ability to assert or claim rights), and because those actions are the result of state action, and because it is within the state's power to disclose the existence of surveillance programs and (more importantly) issue more reasonable legal interpretation, this is a failure of a duty to secure the value of privacy and other rights.

## Transparency

Next, consider transparency, and the right to information about government action. A right to information about the workings of the state is grounded partly in instrumental values, including the role of transparency in preventing corruption and abuse of power, and it is grounded partly in the principle that government is legitimate only with consent of the governed (an autonomy-view). Exactly what consent demands in this case is controversial. Perhaps the most prominent account in recent decades is Rawls's view that legitimate exercise of government power demands that it be consistent with constitutional principles that "all citizens as free and equal may reasonably be expected to endorse in the light of principles and ideals acceptable to their common human reason."[41]

In some ways the secrecy of the metadata program (both the program itself and the legal interpretations on which it is based) would appear only to conflict with rights to information about government. After all, how could the mere lack of transparency *also* diminish the value of rights to government information? What is important here is that the lack of transparency concerns an important moral and legal right. This is not an issue of how a narrow administrative rule or specialized statute is interpreted. Rather, it is a right that has substantial statutory and constitutional protections. While secret actions and obscure interpretations pose problems of transparency and accountability in any case, where they affect basic rights and liberties the problem runs deeper. The weightier the value of the right subject to secret action and secret legal interpretation, the greater the loss of the value of that right due to the secrecy.

Further, such aggressive and secretive legal interpretation infects other rights. Specifically, it allows persons to infer that the government is likely to pursue other aggressive interpretations of the law of which we will be unaware. Part of the value of rights is that they allow individuals to act with some confidence in their belief that the interests grounding the rights are in fact protected, and yet here is a case in which an arm of the executive has received judicial approval in secret for legal interpretations that circumscribe a moral right by narrowing the legal protections for that right. There is, hence, much less reason to think that the government will reasonably, and openly, interpret other statutes and constitutional provisions in a way that tends to protect rather than undermine the interests protected. In light of the interpretations underwriting the program, it is more plausible to believe, and more reasonable to act as if, the government will also aggressively and secretly interpret protections for expression and assembly, religious practice, equal protection, and due process.[42] To the extent that the value of rights includes being able to act on the assumption that they are secured, the metadata program (and the legal interpretations on which it is based) diminishes the value of other rights, too. And that is true regardless of whether those other rights are indeed at risk.

This diminishment of the value of rights conflicts with a key value that justifies transparency in the first place. It is difficult to see that people could endorse a system in which the government interprets laws protecting persons' rights in ways that are at once secret and impossible to anticipate. It would seem, in other words, that persons could not reasonably be expected to endorse principles that preclude their understanding of how their de jure rights are to be treated.

## The Intersection

At this point, it is worth stepping back and considering the intersection of legal interpretation, privacy rights, and transparency. The mere fact that the government has promulgated an aggressive, envelope-pushing interpretation of the law matters. But that alone is not deeply problematic insofar as lawyers and governments often advance such arguments. The nature and extent of information collection in the metadata program is important, too. However, the program's effect on privacy has important limits based on the nature of the information collected, the fact that the information is collected by different parties in any case, and the potential benefits of the program. And transparency itself is important, but some government secrecy is justifiable.

Notice, though, the picture that emerges when we consider the intersection between these issues. First, the secrecy in this case is not just any secrecy; rather, it is secrecy *about* an aggressive, envelope-pushing legal interpretation. And as a result, people were denied the second-order transparency that is crucial to ensure that some secrecy is compatible with democratic governance.

Second, because the privacy loss was secret (both in fact and in legal interpretation), persons were denied the full value of their privacy rights. In other words, the metadata program is not merely about privacy loss, but the inability to actually make use of privacy rights because people did not know their privacy was diminished, and hence, their autonomy was circumvented in that they were unable to fully interpret important facts about their treatment, and people were unable to actually assert their rights. Third, because the secrecy and aggressive legal interpretations were about an important right, it makes less reasonable persons' beliefs in the security of other basic rights, and hence undermines the value of *those* rights to the right-holders. In other words, the importance of metadata program is the way in which problems of legal interpretation, privacy, and transparency work together to render rights less valuable.

## CONCLUSION

My goal in this chapter is to look at several objections to the Section 215 metadata program, each of which is important but limited, and to explain why we need to consider the links between those objections rather than viewing them in isolation. So, while the program presents a legal problem insofar as it is based on aggressive, envelope-pushing legal interpretations, those interpretations are a deeper worry because they are (1) secret, and (2) about an important right. And while the program presents a privacy problem by collecting lots of information about US persons, that privacy issue is a deeper problem because it was (1) secret, and (2) based on legal interpretations that were also secret. Finally, while the secrecy of the program presents a problem of government transparency, that lack of transparency presents a deeper problem because it (1) concerned a legal interpretation that no one could reasonably have anticipated (rather than mere secrecy about the program specifics), and (2) concerned an important right. In the end, one might still argue that the program is justified, all things considered. But such an argument won't be sound unless it addresses the intersection of legal interpretation, privacy, and secrecy, and how that intersection undermines the value of rights.

## NOTES

1. Glenn Greenwald, "NSA Collecting Phone Records of Millions of Verizon Customers Daily," *Guardian*, June 6, 2013, http://www.theguardian.com/world/2013/jun/06/nsa-phone-records-verizon-court-order; Glenn Greenwald and James Ball, "The Top Secret Rules That Allow NSA to Use US Data without a Warrant," *Guardian*, June 20, 2013, http://www.theguardian.com/world/2013/jun/20/fisa-court-nsa-without-warrant.

2. 50 U.S.C. § 1861.

3. 50 U.S.C. § 1861(b)(2)(A). An investigation is "authorized" in turn, if it is approved by the US attorney general under an appropriate executive order and *not* conducted on US persons based on solely on First-Amendment-protected activities; see 50 U.S.C. § 1861(a)(2).

4. 50 U.S.C. § 1861(a)(1)-(2), (b)(2)(B).

5. Privacy and Civil Liberties Oversight Board, *Report on the Telephone Records Program Conducted under Section 215 of the USA PATRIOT Act and on the Operations of the Foreign Intelligence Surveillance Court*, January 23, 2014, 22; Primary Order at 3, *In re Application of the Federal Bureau of Investigation for an Order Requiring the Production of Tangible Things [redacted]*, No. BR 13-158 (FISA Ct. Oct. 11, 2013). There is some dispute about just which phone companies are subject to these ongoing orders.

6. Privacy and Civil Liberties Oversight Board, *Telephone Records Program*, 22.

7. Ibid.

8. 50 U.S.C. § 1861(b)(2)(A); emphasis added.

9. Amended Memorandum Opinion at 20, *In re Application of the Federal Bureau of Investigation for an Order Requiring the Production of Tangible Things [redacted]*, No. BR 13-109 (FISA Ct. Aug. 29, 2013), quoting prior, redacted order.

10. Primary Order.

11. Ibid.

12. 50 U.S.C. § 1861(b)(2)(B).

13. Primary Order, 4.

14. Ibid., 5.

15. Privacy and Civil Liberties Oversight Board, *Telephone Records Program*, 27. The reasonable, articulable suspicion standard is further specified in the Primary Order at 7, as follows: "Based on the factual and practical considerations of everyday life on which reasonable and prudent persons act, there are facts giving rise to a reasonable, articulable suspicion" that the number "is associated with" a terrorist organization identified in the FISA Court's orders.

16. Privacy and Civil Liberties Oversight Board, *Telephone Records Program*, 26, citing Declaration of Teresa H. Shea, Signals Intelligence Director, National Security Agency, ¶23, *ACLU v. Clapper*, 959 F. Supp. 2d 724 (S.D.N.Y. 2013).

17. Declaration of Teresa H. Shea, ¶23.

18. *Katz v. United States*, 389 U.S. 347 (1967).

19. *Katz*, 389 U.S. at 361.

20. *United States v. Miller*, 425 U.S. 435 (1976).

21. *Miller*, 425 U.S. at 443.

22. *Smith v. Maryland*, 442 U.S. 735 (1979)

23. *ACLU v. Clapper*, 959 F. Supp. 2d 724 (S.D.N.Y. 2013); see also David S. Kris, "On the Bulk Collection of Tangible Things," *Journal of National Security Law & Policy* 7, no. 2 (2014): 209–95; Privacy and Civil Liberties Oversight Board, *Telephone Records Program*.

24. *Klayman v. Obama*, 957 F. Supp. 2d 1 (D.D.C. 2013).

25. *United States v. Jones*, 132 S. Ct. 945 (2012).

26. Joel Feinberg, "The Nature and Value of Rights," in *Rights, Justice, and the Bounds of Liberty: Essays in Social Philosophy* (Princeton, NJ: Princeton University Press, 1980), 143–58.

27. Ruth Gavison, "Privacy and the Limits of Law," *The Yale Law Journal* 89, no. 3 (1980): 421–71; Adam D. Moore, *Privacy Rights: Moral and Legal Foundations* (University Park: Pennsylvania State University Press, 2010); Anita L. Allen, *Unpopular Privacy: What Must We Hide?* (Oxford: Oxford University Press, 2011); Judith Wagner DeCew, *In Pursuit of Privacy: Law, Ethics, and the Rise of Technology* (Ithaca, NY: Cornell University Press, 1997); Stanley I. Benn, "Privacy, Freedom, and Respect for Persons," in *Philosophical Dimensions of Privacy: An Anthology*, ed. Ferdinand David Schoeman (Cambridge: Cambridge University Press, 1984), 223–44; Edward Bloustein, "Privacy as an Aspect of Human Dignity: An Answer to Dean Prosser," *New York University Law Review* 39 (1964): 962–1007; Jeffrey H. Reiman, "Privacy, Intimacy, and Personhood," *Philosophy and Public Affairs* 6, no. 1 (1976): 26–44.

28. It is worth pausing to note something about the nature of the argument here. It is possible that the metadata program is a very momentous violation of privacy right, and that that violation is great enough that even very large benefits to most people couldn't justify overriding the rights. Such an argument would not conflict with my arguments here. My strategy is instead to point out why there is something more going on with respect to rights (viz., that the intersection of problems in this case undermines the value of rights to right-holders). By making that case even on the assumption that privacy rights are infringed only slightly, or that they are infringed justifiably, I hope to show that the program is, all things considered, unjustifiable. If I'm right, then the program will also be unjustified (*a fortiori*) if privacy rights infringements are graver, and where there is insufficient grounds to override them.

29. Peter Bergen et al., *Do NSA's Bulk Surveillance Programs Stop Terrorists?* New America Foundation, January 2014, https://static.newamerica.org/attachments/1311-do-nsas-bulk-surveillance-programs-stop-terrorists/IS_NSA_surveillance.pdf.

30. Privacy and Civil Liberties Oversight Board, *Telephone Records Program*, 144–55.

31. Ibid., 212 (separate statement by member Rachel Brand).

32. Dennis F. Thompson, "Democratic Secrecy," *Political Science Quarterly* 114, no. 2 (1999): 181–93.

33. Alan Rubel, "Privacy and the USA Patriot Act: Rights, the Value of Rights, and Autonomy," *Law and Philosophy* 26, no. 2 (2007): 119–59; Alan Rubel, "Profiling, Information Collection and the Value of Rights Argument," *Criminal Justice Ethics* 32, no. 3 (2013): 210–30.

34. Other examples include the right to vote and the right to expression. One might have a fully intact right to vote (access to polls, vote counts the same as others, and one's choice holds sway if it is shared by required proportion of voters), but have that vote be of little value because one does not have sufficient information to distinguish choices. Similarly, one might have a fully intact right to free expression, but that right might be of less value insofar as one lacks financial resources to broadcast or distribute one's expression. See Rubel, "Privacy and the USA Patriot Act," and Rubel, "Value of Rights Argument."

35. This example comes from Rubel, "Value of Rights Argument."

36. Ibid.

37. Benn, "Respect for Persons," 228–29.

38. Bloustein, "Human Dignity."

39. Rubel, "Privacy and the USA Patriot Act"; Thomas Hill Jr., "Autonomy and Benevolent Lies," *Journal of Value Inquiry* 18, no. 4 (1984): 251–97.

40. Feinberg, "Nature and Value of Rights."

41. John Rawls, *Political Liberalism*, The John Dewey Essays in Philosophy, no. 4 (New York: Columbia University Press, 1996), 137.

42. Indeed, there are other cases that fit this pattern. Consider, for example, the particularly aggressive and secret interpretations of laws prohibiting torture. See, for example, memorandum from Jay S. Bybee, assistant attorney general, to Alberto R. Gonzales, counsel to the president, August 1, 2002, National Security Archive, George Washington University, https://www2.gwu.edu/~nsarchiv/NSAEBB/NSAEBB127/02.08.01.pdf (the "Bybee memo"); memorandum from John Yoo, deputy assistant attorney general, and Robert J. Delahunty, special counsel, to William J. Haynes II, general counsel, Department of Defense, January 9, 2002, National Security Archive, George Washington University, http://nsarchive.gwu.edu/NSAEBB/NSAEBB127/02.01.09.pdf; Jeremy Waldron, "Torture and Positive Law: Jurisprudence for the White House," *Columbia Law Review* 105, no. 6 (2005): 1681–1750; "A Guide to the Memos on Torture," *New York Times*, June 25, 2004, http://www.nytimes.com/ref/international/24MEMO-GUIDE.html.

# Chapter Eleven

# Mass Surveillance, Privacy and Freedom

## *A Case for Public Access to Government Surveillance Information*

### Bryce Clayton Newell

Information can provide and facilitate power. Access to information is often a prerequisite to exercising power or seeking redress for potential rights violations stemming from secret activities of others. As such, an imbalance in information access between a people and their government can tip the scales of power and limit the ability of the people to exercise democratic oversight and control of those they have put in power to represent them.[1] Freedom of information laws often provide a great deal of access to government records and serve as a powerful and effective means for empowering oversight by journalists and ordinary citizens. In a very real sense, these laws provide a legal mechanism for citizen-initiated surveillance from underneath (sometimes termed "sousveillance").[2] This form of reciprocal surveillance (which may take numerous forms) grants citizens greater power to check government abuse and force even greater transparency. However, as the recent and ongoing battle for greater transparency in regard to national security intelligence and at the United States' Foreign Intelligence Surveillance Court (FISC) demonstrates, most government records related to mass surveillance for foreign intelligence purposes are strictly guarded, classified, and kept from the people almost *in toto*.

Cross-border intelligence sharing between the global "Five-Eyes" countries (the United States, United Kingdom, Canada, Australia, and New Zealand) has been acknowledged for years, despite the National Security Agency (NSA) only recently declassifying certain historical documents about the

UK–US agreement and its early predecessors in the aftermath of World War II. These collaborative efforts encompass a truly global infrastructure, and they are likely effective at neutralizing a variety of national security threats. They also pose some difficult questions for democratic governance and individual liberty. For example, cross-border information sharing without strict and clearly worded regulations may potentially allow governments to evade domestic restrictions on directly collecting intelligence information about their own citizens. In addition, the string of revelations following Edward Snowden's initial disclosures reinforces the fact that governments are maintaining arguably outdated legal standards about the differences between metadata (or information about information) and the substantive contents of communications. These legal allowances for substantial metadata surveillance pose serious risks to individual privacy and, given the modern reality that information equals (or at least facilitates) power, potentially allow governments to impermissibly interfere with individual liberty and, ultimately, to arbitrarily dominate the citizenry they are supposed to represent.

This chapter explores the relationship between liberty and security implicated by secret government surveillance programs, with an emphasis on the US experience in the near aftermath of Snowden's disclosures in 2013.[3] It includes both doctrinal analysis of case law in the United States and at the European Court of Human Rights (ECtHR) and a normative analysis informed by political philosophy. While examining judicial reasoning in cases where parties have challenged secret government surveillance programs, this chapter will question how liberal and neorepublican conceptions of liberty, defined as the absence of actual interference and the possibility of domination, respectively, can inform the way we think about the proper relationship between security and liberty in the post–9/11, post-Snowden world.

The argument presented in this chapter leads to the conclusion that governments must allow their citizens enough access to information necessary for individual self-government. Greater protections for some types of metadata and aggregate communications data may need to be implemented to effectively reduce the risk of actual interference and domination. Establishing liberal access rights to information about government conduct and mechanisms that ensure that citizens can effectively command noninterference are justified on the grounds that they reduce the possibility of arbitrary, and actual, interference with the right of the people to govern themselves. In an age when technology has "changed the game"[4] by removing barriers to the government's ability to access, aggregate, and utilize the personal information of the people, the law should similarly adapt and provide citizens with rights to counter the otherwise inevitable power imbalance, through greater privacy protections and/or enhanced access to government information.

## MASS SURVEILLANCE AND NATIONAL SECURITY

Mass surveillance is not entirely new, although advances in technology continue to supplement the abilities of governments to gather greater amounts of information much more efficiently. International signals intelligence sharing owes its roots, at least in part, to a British–US intelligence-sharing arrangement that began to take shape as early as 1940. This information-sharing association is often now referred to as Echelon or "Five Eyes." Beginning in the 1940s, the two countries negotiated a number of agreements related to intelligence cooperation and information sharing, establishing a formal agreement on communications intelligence (COMINT) sharing in March of 1946. In 1955 and 1956, the relationship was further formalized in an updated UK–US agreement, which also included reference to the inclusion of Canada, Australia, and New Zealand as "UKUSA-collaborating Commonwealth countries."[5] Subsequent agreements and documents have not been declassified, but the continuing existence of the "Five Eyes" partnership has been confirmed.

In the years between 9/11 and Edward Snowden's leaking documents to the press in 2013, national communications and foreign intelligence programs changed from a "need to know" mentality to a "new culture of 'need to share.'"[6] Based on Snowden's recent revelations and earlier reports, we know that government agencies have been collecting and analyzing vast quantities of telecommunications metadata as well as other online information from social media and online communications providers for quite some time. These disclosures have also led to the Director of National Intelligence (DNI) declassifying a number of surveillance-related documents and legal decisions, as well as to a series of privately initiated lawsuits.[7]

### The (Meta)data Problem

Metadata, commonly defined as "information about information" or "data about data," includes (in the context of electronic communications) information about the time, duration, and location of a communication, as well as the phone numbers or email addresses of the sending and receiving parties. It also may include information about the device used: for example, the make/model and specific device identification number. Metadata is generated whenever a person uses an electronic device (such as a computer, tablet, mobile phone, landline telephone, or even a modern automobile) or an electronic service (such as an email service, social media website, word processing program, or search engine). Often, this results in the creation of considerable amounts of information (metadata). At least with regard to telephone metadata, service providers collect and retain this information in databases that often can be traced directly to an individual person.

## Metadata and Surveillance after Edward Snowden

After Edward Snowden leaked classified NSA documents in 2013, questions about the nature of government collection of communications metadata took a more prominent place on the world stage. Snowden's first revelation was a classified court order from the secretive FISC that compelled Verizon, one of the largest US telecommunications providers, to provide the US government with all of its customers' telephone metadata on an ongoing basis—encompassing landline, wireless, and smartphone communications. Other disclosures indicate that the three major US telecommunications companies were subject to similar orders and that NSA surveillance covered approximately 75 percent of all Internet traffic in the US, including email.[8]

In the months that followed, additional disclosures (approved and otherwise) continued to paint a broader picture of the NSA's domestic and international surveillance activities. The DNI declassified and released additional documents related to current and past surveillance programs. The White House commissioned a Review Group on Intelligence and Communications Technologies to investigate the proper balance between personal security (privacy) and national, or homeland, security, and federal courts have now handed down conflicting decisions about whether the NSA surveillance programs disclosed by Snowden violate the Fourth Amendment rights of American citizens.[9]

In a decision from the FISC, likely rendered in July 2004, Judge Kollar-Kotelly upheld the constitutionality of a prior bulk Internet metadata collection program that had been suspended for a period of months due to concerns about its legitimacy.[10] This decision also marked the point when legal authorization for bulk Internet metadata surveillance transitioned from the President's Surveillance Program, spurred by President Bush's October 4, 2001, authorization memorandum, to FISC jurisdiction. The prior program had been instituted by the NSA after government lawyers concluded the NSA did not "acquire" communications during bulk collection, but only after specific communications were "selected" using "selectors that met certain criteria." In her decision, Judge Kollar-Kotelly recognizes that bulk metadata collection imposes a "much broader type of collection than other pen register/trap and trace applications" than the courts had grappled with before. However, she ultimately concluded that the bulk collection at issue was consistent with the Foreign Intelligence Surveillance Act (FISA) and the First and Fourth amendments to the Constitution, with some modifications (e.g., NSA analysts could only conduct approved queries).[11]

In another FISC decision, a few years later, Judge Bates reauthorized the bulk collection of metadata about Internet communications.[12] In his decision, Judge Bates notes that the NSA acknowledged that it had exceeded the scope of its authorization under earlier orders for a matter of years. However, because the government "asserted that it has a strong national security interest in accessing and using the overcollected information" and "high-level officials" in the Department of Justice and NSA personally promised the FISC that they would "closely monitor" future collection, Judge Bates allowed the NSA to use and query the information collected unlawfully and approved future collection.[13] In a subsequent FISC decision, Judge Walton noted that the government had disclosed a number of additional compliance problems and continued to inadequately conform to the requirements of FISC orders authorizing and regulating intelligence collection under both the Internet surveillance program and a similar metadata surveillance program targeting telephone communications.[14]

## Problems with Binary Fourth Amendment Theory

Much of the metadata surveillance conducted by the NSA, including the harvesting of telephone records of US citizens, is permitted, legally, based on Supreme Court decisions about the appropriate expectation of privacy that individuals may hold in "non-content" (metadata) information.[15] These cases held that citizens cannot claim privacy interests, vis-à-vis the government, in records turned over to a third party (bank records)[16] or in the numbers dialed from a telephone.[17] A recent FISC decision[18] upholding the constitutionality of the FBI/NSA telephone metadata surveillance program authored by Judge Claire Eagan and released on September 17, 2013, failed to take account of potentially important dicta in Supreme Court's decision in *United States v. Jones*.[19] In that case, the justices held that the warrantless application of a GPS tracking device to a suspect's automobile violated the suspect's Fourth Amendment rights. In two concurring opinions signed by five justices, Justices Sotomayor and Alito separately argued that aggregated geolocational metadata ought to raise a reasonable expectation of privacy.[20] Because of the concurring opinions in *Jones*, which signal the possibility that a majority of the justices might be open to revisiting Fourth Amendment theory in light of modern technologically aided police practices, it may be an opportune time to argue for a normative approach to privacy in Fourth Amendment jurisprudence that is more sensitive to context (not bound by purely binary distinctions) and the increasingly revealing capacity of metadata surveillance, especially when such information is collected, stored, and mined in the aggregate.

## SECRET SURVEILLANCE CASE LAW:
## THE UNITED STATES AND EUROPE

Courts around the world have grappled with the legal issues implicated by secret government surveillance programs for a number of years. The two succeeding sections provide a brief overview of some of the important cases in the United States and at the ECtHR.

## The European Court of Human Rights

The ECtHR has a long history of decisions questioning whether secret government surveillance is conducted consistently with the provisions of Article 8 of the European Convention on Human Rights (the "Convention"). The Convention acts (along with individual state constitutions) as one European corollary to the US Constitution, and functions as a basic limit on government authority to conduct domestic (and international) surveillance, albeit at a supranational level.

Article 8 of the Convention states (in relevant part):

1. Everyone has the right to respect for his private and family life, his home and his correspondence.
2. There shall be no interference by a public authority with the exercise of this right except such as is in accordance with the law and is necessary in a democratic society. [21]

The first relevant ECtHR case is *Klass and Others v. Germany*[22] from 1978. In that case, Klass and four other applicants challenged provisions of a German surveillance statute on two primary grounds: first, that the act did not require the government to notify targets of surveillance after the surveillance had concluded and, second, that the act excluded remedies before regular domestic courts. Ultimately, the ECtHR found no violation of the applicants' Article 8 rights, but the court outlined the relevant test to determine when secret surveillance powers might violate a person's basic human rights. This test has been largely adopted in recent cases, with some modifications.

The applicants in *Klass*, lawyers who regularly represented individuals they suspected of being under surveillance, claimed that their own communications might also have been intercepted, and initiated claims to challenge the surveillance as a violation of their Article 8 rights. The European Commission on Human Rights (the "Commission") declared the application admissible to the ECtHR, essentially holding that the applicants had standing, even though they could not provide definite evidence that their communication had actually been intercepted. In its subsequent decision, the ECtHR agreed, holding that "an individual may, under certain conditions, claim to be the victim of a violation occasioned by the mere existence of secret measures or of legislation permitting secret measures, without having to allege that such measures were in fact applied to him." The ECtHR noted that to hold otherwise might reduce Article 8 to a "nullity," since a state could potentially violate a person's rights in secret, without any risk that a person could bring a claim for relief.

Having determined the application admissible, the court found that "the mere existence of the legislation" constituted a "menace" of surveillance which, "necessarily strikes at freedom of communication between users of the postal and telecommunication services and thereby constitutes an 'interference by a public authority' with the exercise of the applicants' right to respect for private and family life and for correspondence." Finding that the surveillance at issue was done in "accordance with [German] law" and that it was conducted for a legitimate purpose, the court conceded that in extraordinary circumstances, legislation that provides for secret surveillance of physical or electronic communication can be "necessary in a democratic society." However, because such laws pose a danger of "undermining or even destroying democracy on the ground of defending it," legislatures may not simply "adopt whatever measures they deem appropriate" in their "struggle against espionage and terrorism." Getting to the heart of whether such surveillance is necessary in a democratic society, the court stated, "Whatever system of surveillance is adopted, there [must] exist adequate and effective guarantees against abuse."

The court concluded that the German law did not violate the applicants' Article 8 rights because the law limited the ability of the government to conduct surveillance "to cases in which there are factual indications for suspecting a person of planning, committing or having committed certain serious criminal acts," and that "[c]onsequently, so-called exploratory or general surveillance is not permitted by the contested legislation." This test has been largely adopted in subsequent ECtHR decisions, with some modifications (including more restrictive requirements when determining whether conduct is "in accordance with law") developing in a few important cases.

Because of the secret nature of the surveillance at issue, the ECtHR has generally allowed applicants' standing in subsequent cases, even without an allegation of facts that would support a finding that the secret surveillance was actually applied to them. In recent cases, the ECtHR continues to adhere to the finding announced in *Klass* that the mere existence of legislation allowing secret surveillance constitutes an interference with a person's Article 8 rights. In *Malone v. the United Kingdom*,[23] the ECtHR reaffirmed this position, holding that because telephone conversations fell within the scope of "private life" and "communications," the existence of legislation that allowed the interception of telephone conversations amounted to an interference with the applicant's rights. This extends to general programs of surveillance as well as targeted eavesdropping on private conversations.[24] Because of the essentially settled nature of this finding, most of the interesting judicial reasoning happens in answering the subsequent questions in the Article 8 analysis.

Initially, with the *Klass* decision, the requirement that an act of interference must be in accordance with the law was also easy to overcome. However, in subsequent cases, the ECtHR has added additional tests to determine the answer to this question. By 1984, the *Malone* court recognized that this requirement also demanded more than just compliance with domestic law; specifically, the law must be accessible, its applicability to a set of circumstances must be foreseeable, and it must be compatible with the rule of law. That is, a citizen "must be able—if need be with appropriate advice—to foresee, to a degree that is reasonable in the circumstances, the consequences which a given action may entail." Finally, if a form of interference (e.g., surveillance) passes all the prior tests (meaning it is otherwise in "accordance with law"), it must still be "necessary in a democratic society" to achieve one or more legitimate aims spelled out in the Convention.

In essence, this inquiry requires a finding of proportionality, and authorities maintain a "fairly wide margin" of discretion, but such discretion is not unlimited.[25] Specifically, there must be adequate and effective guarantees to prevent abuse and, after a finding of proportionality (as the first step of this analysis), the court undertakes a holistic overall assessment (for safeguards against abuse), based on all the facts of the case; the nature, scope, and duration of the possible measures; the grounds required for ordering them; the authorities competent to authorize, carry out, and supervise them; and the kind of remedy provided by the national law.[26]

In *Weber and Saravia v. Germany*,[27] the applicants claimed violations under the same German eavesdropping law that was at issue in *Klass*. Rather than taking issue with targeted interception of telecommunications of specific individuals, however, the applicants in the *Weber* case claimed that their Article 8 rights had been violated by a broader intelligence practice of "strategic monitoring" of telecommunications and the subsequent uses of such information (including information sharing with other agencies). In *Weber*, the ECtHR found that the German law in question did contain adequate safeguards against arbitrary interference.

In *Liberty v. the United Kingdom*,[28] the applicant charity organization alleged that the UK Ministry of Defence operated a facility that was capable of intercepting ten thousand simultaneous telephone channels operating between Dublin and London and from London to the European Continent, as well as a certain amount of radio-based telephone, facsimile, and email communications carried between two British Telecom stations. The government refused to confirm or deny the specific allegations, but agreed, for purposes of the litigation, that the applicants were of the category of legal persons who could be subject to having their communications intercepted by the government under its intelligence-gathering programs. Liberty argued that the secret nature of the Secretary's "arrangements" under the Interception of Communications Act rendered the alleged procedures and safeguards inaccessible to the public and made it impossible for the public to foresee how and in what circumstances the government could intercept their communications. The ECtHR agreed with the government's contentions that all the elements of the accessibility and foreseeability requirements did not need to be specified in primary legislation (for example, they could be specified in administrative orders and other soft law sources), but that secondary sources could satisfy this requirement "only to 'the admittedly limited extent to which those concerned were made sufficiently aware of their contents.'"[29]

However, the ECtHR held that the government had violated the applicants' Article 8 rights in that case. The court came to this conclusion for a few reasons. First, the accessible law did not place any restrictions on the type of external (non-UK) communications that could be included in a warrant, a fact that the court found indicative of "virtually unfettered" executive discretion. Second, the act granted wide discretion to the authorities to determine which of the collected communications to actually review substantively. The secretary of state could issue certificates describing material to be examined, using broad limiting terms and reasons such as "national security" to authorize review of the contents of communications. These certificates could be applied to all communications except those "emanating from a particular address in the United Kingdom," unless the secretary determined such interception was necessary to prevent or detect acts of terrorism. The act also required the secretary to "'make such arrangements as he consider[ed] necessary' to ensure that material not covered by the certificate was not examined and that material that was certified as requiring examination was disclosed and reproduced only to the extent necessary."

Importantly, details of these arrangements were secret and not made accessible to the public. A commissioner did make annual reports stating that the secretary's arrangements were in accordance with the law, but the ECtHR held that, while these reports were helpful, they did not make the details of the scheme any more clear or accessible to the public, since the commissioner was not allowed to reveal details about the arrangements in his public reports. Indeed, the court stated that "the procedures to be followed for examining, using and storing intercepted material, inter alia, should be set out in a form which is open to public scrutiny and knowledge."

The ECtHR dismissed the government's claims that revealing such information publicly would damage the efficacy of the government's intelligence operations because, as indicated in its earlier decision in *Weber*, the German government had included such guidelines and restrictions in its primary (and publicly accessible) legislation itself. In conclusion, the court held that the domestic law did not "provide adequate protection against abuse of power" because of its broad scope and the "very wide discretion conferred on the State to intercept and examine external communications." The court found it particularly important that the government did not make its procedures for "examin[ing], sharing, storing and destroying intercepted material" accessible to the public.

In *Weber*, the court also laid out these requirements in some detail. In that case, the court stated:

> [W]here a power vested in the executive is exercised in secret, the risks of arbitrariness are evident. It is therefore essential to have clear, detailed rules on interception of telephone conversations, especially as the technology available for use is continually becoming more sophisticated. . . . Moreover, since the implementation in practice of measures of secret surveillance of communications is not open to scrutiny by the individuals concerned or the public at large, it would be contrary to the rule of law for the legal discretion granted to the executive or to a judge to be expressed in terms of an unfettered power.[30]

In the case of *Iordachi and Others v. Moldova*,[31] the court also found a violation of Article 8. In that case, the court found that the Moldovan law at issue lacked adequate clarity and detail because (1) there was no judicial control over the granting of applications for interceptions, (2) the law was very open-ended in regard to the persons potentially within its reach, and (3) the requirements for granting warrants were imprecise. Interestingly, the ECtHR also stated that the Moldovan secret surveillance system appeared "overused" since the courts approved "virtually all" of the prosecutor's requests for warrants. The court also noted that the numbers of issued warrants each year over a three-year period (2,300, 1,900, and 2,500, respectively) was indicative of "inadequacy" in the "safeguards contained in the law."

In *Ekimdzhiev*[32] the court found that a Bulgarian law provided sufficient safeguards, at the authorization stage, so that if it were "strictly adhered to," only specifically delineated forms of communications would be intercepted. However, because the law did not provide for any independent review of the intelligence agency's implementation of these measures after the initial authorization stage, it failed to satisfy the requirement that it provide adequate guarantees against the risk of abuse. The ECtHR also found that, although the lack of provisions requiring notification to a person that their communications had been intercepted was not itself unreasonable, a blanket classification of information, in perpetuity, creates the untenable situation where "the persons concerned cannot learn whether they have ever been monitored and are accordingly unable to seek redress for unlawful interferences with their Article 8 rights."

## The United States

Mass communications surveillance by the US federal government's intelligence and law-enforcement agencies has been occurring for decades. In 1978, Congress enacted FISA to check and balance electronic government surveillance and individual rights to privacy under the Fourth Amendment to the US Constitution. FISA allows the government to intercept communications involving foreign powers or "agents of foreign powers," and to maintain secrecy about whose correspondence the government has intercepted. FISA established two courts, FISC and the Foreign Intelligence Surveillance Court of Review (FISCR), drawing upon federal judges from Article III courts to administer secret, nonadversarial, proceedings initiated by government agencies to approve government requests to collect information under FISA. Notably, court proceedings and opinions are generally secret and not available for public scrutiny. Indeed, during the first 24 years of its existence, from its inception until 2002, the FISC only ever publicly released one single opinion (which did not relate to electronic surveillance) and, it turned out, had never rejected a government application to conduct surveillance. [33]

In 2002, the FISC, acting *en banc*, publicly released an opinion signed by all seven judges that refused to allow the government to use the USA PATRIOT Act to enable closer collaboration by intelligence agents and criminal prosecutors to prosecute crimes uncovered through foreign communications intelligence surveillance. Six months later, the FISCR sharply overruled the FISC opinion, holding that the FISC had "not only misinterpreted and misapplied minimization procedures it was entitled to impose . . . [it] may well have exceeded the constitutional bounds that restrict an Article III court."[34] The FISCR also stated that maintaining a divide between criminal and intelligence investigations that walled off certain investigatory and prosecutorial collaboration "was never required and was never intended by Congress."[35] In the intervening years, a number of lawsuits have emerged challenging government powers under FISA and its amending legislation, including the Foreign Intelligence Surveillance Amendments Act of 1978 and the USA PATRIOT Act. The purpose of this section is not necessarily to document each and every case, but rather to explore the judicial reasoning that pervades these decisions.

In February 2013, the US Supreme Court decided *Clapper v. Amnesty International USA*,[36] which stands in fairly sharp contrast to the line of ECtHR cases beginning with *Klass*, as discussed above. In *Clapper*, the court rejected a challenge to the constitutionality of FISA mounted by a number of attorneys and a variety of other human rights, legal, media, and labor organizations. In that case, the plaintiffs sued the US government, claiming that surveillance authorized under Section 1881a (otherwise known as Section 702, enacted in 2008 by the FISA Amendments Act) violated their constitutional rights. The organizations claimed, as did the attorneys in *Klass*, that, because of their regular communications with overseas persons, there was an "objectively reasonable likelihood that their communications will be acquired under Section 1881a at some point in the future," and that the threat of this acquisition had caused them to take costly preventive measures aimed at preserving the confidentiality of their communications.

Despite the fact that, due to the law's secrecy requirements, the government is the only entity that knows which communications have been intercepted, the court held that third parties like Amnesty International do not have standing to challenge the act because they cannot show that they have been harmed (precisely because they don't have access to information about the government's surveillance activities). Unlike at the ECtHR, the Supreme Court held that the mere existence of secret surveillance did not grant standing, effectively blocking any challenge to secret programs absent some form of prior disclosure.

## Enter Edward Snowden

In May 2013, Snowden leaked a secret FISC order to *Guardian* journalist Glenn Greenwald, which was published on June 5. In that order, the FISC directed Verizon, one of the largest telecommunications providers in the United States, to turn over phone call metadata on millions of Americans to the NSA on an ongoing and daily basis. Justice Claire Eagan's decision, released September 17, 2013, upheld a subsequent order requiring similar, continued compliance by an unnamed telecommunications provider.[37] Following the *Guardian*'s publication of the Verizon order, the American Civil Liberties Union (ACLU) and New York Civil Liberties Union (NYCLU) filed a lawsuit against the NSA. Both the ACLU and NYCLU claimed standing in their complaint because they were actually Verizon customers during the dates covered by the FISC order.

Years earlier, in 2006, the Electronic Frontier Foundation (EFF) had sued AT&T for violating its customers' privacy by collaborating with the NSA to conduct electronic surveillance of its customers.[38] In response to this case, and dozens of other lawsuits fueled by news reports of the government's warrantless surveillance program, Congress enacted Section 802 of the FISA Amendments Act to grant these corporations retroactive immunity. Subsequently, in 2008, EFF filed suit against the NSA and various other federal entities in *Jewel v. NSA*, claiming that the same warrantless dragnet surveillance program violated the plaintiffs' constitutional rights.[39] Although this case was based on leaked documentation of the alleged practices, unlike *Clapper*, the case was also originally dismissed on standing grounds.

However, the Ninth Circuit later reversed and allowed the plaintiffs standing to continue their suit.[40] In July 2013, the US District Court for the Northern District of California rejected the government's state secrets defense, allowing the plaintiffs' First and Fourth Amendment claims to move forward. The district court did, however, conclude that the plaintiffs might have an uphill battle to overcome standing after *Clapper*.[41] Subsequently, on

February 10, 2015, the district court dismissed the plaintiffs' claims in regards to the interception of their Internet communications on summary judgment, holding that they had "failed to establish a sufficient factual basis" to gain standing and, in any event, "even if Plaintiffs could establish standing, a potential Fourth Amendment Claim would have to be dismissed on the basis that any possible defenses would require impermissible disclosure of state secret information."[42]

Similarly, in *CCR v. Obama*, the Ninth Circuit affirmed dismissal of a case challenging the Terrorist Surveillance Program, which ended in 2007.[43] The court found that the plaintiffs lacked standing, much like the plaintiffs in *Clapper v. Amnesty International USA*.

In two recent district court decisions at the end of 2013, the District Court for the District of Columbia and the District Court for the Southern District of New York came to opposite conclusions about the legality of the NSA's bulk telephone metadata surveillance activities.[44] Also in 2013, the Supreme Court declined to hear a case filed directly with the high court by the Electronic Privacy Information Center.[45] In the *ACLU v. Clapper* case, the plaintiffs overcame the standing issue that plagued Amnesty International USA in *Clapper v. Amnesty International USA* because they could show, thanks to the Snowden disclosures, they were, in fact, the subjects of the government's phone call metadata surveillance. However, in reliance on the third-party doctrine, the court concluded that telephone service subscribers maintained no legitimate expectation of privacy in their call metadata. Conversely, in *Klayman v. Obama*, the court found that the "plaintiffs have a very significant expectation of privacy in an aggregated collection of their telephony metadata covering the last five years, and the NSA's Bulk Telephony Metadata Program significantly intrudes on that expectation."[46] However, despite this positive finding in favour of individual Fourth Amendment privacy, the court stayed its holding pending an appeal.

These cases demonstrate that US courts are often exercising restraint when confronting challenges to the federal government's claims of secrecy in the name of national security. This restraint is in fairly sharp contrast to the willingness of the ECtHR to allow challenges and hold governments accountable for secret surveillance.[47] These situations clearly represent the nature and existence of potentially dominating activity by the state. As elaborated in the overall argument advanced in this chapter, because the holdings effectively immunize the federal government from citizen review of the procedures and substance of government action, they are highly suspect and problematic.

## LIBERTY: INTERFERENCE OR DOMINATION?

### Liberal Liberty: Berlin's Negative Conception of Freedom

One of the most seminal essays in modern political philosophy on the topic of political liberty is Isaiah Berlin's *Two Concepts of Liberty*.[48] In that essay, Berlin outlines the trajectory of two different conceptions of liberty, what he calls "negative" and "positive" liberties. On one hand, negative liberty "is simply the area within which a [person] can act unobstructed by others."[49] A person's *degree* of freedom rests on whether, or how thoroughly, that person is prevented from doing something by another person. A certain level of interference by another with one person's freedom to do something, in Berlin's view, can equate to coercion or slavery, and thus ought to be avoided. On the other hand, Berlin defines positive liberty as a form of self-mastery; to have one's decisions depend on no other person or any other force. Berlin's conception of negative liberty has provided the basis for much contemporary work on philosophical liberty in the liberal tradition. Berlin himself noted that his version of negative liberty was not "logically . . . connected with democracy or self-government," although democratic self-government may admittedly guarantee liberty better than other forms of rule.[50] Berlin states that "[t]he answer to the question 'Who governs me?' is logically distinct from the question 'How far does the government interfere with me?'"[51] Other writers have distinguished between "effective freedom" and "formal freedom" as a way to clarify Berlin's distinctions between positive and negative and to make the point that the absence of restraint (defined in terms of *legal* restraints) does not always guarantee the actual ability of an individual to do something he or she is legally entitled to do (for example, a person may not be able to take an expensive international vacation because of economic hardship).[52] On one hand, negative freedom is concerned with the absence of state restraint (or interference), while positive freedom is concerned about equalizing the effective freedoms of everyone in a society (e.g., international vacations might be assured by a state mandating a certain level of basic income). Some forms of positive freedom might also privilege the value of political engagement and self-government, as opposed to viewing laws as an interference (whether justified or not) on personal liberty.[53]

### Neorepublican Liberty: Pettit's Theory of Nondomination

In recent decades, republicanism, as an alternative to liberalism, has received renewed attention. Philip Pettit, a champion of one form of republicanism, often termed neorepublicanism or civic-republicanism, proposes a conceptualization of freedom as the opposite of "defenseless susceptibility to interference by another"—or put more simply, nondomination or "antipower."[54]

This proposition is part of a larger neorepublican research agenda based on three primary tenets: individual freedom (conceptualized as freedom as non-domination), limited government power over its citizens based on a mixture of constitutionalism and the rule of law (with an emphasis on the importance of the free state promoting the freedom of its citizens without dominating them), and a vigilant commitment by citizens to preserve the freedom-pre-serving structure and substance of their government through active democratic participation.[55]

Contrary to Berlin's account of negative liberty—that a person is free to the extent that no other entity actually interferes with that person's activity—Pettit's neorepublican position does away with the requirement of actual interference, focusing on eliminating the danger (or potential danger) of arbitrary interference from others.[56] Rather than predicating freedom on ideas of self-mastery, autonomy, or a person's ability to act in accordance with their higher-order desires, an account of Berlin's positive liberty, neorepublican theory is more concerned with ensuring the ability of the people to self-govern, by reducing domination and arbitrary interference. Pettit bases his account on the idea that the opposite of freedom is slavery (or the subjugation to arbitrary exercise of power).[57] Pettit is concerned that a conception of liberty limited to noninterference restricts our potential for appropriate emancipation from domination. Lovett argues that since political liberty ought to be "understood as a sort of structural relationship that exists between persons or groups, rather than as a contingent outcome of that structure," freedom is properly seen "as a sort of structural independence—as the condition of not being subject to the arbitrary power of a master."[58]

On some republican accounts, power and domination are built into the structure of social institutions, and this structure, if constructed improperly, potentially allows institutions to dominate and subjugate the people systemically. This, in turn, makes it difficult for "individuals and groups to possess political control over the institutions which govern their lives," a serious problem for republican politics.[59] Domination, then, can become institution-alized and integrated into our social and political institutions in a way that creates systemic domination, as well as evidenced in the relationships between agents of government and individuals or groups of citizens.

But what exactly is domination, from the neorepublican position? Domination requires the capacity to interfere, with impunity and in an arbitrary fashion, with certain choices that the dominated agent otherwise has the capacity to make. I say "certain choices" because the scope of the interference need not impinge on all of the dominated agent's choices, but may be limited to just a subset of choices of varying centrality or importance. Interference requires "an intentional attempt to worsen an agent's situation of choice."[60] Unintentional or accidental interference is not freely exercised subjugation. However, interference does encompass a wide variety of possible actions, including restraint, obstruction, coercion, punishment (or threat of punishment), and manipulation (which includes, in Pettit's view, "agenda fixing, the deceptive . . . shaping of people's beliefs or desires, [and] rigging . . . the consequences of people's actions").[61]

If an agent is capable of interfering with impunity and at will (or arbitrarily) to dominate another, without risk of penalty for interfering—whether from the victim themselves (directly or indirectly) or society at large—then the agent has "absolutely arbitrary power."[62] The only check on the exercise of such power is in the agent itself—in that agent's free and capricious will. Thus, it follows that a person (X) is dominated by another (Y) when X has no legal recourse to contest actions by Y that interfere with X's situation of choice. Thus, because widespread state surveillance of the communications of its citizens has the potential to interfere with individual citizens' situations of choice (for example, by chilling free expression), this relationship exhibits domination.

In response to this conception of domination as the antithesis of liberty, the neorepublican project places a great premium on emancipation—through balancing power and limiting arbitrary discretion—and active political participation. Importantly, reversing roles would not solve the problem of domination but merely relocate it. Fairly allocating power to both sides, on the other hand, does not just equalize the subjugation; if both sides—say, the people and their government—may interfere with the other's affairs, then neither may act with impunity since the other may exact something in return. Thus, "neither dominates the other."[63] This is an exemplification of what Pettit terms "antipower." According to Pettit, "Antipower is what comes into being as the power of some over others—the power of some over others in the sense associated with domination—is actively reduced and eliminated."[64] Antipower, then, subjugates power and, as a form of power itself, allows persons to control the nature of their own destiny. In this sense, the "person enjoys the noninterference resiliently" because they are not dependent on the arbitrary use of power, precisely because they have the power to "command noninterference."[65] Because access to information is a prerequisite to seeking legal recourse for potentially dominating activities of another, this aspect of power regulation should take an important place in our domestic and international information policies, and might be seen as instrumental to achieving robust antipower.

## CONCLUSION

Government surveillance can be detrimental to individual liberty. It may chill the exercise of civil liberties, such as free speech, or may violate subjective and/or objective expectations of privacy that ought to be protected under the

Fourth Amendment. Secret surveillance laws pose a danger of "undermining or even destroying democracy on the grounds of defending it" in their "struggle against espionage and terrorism."[66] Fully realizing a situation of more equalized reciprocal surveillance and rights to access information about government activities (with temporary exceptions as may be needed to protect national security) would give citizens greater ability to ensure their government is not overreaching and abusing its authority, to hold the state and state actors accountable for rights violations, and to maintain government as an entity that protects its citizens' freedoms without coming to subjugate them to arbitrary exercises of power.

The primary point of this argument, then, is not that we eliminate or unduly restrict the ability of government and law enforcement to conduct surveillance (or to restrict access to certain information in some cases), but rather that we recognize the bargain we have struck, in our representative democratic society, that the government assumes some surveillance powers—and thus encroaches on our individual negative freedoms to some degree—because it has the ability (and the responsibility) to use these powers for the public good. Our contract, and our consent, does not negate the possibility of domination or the relevance of freedom (including its attendant needs for personal privacy and free speech). However, this power cannot be granted without strings attached.

An imbalance in information access between a people and their government will tip the scales of power and limit the ability of the people to exercise democratic oversight and control over those they have put in power to represent them. Freedom of information laws provide one way to access government records and serve as a powerful and effective means for empowering oversight by journalists and ordinary citizens. These laws, which provide a legal mechanism for citizen-initiated reciprocal surveillance, must capture more information about the legal bases and secret surveillance programs to ensure that "adequate and effective guarantees against abuse" exist.[67] The violation of our rights should not hinge on our *awareness* of government overreaching, but whether the government has in fact acted impermissibly, visibly, or in secret. As such, our access to remedies (and information) should not similarly be limited solely to cases involving nonsecret government action.

Strict limitations on standing in cases challenging secret government surveillance activities constitute an interference with individual freedom, as the ECtHR has held. The stark differences in the ability of plaintiffs to claim violations of their constitutional or basic human rights in the United States and at the ECtHR provides a suggestive critique of the nature of the current judicial politics of surveillance and transparency in domestic US courts. The unwillingness of US courts to allow challenges to secret government surveillance programs on standing grounds is a failure of the judicial system to check the ability of the executive to usurp arbitrary domination over the people. It is a failure of antipower in America.

## NOTES

1. Craig Forcese and Aaron Freeman, *The Laws of Government: The Legal Foundations of Canadian Democracy* (Toronto, ON: Irwin Law, 2005), 481–84.
2. Steve Mann, Jason Nolan, and Barry Wellman, "Sousveillance: Inventing and Using Wearable Computing Devices for Data Collection in Surveillance Environments," *Surveillance & Society* 1, no. 3 (2003): 331; Jean-Gabriel Ganascia, "The Generalized Sousveillance Society," *Social Science Information* 49, no. 3 (2011): 489.
3. An extended version of this chapter was previously published as Bryce Clayton Newell, "The Massive Metadata Machine: Liberty, Power, and Secret Mass Surveillance in the U.S. and Europe," *I/S: A Journal of Law and Policy for the Information Society* 10, no. 2 (2014): 481.
4. Adam D. Moore, *Privacy Rights: Moral and Legal Foundations* (University Park: Pennsylvania State University Press, 2010), 4.
5. National Security Agency, "U.K.–U.S. Communications Intelligence Agreement, U.S.-U.K.," May 10, 1955, http://www.nsa.gov/public_info/_files/ukusa/new_ukusa_agree_10may55.pdf.
6. Peter P. Swire, "Privacy and Information Sharing in the War on Terrorism," *Villanova Law Review* 51, no. 4 (2006): 951.
7. See *ACLU v. Clapper*, 2013 WL 6819708 (S.D.N.Y. Dec. 27, 2013); *Klayman v. Obama*, 2013 WL 6571596 (D.D.C. Dec. 16, 2013); In re Electronic Privacy Information Center, 134 S. Ct. 638 (2013); *First Unitarian Church of Los Angeles v. NSA*, First Amended Complaint, 2013 WL 5311964 (N.D. Cal. Sept. 10, 2013).
8. Siobhan Gorman and Jennifer Valentino-DeVries, "NSA Reaches Deep into U.S. to Spy on Net," *Wall Street Journal*, August 21, 2013, A1.
9. Compare *ACLU v. Clapper*, 2013 WL 6819708, with *Klayman v. Obama*, 2013 WL 6571596.
10. [Case name redacted], No. PR/TT [redacted], slip op. at 80 (FISA Ct.) (opinion of Kollar-Kotelly, J), http://www.dni.gov/files/documents/1118/CLEANEDPRTT%201.pdf.
11. [Case name redacted], No. PR/TT [redacted], slip op. at 2 (FISA Ct.) (opinion of Kollar-Kotelly, J).
12. [Case name redacted], No. PR/TT [redacted], slip op. at 2 (FISA Ct.) (opinion of Bates, J.), http://www.dni.gov/files/documents/1118/CLEANEDPRTT%202.pdf.
13. [Case name redacted], No. PR/TT [redacted], slip op. at 115–16 (FISA Ct.) (opinion of Bates, J.).
14. In re Application of the Federal Bureau of Investigation for an Order Requiring the Production of Tangible Things from [redacted], no. BR 09-06, slip op. at 2, available at http://www.dni.gov/files/documents/1118/CLEANED101.%20Order%20and%20Supplemental%20Order%20%286-22-09%29-sealed.pdf.
15. See Bryce Clayton Newell, "Rethinking Reasonable Expectations of Privacy in Online Social Networks," *Richmond Journal of Law & Technology* 17, no. 4, art. 12 (2011): 32.
16. *United States v. Miller*, 425 U.S. 435 (1976).
17. *Smith v. Maryland*, 442 U.S. 735 (1979).
18. In re Application of the Federal Bureau of Investigation for an Order Requiring the Production of Tangible Things from [redacted], no. BR 13-109, slip op. at 2 (as amended and released on Sept. 17, 2013), http://www.fisc.uscourts.gov/sites/default/files/BR%2013-109%20Order-1.pdf.
19. *United States v. Jones*, 132 S. Ct. 945 (2012).
20. *United States v. Jones*, 132 S. Ct. at 954 (Sotomayor, J. concurring), 958 (Alito, J. concurring).

21. Council of Europe, European Convention for the Protection of Human Rights and Fundamental Freedoms, art. 8, Apr. 11, 1950, 213 U.N.T.S. 221 (as amended), available at http://conventions.coe.int/Treaty/en/Treaties/Html/005.htm.

22. *Klass v. Germany*, App. No. 5029/71, 2 Eur. H.R. Rep. 214 (ser. A) (1978).

23. *Malone v. United Kingdom*, App. No. 8691/79, 7 Eur. H.R. Rep 14 (1984).

24. *Liberty v. United Kingdom*, App. No. 58243/0, 2008 Eur. Ct. H.R. 568 (2008), para. 63.

25. *Weber and Saravia v. Germany*, App. No. 54934/00, 2006-XI Eur. Ct. H.R. 1173 (2006), para. 106.

26. *Association for European Integration and Human Rights and Ekimdzhiev v. Bulgaria*, App. No. 62540/00, 2007 Eur. Ct. H.R. 533 (2007), para. 91.

27. *Weber and Saravia v. Germany*, 2006-XI Eur. Ct. H.R. 1173 (2006).

28. *Liberty v. United Kingdom*, 2008 Eur. Ct. H.R. 568 (2008).

29. *Liberty v. United Kingdom*, 2008 Eur. Ct. H.R. 568 (2008), para. 61, quoting *Malone v. United Kingdom*, 7 Eur. H.R. Rep 14.

30. *Weber and Saravia v. Germany*, 2006-XI Eur. Ct. H.R. 1173 (2006), paras. 93–94.

31. *Iordachi v. Moldova*, App. No. 25198/02, 2009 Eur. Ct. H.R. 256 (2009).

32. *Association for European Integration and Human Rights and Ekimdzhiev v. Bulgaria*, 2007 Eur. Ct. H.R. 533 (2007).

33. Diane Carraway Piette and Jesslyn Radack, "Piercing the Historical Mists: The People and Events behind the Passage of FISA and the Creation of the Wall," *Stanford Law & Policy Review* 17, no. 2 (2006): 439.

34. In re Sealed Case No. 02-001, 310 F.3d 717, 731 (FISA Ct. Rev. 2002).

35. Neil A. Lewis, "Court Overturns Limits on Wiretaps to Combat Terror," *New York Times*, November 19, 2002; Piette and Radack, "Piercing the Historical Mists," 440.

36. *Clapper v. Amnesty International USA*, 133 S.Ct. 1138 (2013).

37. In re Application of the Federal Bureau of Investigation for an Order Requiring the Production of Tangible Things from [redacted], no. BR 13-109, slip op. at 3.

38. *Nat'l Sec. Agency Telecommunications Records Litigation v. AT&T Corp.*, 671 F.3d at 890–91.

39. *Jewel v. NSA*, 2013 U.S. Dist. LEXIS 103009 (N.D. Cal. July 23, 2013), *9–*11.

40. *Jewel v. NSA*, 673 F.3d 902.

41. *Jewel v. NSA*, 2013 U.S. Dist. LEXIS 103009, *21.

42. *Jewel v. NSA*, 2015 WL 545925, *1.

43. In re NSA Telecommunications Records Litigation, 522 F.App'x 383 (9th Cir. 2013).

44. *ACLU v. Clapper*, 2013 WL 6819708; *Klayman v. Obama*, 2013 WL 6571596.

45. In re Electronic Privacy Information Center, 134 S.Ct. 638.

46. *Klayman v. Obama*, 2013 WL 6571596, *23.

47. To be sure, the ECtHR has a different relationship to its relevant state governments than the Supreme Court has to the executive branch of the US government, but the difference in approaches and outcomes is still striking.

48. Isaiah Berlin, "Two Concepts of Liberty," in *Liberty: Incorporating Four Essays on Liberty*, ed. Henry Hardy, 2nd ed. (Oxford: Oxford University Press, 2002).

49. Ibid., 169.

50. Ibid., 177.

51. Ibid.

52. Adam Swift, *Political Philosophy: A Beginner's Guide for Students and Politicians*, 2nd ed. (Cambridge: Polity, 2006), 55.

53. Swift, *Political Philosophy*, 64.

54. Philip Pettit, "Freedom as Antipower," *Ethics* 106, no. 3 (1996): 576–77.

55. Frank Lovett and Philip Pettit, "Neorepublicanism: A Normative and Institutional Research Program," *Annual Review of Political Science* 12 (2009): 11–29.

56. Frank Lovett, "Republicanism," in *The Stanford Encyclopedia of Philosophy*, ed. Edward N. Zalta, Spring 2013 edition, sec. 3.2, http://plato.stanford.edu/archives/spr2013/entries/republicanism/.

57. Pettit, "Freedom as Antipower," 576; Lovett, "Republicanism," sec. 1.2.

58. Lovett, "Republicanism," sec. 1.2.

59. Michael J. Thompson, "Reconstructing Republican Freedom: A Critique of the Neo-Republican Concept of Freedom as Non-Domination," *Philosophy & Social Criticism* 39, no. 3 (2013): 279.

60. Pettit, "Freedom as Antipower," 578.

61. Ibid., 579.

62. Ibid., 580.

63. Ibid., 588.

64. Ibid.

65. Ibid., 589.

66. Forcese and Freeman, *Laws of Government*, 49.

67. *Klass and Others v. Germany*, 2 Eur. H.R. Rep. 214, para. 50.

## Chapter Twelve

# Post–9/11 Government Surveillance, Suppression and Secrecy

## Nadine Strossen

In the wake of the 9/11 terrorist attacks, the U.S. government stepped up its policies of secrecy and surveillance, which had been widely criticized as excessive even before 9/11. The undue secrecy and surveillance propel a vicious spiral. The secrecy shields the surveillance from oversight, and both of them suppress free speech, dissent, and democracy. To quote our Constitution's opening words, "We the People" are the ultimate governors, but we cannot hold those we elect accountable if we do not know what they are doing. Moreover, when we have reason to fear that the government will spy on our communications, we engage in self-censorship.

Thanks to undue secrecy and surveillance, we have exactly the opposite information flow that we should have between We the People and those we elect—they have too much information about us, and we have too little information about them. In 2014, the American Civil Liberties Union (ACLU) and Human Rights Watch issued a joint report that documents how undue surveillance and secrecy are undermining press freedom and the public's right to information.[1] It was based on extensive interviews with dozens of journalists, including many Pulitzer Prize winners. They attest that sources of valuable information have been intimidated by the combination of surveillance, increased leak prosecutions, and new government restrictions on press contacts. As a result, sources hesitate to discuss even unclassified matters of public concern. Describing his ongoing struggle to obtain and publish essential information about the "War on Terror," and to maintain the confidentiality of his sources, *New York Times* reporter James Risen said, "The whole global war on terror has been classified. If we, today, only had that information that was officially authorized from the U.S. government, we would know virtually nothing about the war on terror."[2]

The first part of this chapter discusses excessive surveillance, focusing on the dragnet communications surveillance programs that Edward Snowden revealed. It outlines the fundamental Fourth Amendment principles that this sweeping suspicionless surveillance violates, and explains why this constitutional protection is of utmost importance for everyone, including the vast majority of us who "have nothing to hide" in the sense of illicit activities. It also explains why even communications "metadata," or information about our communications, reveals sensitive personal information about people who are not even suspected of any wrongdoing, and hence is none of the government's business. Finally, it rebuts the major defenses that the government has offered for this bulk communications surveillance: that it has played a vital role in countering terrorism; that it is subject to effective oversight by the Foreign Intelligence Surveillance Court; and that it is consistent with the Supreme Court's Fourth Amendment rulings.

The next section of this chapter discusses the unwarranted secrecy that has facilitated the unwarranted communications surveillance, as well as undermining democratic accountability and the rule of law more generally. It focuses on one especially egregious type of undue secrecy: secret laws. Both post–9/11 presidents have relied on secret laws to carry out, free from any meaningful oversight, not only the dragnet communications surveillance programs but also other post–9/11 executive branch programs that likewise pose serious constitutional problems.

Finally, the chapter briefly outlines some pending countermeasures that could rein in unjustified surveillance and secrecy.

## SURVEILLANCE

Government agencies at all levels have rapidly been deploying burgeoning surveillance technologies to gain ever more information about us and, hence, power over us. Some such high-tech surveillance programs include cell phone location tracking, drone surveillance, GPS tracking, and license plate readers, which have been increasingly used by multiple local, state, and national law enforcement agencies; the CIA's collection of business records regarding our international money transfers; the National Security Agency's (NSA) collection of online address books and contact lists; the NSA's collection of millions of faces from web images for use in sophisticated facial recognition programs; and the U.S. Postal Service's photographing of all mail.

The surveillance that has understandably provoked the most concern is the NSA's suspicionless spying on the phone and Internet communications of everyone in this country, as well as people all over the world, even if we are not suspected of any wrongdoing. As the Supreme Court has recognized, surveillance of communications threatens not only privacy rights but also free speech rights, because of the "chilling" or deterrent impact that surveillance has on our communications. This chapter accordingly focuses on these doubly dangerous communications surveillance programs.

## Fourth Amendment Principles

These programs violate the fundamental Fourth Amendment limits on any "search and seizure"—that is any government intrusion into our privacy. Although Fourth Amendment privacy rights are no more absolute than any other constitutional rights, the government bears a heavy burden of proof to justify any rights restriction. In general, the Supreme Court has held that any freedom-restricting measure must be necessary to promote a countervailing goal of compelling importance, such that no "less restrictive alternative" would suffice. In other words, the government may not impose a liberty-restricting measure if it could promote its goal through a measure that restricts liberty less. These general constitutional law standards reflect just plain common sense. After all, why should we give up our cherished liberty if we did not gain security in return? Or if we could gain as much security without giving up as much liberty?

Of course, national security is a goal of compelling importance. However, too many of the post–9/11 measures that the government touts as promoting national security are not even effective at doing so, let alone necessary. Therefore, many such measures have been critiqued not only by civil libertarians as unjustifiably undermining our freedom but also by national security experts as ineffective at best, counterproductive at worst. This is true of the dragnet surveillance programs. They sweep in too much information about too many innocent people, thus making it harder to hone in on the dangerous ones. As critics have put it, "The government is trying to find a needle in the haystack by adding more hay to the stack." Some of the harshest critics of dragnet communications surveillance include FBI agents who complain about the huge amount of time they have wasted in tracking down the thousands of completely innocent Americans whose communications have been caught in these fishing expeditions.

The same ineffectiveness problem plagues the government's asserted rationale for collecting all data about all of our phone calls. The government says that it uses these massive customer calling records for "data mining," looking for patterns of calls and keywords according to certain mathematical formulas that, it says, might point to suspected terrorists. However, prominent experts have denounced such data mining as "junk science." For example, Jonathan Farley, a math professor at Harvard and a Science fellow at

Stanford's Center for International Security, wrote, "[This] entire spying program [is] based on a false assumption: that you can work out who might be a terrorist based on calling [and keyword] patterns. . . . [B]ut guilt by association is not just bad law, it's [also] bad mathematics."[3]

Beyond the foregoing general constitutional limits on liberty-restricting measures, the Fourth Amendment also lays out two specific limits on government's surveillance power, one substantive and one procedural. It reads as follows:

> The right of the people to be secure in their persons, houses, papers, and effects, against unreasonable searches and seizures, shall not be violated, and no Warrants shall issue, but upon probable cause, supported by Oath or affirmation, and particularly describing the place to be searched, and the persons or things to be seized.

Substantively, the Fourth Amendment requires that any search or seizure must be based on "probable cause"—that is, individualized suspicion that the targeted person had engaged in illegal activity or is about to do so. The Fourth Amendment bars suspicionless searches because the government should not engage in fishing expeditions based on mere hunches or, worse yet, discriminatory stereotypes or guilt by association. Procedurally, the Fourth Amendment requires that any search or seizure must be based on a judge-issued warrant, which is a key element in the Constitution's overall scheme of checks and balances. It prevents executive officials from engaging in surveillance on their own initiative, instead requiring an independent judicial assessment that the probable cause standard is indeed satisfied.

Important as the Fourth Amendment requirements are in general, the Supreme Court has stressed that they are especially important when the government's search and seizure power is directed at expressive materials,[4] thus also raising First Amendment free speech concerns. In light of these dual constitutional concerns, the courts and Congress have strictly limited government's electronic surveillance of communications. Until the 9/11 terrorist attacks, even when such surveillance sought foreign intelligence, it still had to comply with the Fourth Amendment's core warrant and individualized suspicion requirements, albeit in somewhat modified forms. Under the 1978 Foreign Intelligence Surveillance Act or "FISA," the government had to seek an order from the special FISA Court, which could issue the order only if it found that there was "probable cause to believe that the target . . . [was] a foreign power or agent of a foreign power," and also that "each of the facilities or places at which the electronic surveillance [was] directed [was] being used, or about to be used, by a foreign power or an agent of a foreign power."[5] In short, there still was individualized targeting of both the surveillance subject and the specific communications devices. Since 9/11, however, the government has implemented multiple surveillance programs which abandon Fourth Amendment principles, as well as the FISA standards that reflected these principles.

## Dragnet Suspicionless Communications Surveillance

Thanks to Edward Snowden, we know much more about these programs than we could have learned in any other way, given the government's excessive secrecy and outright lies. Even members of Congress and FISA Court judges, who were supposedly overseeing and checking surveillance, were in fact kept largely in the dark about these programs. Oregon senator Ron Wyden played a key role in calling attention to this problem. As a member of the Senate Intelligence Committee, he knew that the U.S. government was spying on unsuspected—and unsuspecting—Americans and lying about it to Congress. Wyden honored his duty to preserve the confidentiality of what he had learned through his committee position, but he did everything short of breaching that duty to force the government to come clean. That culminated in his now-infamous exchange with James Clapper, director of national intelligence, during a Senate hearing on March 12, 2013. When Wyden pressed Clapper about whether the NSA was engaging in bulk surveillance of Americans' communications, Clapper said, "No." After the Snowden revelations confirmed that this was a flat-out lie, Clapper dissembled yet again, explaining that this was "the least untruthful" answer he could give.[6] Finally, under pressure of continuing revelations from Snowden, on June 21, 2013, Clapper wrote a letter to the Senate Intelligence Committee apologizing for his "clearly erroneous" testimony.

Snowden's disclosures provided vital information that Clapper and other officials hid, when all other supposed oversight mechanisms had failed. In fact, the dramatic exchange between Ron Wyden and James Clapper was what Snowden called his "breaking point." As he said, "Seeing the Director of National Intelligence . . . lie under oath to Congress . . . meant for me there was no going back. . . . [I]t brought . . . the . . . realization that no one else was going to do this," to honor "[t]he public . . . right to know about these programs."[7]

Through the Snowden revelations and other sources, the American public has been learning about multiple dragnet communications surveillance programs, although we still lack crucial details about them, and there are probably more programs about which we are still completely ignorant. For example, as this chapter was being written, in January 2015, the government acknowledged yet another mass database of U.S. citizens' telephone records that it collected without any individualized suspicion or judicial authorization; the government maintained these records, even if there was no evidence that the callers were involved in illegal activity, until at least September

2013. Maintained by the Drug Enforcement Administration and available to other law enforcement agencies, this database contained information about calls between people in the United States and people in foreign countries "that . . . have a demonstrated nexus to international drug trafficking and related criminal activities." The stored information consisted of the same kind of call data that the NSA has been collecting: phone numbers, time and date, and length. As Vermont senator Patrick Leahy stressed, in a letter to attorney general Eric Holder, "I am deeply concerned about this suspicion-less intrusion into Americans' privacy in any context, but it is particularly troubling when done for routine criminal investigations."[8]

## PATRIOT Act Section 215

One bulk surveillance program that Snowden disclosed arises under Section 215 of the PATRIOT Act. Section 215 eliminated even the watered-down individualized suspicion requirement that had existed under FISA since 1978, summarized above. It empowers the government to seize anything that it deems "relevant" to a terrorism investigation. This new "relevance" standard is diametrically different from the Fourth Amendment's (and FISA's) strict but sensible "probable cause" standard. In fact, "relevance" is by definition the lowest possible standard; after all, the government indisputably is not entitled to information that is irrelevant to an investigation.

Overreaching as Section 215 was, for several years prior to Snowden's revelations, a couple members of the Senate Intelligence Committee had been warning that the executive branch had been engaging in surveillance that exceeded even these loose standards, through secret interpretations—actually, misinterpretations—of Section 215. Their confidentiality obligations barred them from disclosing any details, even to other members of Congress. For example, in 2011, Senator Wyden declared, "When the American people find out how their government has secretly interpreted the PATRIOT Act, they will be stunned and they will be angry."[9]

Sure enough, beginning in June 2013, the Snowden revelations documented that the government had been relying on Section 215 to gather copious data about literally all telephone users, which was indeed irrelevant to any terrorism investigation—nor did the government dispute this. Rather, the government's rationale is that the information might become relevant in the future. In short, the government's approach is to collect all our data first, and then hope to use it to solve or prevent some crime that might occur sometime in the future. This approach could not be further from the Fourth Amendment's requirements. Moreover, this misreading of Section 215 is completely inconsistent with its language, and has accordingly been denounced by many members of Congress who voted for the PATRIOT Act, including Wisconsin Republican congressman Jim Sensenbrenner, its chief author.

Under the government's unbounded misconstruction of Section 215, it has been collecting "metadata" about all of our phone calls at least since 2006, and perhaps earlier. This metadata includes the phone numbers to and from which we place and receive calls, also revealing the names of the parties to the call; when the calls are made; how long they last; and from what locations they are made. In addition to collecting this information about all of our phone calls, the government swept up this same information about all of our Internet communications from 2001 until 2011. Notably, the government ended this bulk Internet surveillance because it did not produce useful intelligence, as the government was forced to acknowledge under questioning from congressional intelligence committee members.

## FISA Section 702

A second communications surveillance program that came to light thanks to the Snowden disclosures, the "PRISM" program, arises under Section 702 of FISA, which codifies the FISA Amendments Act of 2008. Section 702 revolutionized the FISA regime by permitting the mass acquisition of American's international communications—their actual contents—without individualized judicial oversight.

Since Edward Snowden brought PRISM to light, its defenders, including President Obama, have been asserting that it does not apply to any U.S. citizen or resident.

However, that assertion is misleading at best. Section 702 does provide that Americans' domestic calls may not be the direct target of the surveillance, but the government may and does retain Americans' domestic calls that are obtained "incidentally," a potentially boundless group. After all, communication is a two-way street. So if an American is communicating with a foreign "target," no matter how innocently, the government may collect, inspect, and keep the content of that communication. Moreover, the definition of a foreign target is so broad that it inevitably encompasses many innocent Americans as well. First, the government may target anyone it believes to be a foreigner, even if that person is actually an American. Second, the government may target people who are not even suspected of any crime, let alone terrorism. Rather, it may target anyone who is communicating about "foreign affairs," which it defines broadly to include everything from trade to travel, thus putting U.S. businesspeople in the crosshairs, as well as journalists, human rights researchers, academics, and attorneys.

Worse yet, under PRISM, the NSA was automatically searching the phone communications of anyone who was within "three hops" from a targeted person: anyone who had a phone communication with the target during the last five years ("the first hop group"), plus anyone who had a phone communication with anyone in the first hop group during the last five years ("the second hop group"), plus anyone who had a phone conversation with anyone in the second hop group during the last five years. Even if one assumes that, in that time period, each targeted individual had phone communications with just 100 other people, and that each person involved in each "hop" also had phone communications with just 100 other people, that would mean that for each target, the NSA would search the phone communications of 1,000,000 people. In response to the public outcry about this vacuuming up of Americans' communications, President Obama trimmed back the collection to two hops. However, this means that for every target believed to be foreign, the NSA searches the content of the phone communications of ten thousand people.

In 2014, the *Washington Post* ran a chilling expose, analyzing a large cache of phone communications that the NSA had intercepted under Section 702. Edward Snowden said he had provided these communications so the public could assess the actual costs and benefits of Section 702 surveillance. The chief author of the *Washington Post* analysis was the respected national security journalist Barton Gellman. As he observed, "No government oversight body . . . has delved into a comparably large sample of what the NSA actually collects—not only from its targets but also from people who may cross a target's path," even tangentially. The upshot? A full 90 percent of the intercepted communications came from "ordinary Internet users," including Americans, rather than legally targeted foreigners. Describing the highly personal, sensitive nature of the spied-upon communications, the article went on to say:

> Many . . . have a startlingly intimate . . . quality. They tell stories of love and heartbreak, illicit sexual liaisons, mental-health crises, political and religious conversions, financial anxieties and disappointed hopes. . . . [They include] medical records sent from one family member to another . . . pictures [of] infants and toddlers in bathtubs . . . and photos [of] men show[ing] off their physiques, [and of] women model[ing] lingerie. [10]

## Executive Order 12333

Another bulk communications surveillance program is based on an executive order that president Ronald Reagan issued in 1981, which authorizes surveillance of the content of communications intercepted on foreign soil, with virtually no limits or oversight. It was designed for communications between non-Americans but it now also sweeps up countless American communications, given technological changes since 1981—specifically, that most purely domestic communications now are located on servers in other countries. In 2014, former State Department official John Tye blew the whistle on this essentially secret surveillance power, in the tradition of Ron Wyden's earlier warnings about NSA surveillance: sounding a general alarm but honoring confidentiality duties, and hence not revealing details. Ominously, Tye warned, "Based in part on classified facts that I am prohibited by law from publishing, I believe that Americans should be even more concerned about the collection and storage of their communications under [this] Executive Order . . . than under [the PATRIOT Act]."[11]

## Why Privacy Matters

Many fellow Americans ask why we should care about these sweeping communications surveillance programs, saying, "I have not done anything wrong, so I have nothing to hide." The fallacious premise is that the only things we would want to hide from government spies would be evidence of wrongdoing. To the contrary, all of us law-abiding folks have compelling reasons to hide completely lawful actions and interactions—indeed, some of our most important, positive, and cherished actions and interactions—simply because they are no one else's business.

George Orwell's prescient dystopian novel, *1984*, powerfully demonstrates the oppression that results from pervasive surveillance; as the novel puts it, Big Brother is always watching us. It shows how such surveillance demeans our dignity and destroys our relationships. This surveillance causes the very same harms that also result from more overtly coercive authoritarian tactics, such as torture and imprisonment. Psychological studies have confirmed that people who are being watched tend to behave differently, and to make different decisions, than when they are not being watched. This effect is so great that a recent study found that "merely hanging up posters of staring human eyes is enough to significantly change people's behavior"[12]— the very type of "Big Brother is Watching" poster that Orwell imagined.

## Why Government Metadata Collection Violates Privacy

Defenders of the Section 215 bulk metadata collection program contend that this entails an insignificant privacy invasion, in contrast to surveillance of communications' actual content. As one government official correctly concluded, though, government collection of communications metadata under Section 215 is "very, very intrusive."[13] Ironically, the official I have quoted is Vice President Joe Biden, speaking while he was still in the Senate, and critiquing the Bush administration's collection of metadata. Metadata disclosing with whom we communicate, and when, can well be at least as revealing as what we say or write. Consider, for example, calls between a reporter and a government whistleblower, and calls to Alcoholics Anonymous, a gambling bookie, abortion clinic, or hotline for gay teens. An MIT study found that from reviewing people's social networking contacts, which metadata reveal, one can identify their sexual orientation.[14] Likewise, metadata from e-mails were sufficient to identify the mistress of the then CIA director David Petraeus, which drove him out of office. The NSA's super-computers can employ sophisticated data-mining technologies to analyze te-rabytes of metadata, and thus construct detailed portraits of us and our rela-tionships.

A leading computer expert, Princeton University professor Edward Fel-ten, has explained that the communications metadata that the NSA has been sweeping up conveys highly sensitive information, which traditionally could be obtained only by reviewing communications' content: "The government can learn our religion . . . our work habits . . . our civi[c] and political affiliations . . . the rise and fall of intimate relationships, the diagnosis of a life-threatening disease, the telltale signs of a corporate merger . . . and the identities of a prospective government whistleblower and an anonymous liti-gant."[15]

In fact, as technology advances, the distinction between a communica-tion's content and metadata blurs. For example, the government has argued that a website address is only metadata, and hence should be less protected against surveillance. But the sites we visit online are comparable to the list of books we check out of a library. The very fact that we have visited a certain webpage can be every bit as revealing as the content of an e-mail message. After all, the very reason the government is so eager to sweep up metadata is precisely because it is a treasure trove of information.

## Rebutting Government's Defenses of Dragnet Communications Surveillance

The government has offered three major defenses for its sweeping communi-cations surveillance: that it is essential for countering terrorism; that it is subject to oversight by the special FISA Court; and that it comports with Supreme Court decisions construing the Fourth Amendment.

### It Is Not Essential for Countering Terrorism

Experts concur that the NSA's indiscriminate communications surveillance has not made any contribution to U.S. counterterrorism efforts. That was the conclusion of both high-level commissions that issued detailed reports on point in 2013 and 2014: the President's Review Group on Intelligence and Communications Technologies[16] and the Privacy and Civil Liberties Over-sight Board.[17] For example, in the latter's 2014 report, which reflected an in-depth examination of classified information, it concluded:

> The [NSA's phone records] program has shown minimal value in safeguarding
> the nation from terrorism. Based on the information [the government] pro-
> vided . . . including classified briefings and document[s], we have not iden-

tified a single instance . . . in which the program made a . . . difference in the outcome of a counterterrorism investigation. Moreover, we are aware of no instance in which the program directly contributed to the discovery of a previously unknown terrorist plot or the disruption of a terrorist attack.[18]

A federal judge who ruled that this program was unconstitutional reached the same conclusion: "[T]he Government does *not* cite a single instance in which . . . the NSA's bulk . . . collection actually . . . aided in achieving any time-sensitive objective."[19] Likewise, a 2014 report by the New America Foundation, which analyzed all the terrorist plots that the government initially claimed had been thwarted in part due to the NSA's dragnet surveillance—before the evidence forced it to back away from these claims—concluded that such surveillance in fact had had "no discernible impact on preventing acts of terrorism."[20]

## FISA Court Supervision Is Insufficient

The government's second major defense of the NSA's massive surveillance is that the FISA Court provides oversight. In fact, though, that court functions more like a rubber stamp for the government than an independent court. Among many other limits, it operates completely in secret, and hears completely one-sided arguments, only from the government.

Thanks to post-Snowden disclosures, we have learned that the FISA Court has repeatedly rebuked the NSA for repeatedly misleading the court about its bulk surveillance, and for repeatedly violating FISA Court orders imposing some modest curbs on that surveillance. In 2009, FISA Court judge Reggie Walton concluded that, since the inception of this surveillance three years earlier, the NSA had engaged in "systematic noncompliance" with court orders designed to minimize the suspicionless collection and review of Americans' communications. Judge Walton also concluded that the NSA had repeatedly made misrepresentations about the program to the FISA Court judges.[21] Stating that he had no confidence that the government was doing its best to comply with the FISA Court's orders, Judge Walton imposed a six-month sanction. Nonetheless, the government persisted in violating FISA Court orders. In 2011, FISA Court presiding judge John Bates said, "The Court is troubled that [this is] the third instance in less than three years in which the government has disclosed substantial misrepresentations regarding the scope of a major collection program."[22] One FISA Court judge actually resigned in protest over the dragnet communications surveillance programs, and testified in Congress about the court's inability to provide any meaningful check.

To put the FISA Court judges' strong reprimands in context, it should be noted that the FISA Court has been critiqued because of its judges' pro-government tilt. Therefore, it is especially troubling that even this court has repeatedly concluded that the government had not only violated the Constitution and court orders but also lied about its actions.

This repeated government lying about surveillance is an aspect of the government's excessive secrecy. The government has too often been providing either no information or misleading or false information, not only to We the People, but even to the handful of members of Congress on the intelligence committees and to the FISA Court judges, who are supposed to act as watchdogs in our stead. Thanks to some successful Freedom of Information Act lawsuits, we have recently seen some of the FISA Court opinions that authorize this surveillance, which in turn quote the government's arguments. The ACLU's deputy legal director, Jameel Jaffer, compared the government's arguments in the one-sided, secret proceedings before the FISA Court with the government's arguments in the regular federal court system, in which the ACLU and others have been challenging this surveillance post-Snowden.

In the FISA Court, the government made extravagant claims about the supposed necessity and efficacy of such surveillance. For example, it said that this surveillance was "the only effective means" for "keep[ing] track" of suspected terrorists.[23] There is no opponent in the FISA Court, so these bold claims went unchallenged. By contrast, in the open federal court system, the government's claims are subject to rebuttal by opposing parties, and to meaningful scrutiny by independent judges, as well as the public and press. Not surprisingly, in this context, the government's claims about the importance of bulk surveillance are much more modest. Specifically, in open federal court the government has said only that such surveillance is "one method . . . that can "complement . . . other[s]" and "can contribute" to counterterrorism efforts.[24] Surely such a limited security benefit can hardly justify the huge costs to privacy, freedom of speech and press, and democracy.

*The Supreme Court's Fourth Amendment Jurisprudence*
*Does Not Authorize This Surveillance*

At the time this chapter is being written, there is ongoing litigation in several courts in which the dragnet communications surveillance programs are being challenged, and to date the lower court judges have reached inconsistent results. This chapter will focus on the constitutional principles in general, including as they have been enforced by the Supreme Court rulings that are generally on point, since the high court has not yet ruled on a Fourth Amendment challenge specifically to the communications surveillance.

As discussed above, the Fourth Amendment's plain language requires that all searches and seizures must be based on individualized suspicion and a judicially issued warrant, both of which are absent from the dragnet communications surveillance programs. Moreover, the original understanding of the Fourth Amendment framers reinforces the conclusion that such surveillance is unconstitutional. This is significant, because the Constitution's text and original understanding are the two methods of constitutional interpretation that tend to be favoured by conservatives. Accordingly, the constitutional analysis provides a persuasive reason for conservatives to oppose this surveillance, and in fact many conservative members of Congress have voted to curb it.

By contrast, the government defends such surveillance not by invoking the Fourth Amendment's language or original understanding, but rather by invoking Supreme Court decisions that have cut back on the Fourth Amendment's scope in what the government views as analogous situations. Since these cases involve facts that are materially distinguishable from the bulk surveillance program, they are not controlling. On the contrary, more recent Supreme Court decisions involving other high-tech surveillance indicate that the court will likely enforce the Fourth Amendment robustly in the bulk surveillance context.

In 2013, federal judge Richard Leon, a respected conservative, granted a preliminary injunction against the NSA's dragnet phone records collection, stressing the original understanding of the Fourth Amendment's framers. As he said:

> I cannot imagine a more "indiscriminate" and "arbitrary invasion" than this . . . high-tech collection and retention of personal data on virtually every single citizen . . . without prior judicial approval. Surely such a program infringes on [the] privacy that the Founders enshrined in the Fourth Amendment. Indeed, I have little doubt that the author of our Constitution, James Madison . . . would be aghast.[25]

The Fourth Amendment expressly bars the type of dragnet phone record program that the NSA has been conducting, without any individualized probable cause warrants. On the contrary, this program proceeds under blanket FISA Court warrants, which purport to authorize wholesale, suspicionless collection of all our records. This is the very kind of hated general warrant and general search that fueled both the American Revolution and the Fourth Amendment. Citing this history, the Supreme Court has consistently held that suspicionless, warrantless searches and seizures are almost automatically unconstitutional, and there are powerful originalist arguments that they should always be automatically unconstitutional.

The government argues that bulk phone records collection should instead be judged under the "special needs" exception to the warrant and suspicion requirements, which the Supreme Court created in 1985. It applies only in "exceptional circumstances" where "special needs, beyond the normal need for law enforcement, make the warrant and probable cause requirements impracticable."[26] However, many experts concur that the government could practicably comply with these requirements in seeking terrorism-related communications. Indeed, even the director of national intelligence has recently "signaled that the information the NSA needs about terrorist connections might be obtainable without first collecting . . . 'the whole haystack' of U.S. phone data."[27]

Even assuming for the sake of argument that the special needs exception did apply to the bulk phone record collection, it would still be unconstitutional. Even under the special needs exception, the court has held that a suspicionless search or seizure is unconstitutional unless "the privacy interests [it] implicate[s] are minimal, "and . . . an important government[] interest . . . would be . . . jeopard[ized] by [an] individualized suspicion requirement."[28] On the contrary, though, the privacy interests that bulk collection implicates are maximal, not minimal: sweeping up countless records about hundreds of millions of innocent Americans, containing the most intimate personal details. Likewise, as also discussed above, dragnet phone records collection also fails the second prong of the "special needs" test, because experts have concluded that the indiscriminate communications surveillance has not advanced our counterterrorism efforts.

In the lawsuits challenging the NSA's bulk phone records program, the government's main defense rests on the "third-party doctrine," which is based on some Supreme Court cases in which the court has held that when we voluntarily disclose data to third parties, we forfeit a "reasonable expectation of privacy" in that data, and hence have no Fourth Amendment claim when the third party gives that data to the government. However, the court has never held that the third-party doctrine always bars Fourth Amendment claims, as the government itself recognizes. For instance, even the government recognizes that we do have a reasonable expectation of privacy in the contents of our calls or e-mails, even though phone companies also have access to them.

The government's third-party argument centers on a 1979 case, *Smith v. Maryland*,[29] which also involved phone records. Beyond that single fact, though, *Smith* is light years apart from the mass surveillance programs now at issue. The court held that Michael Smith, a criminal suspect, had no reasonable expectation of privacy in the list of phone numbers he had called during just two days, which the government did not retain. By contrast, indiscriminate metadata collection presents the following, completely different, question: whether hundreds of millions of Americans who are not criminal suspects have a reasonable expectation of privacy in a complete catalog of the phone numbers, date, time, duration, and location for every call we have made or received since 2006, or even earlier, and continuing on indefinitely, all of which the government will retain for at least five years.

Most Americans probably are not even aware that their phone companies are collecting this detailed information, and we certainly have not consented to our phone companies systematically turning it all over to the government, in violation of their written privacy policies.

As Professor Felten explained, "The only . . . way to avoid creating such metadata [which is available to the phone companies] is to avoid telephon[e] communication altogether"[30]—in other words, not a real choice, given the vastly increased importance of such communication in our twenty-first-century world. Moreover, as Judge Leon wrote, in support of his holding that the sweeping NSA phone surveillance violates the Fourth Amendment, "It's one thing to say that people expect phone companies to occasionally provide information to law enforcement; it is quite another to suggest that our citizens expect all phone companies to operate what is effectively a joint intelligence-gathering operation with the Government."[31]

The key technological changes since 1979, when *Smith* was decided, constitute another reason why that ruling does not apply to bulk phone record collection. As Justice Scalia wrote in a 2001 majority opinion striking down warrantless thermal imaging, our Fourth Amendment privacy should not be left to "the mercy of advancing technology." In the court's 2012 case striking down GPS surveillance under the Fourth Amendment, five justices expressly questioned whether *Smith* applies to new technology, in opinions by Justices Alito and Sotomayor—notably, among the court's most conservative and liberal members, respectively. Likewise, in a 2014 decision concerning cell phones, the justices unanimously recognized that, in effect, "digital is different," so that prior cases allowing searches and seizures incident to arrest do not apply to cell phones, given the vast differences between such digital devices and other items. The same conclusion applies to the *Smith* decision; it simply does not govern dragnet metadata collection. The argument that bulk metadata collection is not materially distinguishable from the *Smith* facts is wrong for the same reason that the Supreme Court in 2014 unanimously rejected the government's argument that cell phone seizures are "materially indistinguishable" from other seizures: "That is like saying a ride on horseback is materially indistinguishable from a flight to the moon."[32]

The government's other major argument in the NSA litigation is that the Fourth Amendment does not apply when it vacuums up this massive, sensitive data, but rather only when it examines the data. This is dead wrong for many reasons starting with, again, the Fourth Amendment's plain language and original meaning. On these points, I will quote two respected conservative scholars, Randy Barnett and Jim Harper: "The Founders thought that the seizure of 'papers' [or data] for later perusal . . . was an abuse distinct from, but equivalent to the use of" the reviled "general warrants."[33] To allow the government to seize first and show probable cause later is exactly the opposite of what the Fourth Amendment explicitly requires, and the opposite of what it meant to our nation's founders.

If the government's contrary position prevailed, it could collect any of our data, including the contents of our communications, on the pledge that we should trust government employees not to actually look at it without first getting a warrant. This "trust us" argument is risible given government's track record of negligently and intentionally failing to protect the confidentiality of our data. As discussed above, the FISA Court has harshly chided the NSA for repeatedly violating even the modest limits that the FISA Court had imposed on the bulk phone record program. The government is not even able to protect its own data against leakers and hackers. To cite one recent example, we learned in late 2014 of a massive online data breach of the U.S. Postal Service, disclosing sensitive information about more than 800,000 USPS employees, including their Social Security numbers. Moreover, government employees have consistently snooped on and used data that is supposed to be maintained as confidential for a host of personal and political reasons. Therefore, the government's "trust us" argument flies in the face of the facts, as well as Fourth Amendment principles.

## SECRECY

### Overview

As discussed above, the argument that dragnet communications surveillance is no problem for anyone who has "nothing to hide" is deeply flawed. Moreover, the nothing-to-hide argument is a double-edged sword. If it were true that you have nothing to hide unless you are doing something wrong, then the *government* should declassify everything and end all of its secrecy policies! Of course, though, even the most ardent transparency advocate recognizes that government has legitimate secrets, such as the names of undercover agents and battle plans. On the other hand, even the most ardent security hawk recognizes that the United States now is enforcing egregiously excessive secrecy policies, covering material that posed no real security risk. For example, in 1970, a Defense Department report concluded that the amount of classified information "could profitably be decreased perhaps as much as 90 percent,"[34] but instead, the trajectory since then has been towards even more overclassification. It is also widely acknowledged that too often, officials hide information from the public only to protect themselves from political embarrassment.

Many studies have documented how the already excessive secrecy policies pre–9/11 became enormously more so after 9/11. For example, in 2010, the *Washington Post* published an article entitled "Top Secret America," which summarized the findings of its two-year investigation as follows:

The top-secret world the government created in response to the [911] attacks . . . has become so large . . . and so secretive that no one knows how much money it costs, how many people it employs, [and] how many programs exist within it. . . . [It] amounts to an alternative geography . . . a Top Secret America hidden from public view and lacking in thorough oversight.[35]

Some examples of the Obama administration's unwarranted secrecy include:

- rampant overclassification;
- a crackdown on whistle-blowers;
- imposing severe restrictions on officials' press contacts;
- in overly aggressive leak investigations, subpoenaing reporters, wiretapping media outlets, spying on journalists' private e-mail accounts, and even threatening reporters with potential prosecution;
- resisting the Freedom of Information Act (FOIA);
- refusing to disclose basic information to Congress;
- secret lawmaking; and
- aggressive assertion of the "state secrets privilege" to dismiss lawsuits that challenge unconstitutional and illegal actions in the "War on Terror."

This chapter will now expand on a couple of these unjustified secrecy policies, by way of example.

## The War on Whistleblowers and Investigative Journalists

The Obama administration has prosecuted more whistleblowers under the infamous 1917 Espionage Act than all prior administrations added together. In its first ninety-two years, the act was used only three times to prosecute government officials for press leaks. By contrast, the Obama administration has pursued eight such prosecutions. Moreover, a less well-known statistic underscores an even more dramatic disparity between the Obama administration and all others in its persecution of leakers; as summarized by ACLU legislative counsel Gabe Rottman, "the Obama administration has secured 526 months of prison time for national security leakers, versus only twenty-four months total jail time for [all such leakers] since the American Revolution."[36] As Rottman explains, the historically light sentencing in media leak cases reflected at least in part press freedom concerns.

Not surprisingly, the administration's aggressive stance towards whistleblowers has chilled government sources, hence freezing access to vital information for journalists and the public, as documented in the 2014 ACLU/ Human Rights Watch report noted in the introduction. For example, *New York Times* journalist Scott Shane, who covers national security, said that "government officials who might otherwise discuss sensitive topics . . . refer to these [Espionage Act] cases in rebuffing a request for background information."[37] The administration's overbearing policies in this area have been criticized by even such a strong proponent of strong executive power and national security policies as the *Wall Street Journal*. It said that the administration is engaging in "a pattern of anti-media behavior," and that its leak investigations "are less about deterring leakers and more about intimidating the press."[38]

Especially troubling is the Administration's prosecution of Pfc. Chelsea (formerly Bradley) Manning for the potential capital offense of "aiding the enemy," when he leaked documents to WikiLeaks.

Under the prosecution's theory, because Manning knew the materials would be published and that al-Qaeda could then read them, she indirectly communicated with the enemy. In response to the judge's inquiry, the prosecutors said that they would have brought the same charges if Manning had leaked the materials to the *New York Times* rather than WikiLeaks. Even the noted First Amendment attorney Floyd Abrams, who has criticized both Chelsea Manning and WikiLeaks, nonetheless condemned this prosecution, stating, "Anyone who holds freedom of the press dear should shudder at the threat that the prosecution's theory presents to journalists, their sources and the public that relies on them."[39]

By contrast to the administration's prosecution and punishment of those who have leaked information about illegal government conduct, it has done nothing at all to punish those who committed the illegal conduct. For example, the only person to do time for the CIA's torture policies is the whistleblower who brought them to light. Likewise for the illegal NSA surveillance program in the Bush administration—the only person to be penalized was the whistleblower who told the *New York Times* about it, then had his life ruined with vindictive investigations. Moreover, the telecoms that illegally cooperated were retroactively immunized from all legal accountability.

In addition to the Obama administration's double standard towards whistleblowers and the wrongdoers on whom they blow the whistle, it also has a double standard about leaks. As is consistently the case in any presidential administration, top officials selectively leak information about sensitive matters that reflect positively on it or serve other strategic purposes, while decrying and punishing leaks that reflect negatively on it or otherwise undermine its goals. As one commentator summed it up, the Obama administration is "trumpeting information that makes [it] look good while suppressing with the force of the criminal law anything that does the opposite."[40]

The adverse impact of the Obama administration's "War on Whistleblowers" was well summarized by the following statement: "Often the best source of information about waste, fraud, and abuse in government is an existing government employee committed to public integrity and willing to speak out. Such acts of courage and patriotism, which can sometimes save lives and often save taxpayer dollars, should be encouraged rather than stifled."[41]

Sadly, this statement came in 2009 from president-elect Obama.

## Excessive Secrecy Undermines National Security

All of this unwarranted secrecy obviously is antithetical to First Amendment values, democratic accountability, and the rule of law. Worse yet, it also has an adverse impact on national security. Of course, the asserted justification for such secrecy is to advance national security. In fact, though, experts concur that excessive secrecy actually undermines security by preventing effective information sharing among government officials, as well as between the public and private sectors, thus leading to flawed intelligence. This point was underscored, for example, by none other than a former head of the whole classification system, J. William Leonard, who served as director of the Information Security Oversight Office from 2002 until 2011. As he said, "Government secrecy just about guarantees the absence of an optimal decision on the part of our nation's leaders, often with tragic consequences for our nation."[42] In the same vein, the staff director of the bipartisan 9/11 Commission, Eleanor Hill, declared that the intelligence community's "most potent weapon" is "an alert and informed American public."[43] Conversely, the commission concluded that excessive secrecy was one of the factors that could well have contributed to the 9/11 attacks, which it indicated could have been foiled with more information sharing. Indeed, the commission expressly asserted, "Had KSM known that Moussaoui had been arrested, he would have cancelled the attacks."[44]

## Secret Laws

Of all the forms of unjustified secrecy, none is more inconsistent with democratic self-government than secret laws. When Senator Wyden first warned Americans about the government's secret interpretation of the PATRIOT Act in 2011, the whole concept of a secret law was shocking, inherently antithetical to our form of government by the people. Indeed, a prominent conservative federal judge, Richard Posner, wrote, "The idea of secret laws is repugnant."[45] Sadly, as with so many post–9/11 abuses that at first seemed like something out of a dystopian novel, secret laws have come to seem almost routine, even though still repugnant.

Post–9/11, both the Bush and the Obama administrations have been relying on two major sources of secret law, which are secret not only from the American people but also from members of Congress, including even members of the intelligence committees, who are supposed to be overseeing intelligence operations, and who are given top-secret security clearances for that purpose. Nonetheless, as Senator Wyden told the *New Yorker*, when people ask him about sensitive national security issues, he answers, "What do I know? I'm only on the [Senate] Intelligence Committee."[46]

The first major source of secret law comes from the Department of Justice's Office of Legal Counsel, which writes memos that guide the executive branch. These memos have purported to authorize multiple measures that are widely considered illegal and unconstitutional, including torture and targeted killing of U.S. citizens away from any battlefield, as well as dragnet NSA surveillance. To its credit, the Obama administration did disclose the torture memos that were written during the Bush administration, but it has fought against release of other memos, which have authorized its own controversial policies.

The second major source of secret law about dragnet communications surveillance consists of the FISA Court opinions that have interpreted federal statutes and the Constitution as allegedly authorizing dragnet surveillance. Again, public interest organizations and journalists have been fighting for disclosure of these opinions. While some have been released, others have not. To be sure, these opinions should be redacted to the extent that they reveal security-sensitive facts. By contrast, what should not be kept secret is the legal reasoning that allegedly justifies the NSA's sweeping surveillance. This is especially critical because the Supreme Court has not reviewed any of these FISA Court opinions. Therefore, as the *New York Times* observed, "[The FISA Court] has . . . become . . . a parallel Supreme Court, serving as the ultimate arbiter on surveillance issues."[47] In short, these secret FISA Court opinions are tantamount to secret Supreme Court rulings, underscoring why such secrecy is anathema.

## POTENTIAL REFORMS

In the wake of the Snowden revelations, there has been more positive momentum to rein in excessive surveillance and secrecy than there has been since 9/11. There have been meaningful steps in the right direction on two major fronts: litigation and legislation.

On the litigation front, there have been some significant pro-privacy victories in lower courts. Furthermore, while the Supreme Court has not directly ruled on communications surveillance in particular, it has issued a couple recent rulings about other high-tech forms of surveillance that strongly protect privacy rights, and could certainly be the basis for positive rulings on communications surveillance too.

On the legislative front, bipartisan bills have been introduced in both houses of Congress that would rein in NSA surveillance as well as excessive secrecy. Since the Snowden disclosures, a couple bills constraining NSA surveillance have received majority votes in the House of Representatives;

this is the first time since 9/11 that either house of Congress has voted to curb government surveillance at all. Even the Obama administration has expressed support for some of these reforms. Important support is also coming from U.S. tech companies, whose business has been greatly harmed by NSA surveillance and the worldwide mistrust it is creating about the security of U.S. products and services. A recent report projected that, in 2015–2016 alone, U.S. tech companies could lose up to $35 billion in canceled contracts and missed opportunities.[48]

## CONCLUSION

As the Supreme Court has repeatedly reminded us, we must never let our concern for security blind us to what exactly we are striving to secure. For example, during the Cold War, the court declared, "It would indeed be ironic if, in the name of national defense, we would sanction the subversion of . . . those liberties . . . which make the defense of the Nation worthwhile."[49] In the case of excessive surveillance and secrecy, the irony is compounded because, in national security terms, these policies are at best ineffective and at worst counterproductive.

## NOTES

1. G. Alex Sinha, Human Rights Watch, and American Civil Liberties Union, *With Liberty to Monitor All: How Large Scale US Surveillance is Harming Journalism, Law, and American Democracy* (New York: Human Rights Watch, 2014).

2. James Risen, interview by Lesley Stahl, *CBS 60 Minutes*, October 12, 2014, http://www.cbsnews.com/news/war-on-leaks-national-security-press-freedom/.

3. Jonathan David Farley, "The N.S.A.'s Math Problem," *New York Times*, May 16, 2006, http://www.nytimes.com/2006/05/16/opinion/16farley.html?_r=0.

4. See, e.g., *Zurcher v. Stanford Daily*, 436 U.S. 547, 564 (1978).

5. Foreign Intelligence Surveillance Act of 1978, 50 U.S.C. §§ 1801 et seq. (2008).

6. James Clapper, interview by Andrea Mitchell, *NBC Nightly News*, June 8, 2013, http://www.dni.gov/index.php/newsroom/speeches-and-interviews/195-speeches-interviews-2013/874-director-james-r-clapper-interview-with-andrea-mitchell.

7. "Snowden Exklusiv: Das Interview," video, 30:28, interview of Edward Snowden by Hubert Siebel from Norddeutscher Rundfunk, broadcast by ARD TV on January 26, 2014, posted by "ARD_Stinkt," January 27, 2014, http://liveleak.com/view?i=f93_1390833151.

8. Michael S. Schmidt and Matt Apuzzo, "U.S. Discloses New Trove of Phone Call Records," *New York Times*, January 16, 2015, http://www.nytimes.com/2015/01/17/us/dea-kept-telephone-records-on-americans-justice-department-says.html.

9. Senator Wyden of Oregon, speaking during a debate about the official interpretation of the Patriot Act on May 26, 2011 (157 Cong. Rec. 8179 [2011]).

10. Barton Gellman, Julie Tate, and Ashkan Soltani, "In NSA-Intercepted Data, Those Not Targeted Far Outnumber the Foreigners Who Are," *Washington Post*, July 5, 2014, http://www.washingtonpost.com/world/national-security/in-nsa-intercepted-data-those-not-targeted-far-outnumber-the-foreigners-who-are/2014/07/05/8139adf8-045a-11e4-8572-4b1b969b6322_story.html.

11. John Napier Tye, "Meet Executive Order 12333: The Reagan rule that lets the NSA spy on Americans," *Washington Post*, July 18, 2014, http://www.washingtonpost.com/opinions/meet-executive-order-12333-the-reagan-rule-that-lets-the-nsa-spy-on-americans/2014/07/18/93d2ac22-0b93-11e4-b8e5-d0de80767fc2_story.html.

12. Sander van der Linden, "How the Illusion of Being Observed Can Make You a Better Person," *Scientific American*, May 3, 2011, http://www.scientificamerican.com/article/how-the-illusion-of-being-observed-can-make-you-better-person/.

13. "Sen. Biden on NSA Database," CBS News video, 3:38, May 12, 2006, https://www.youtube.com/watch?v=8T4EPYSt5Dk.

14. Carter Jernigan and Behram F. T. Mistree, "Gaydar: Facebook Friendships Expose Sexual Orientation," *First Monday* 14, no. 10 (October 2009), doi: 10.5210/fm.v14i10.2611.

15. Declaration of Professor Edward W. Felten, ¶ 56–58, *ACLU v. Clapper*, 959 F Supp. 2d 724 (S.D.N.Y. 2013).

16. Review Group on Intelligence and Communications Technologies, *Liberty and Security in a Changing World* (2013), 33.

17. Privacy and Civil Liberties Oversight Board, *Report on the Telephone Records Program Conducted under Section 215 of the USA PATRIOT Act and on the Operations of the Foreign Intelligence Surveillance Court* (2014), 146, 169n.

18. Ibid., 11.

19. *Klayman v. Obama*, 957 F. Supp. 2d 1, 40 (D.D.C. 2013).

20. Peter Bergen et al., *Do NSA's Bulk Surveillance Programs Stop Terrorists?* New America Foundation, January 2014, https://static.newamerica.org/attachments/1311-do-nsas-bulk-surveillance-programs-stop-terrorists/IS_NSA_surveillance.pdf.

21. In re Production of Tangible Things From [redacted], Order, No. BR 08-13, 2009 WL 9150913, at *5 (FISA Ct. Mar. 2, 2009).

22. [Redacted], 2011 WL 10945618, at *5, n14 (FISA Ct. Oct. 3, 2011).

23. Judge Reggie Walton cited in Jameel Jaffer, "The Basis for the NSA's Call-Tracking Program Has Disappeared, If It Ever Existed," https://www.aclu.org/blog/basis-nsas-call-tracking-program-has-disappeared-if-it-ever-existed.

24. Declaration of Acting Assistant Director of FBI Robert J. Holley, 2, 4, *ACLU v. Clapper*, 959 F. Supp. 2d 724 (S.D.N.Y. 2013).

25. *Klayman*, 957 F. Supp. 2d at 42.

26. *New Jersey v. T.L.O.*, 469 U.S. 325, 351 (1985). (Blackmun, J., concurring).

27. Siobhan Gorman, "NSA Chief Opens Door to Narrower Data Collection," *Wall Street Journal*, February 27, 2014, http://www.wsj.com/news/articles/SB10001424052702304071004579409582715306814?mod=rss_Technology&mg=reno64-wsj. ("But Gen. Alexander . . . signaled that the information the NSA needs about terrorist connections might be obtainable without first collecting what officials have termed 'the whole haystack' of U.S. phone data.")

28. *Skinner v. Ry. Labor Execs' Ass'n*, 489 U.S. 602, 624 (1989).

29. *Smith v. Maryland*, 442 U.S. 735 (1979).

30. Declaration of Professor Edward W. Felten, 13, *ACLU v. Clapper*, 959 F. Supp. 2d 724 (S.D.N.Y. 2013).

31. *Klayman v. Obama*, 957 F. Supp. 2d 1, 33 (D.D.C. 2013).

32. *Riley v. California*, 134 S. Ct. 2473, 2489 (2014).

33. Randy E. Barnett and Jim Harper, "Why NSA's Bulk Data Seizures are Illegal and Unconstitutional," *Federalist Society for Law and Public Policy Studies*, October 21, 2013, http://www.fed-soc.org/publications/detail/why-nsas-bulk-data-seizures-are-illegal-and-unconstitutional.

34. Memorandum from the Office of the Director of Defense Research and Engineering to the Chairman of the Defense Science Board on the Report of the Defense Science Board Task Force on Secrecy, July 1, 1970, http://www.fas.org/sgp/othergov/dsbrep.html.

35. Dana Priest and William M. Arkin, "A Hidden World, Growing Beyond Control," *Washington Post*, July 19, 2010, http://projects.washingtonpost.com/top-secret-america/articles/a-hidden-world-growing-beyond-control/.

36. Gabe Rottman, "On Leak Prosecutions, Obama Takes it to 11. (Or Should We Say 526?)," *Washington Markup* (blog), ACLU, October 14, 2014, https://www.aclu.org/blog/free-speech/leak-prosecutions-obama-takes-it-11-or-should-we-say-526.

37. Margaret Sullivan, "The Danger of Suppressing the Leaks," *New York Times*, March 9, 2013, http://www.nytimes.com/2013/03/10/public-editor/the-danger-of-suppressing-the-leaks.html.

38. "A Journalist 'Co-Conspirator,'" *Wall Street Journal*, May 20, 2013, http://www.wsj.com/articles/SB10001424127887324102604578495253824175498.

39. Floyd Abrams and Yochai Benkler, "Death to Whistle-Blowers?," *New York Times*, March 13, 2013, http://www.nytimes.com/2013/03/14/opinion/the-impact-of-the-bradley-manning-case.html.

40. Jennifer Lynch and Trevor Timm, "The Dangers in Classifying the News," *Deeplinks* (blog), Electronic Frontier Foundation, October 18, 2011, https://www.eff.org/deeplinks/2011/10/dangers-classifying-news.

41. "The Obama-Biden Plan," Change.gov, http://change.gov/agenda/ethics_agenda/.

42. See William Leonard, "Classification: Radical, Let Alone Incremental, Reform Is Not Enough!," *Informed Consent*, August 9, 2009 (on file with author).

43. "Joint Inquiry into the Terrorist Attacks of September 11, 2001: Hearing Before the House Permanent Select Committee on Intelligence and the Senate Select Committee on Intelligence," 107th Cong. 683 (2002) (statement of Eleanor Hill, Staff Dir. of Joint Inquiry Comm.), http://www.intelligence.senate.gov/pdfs/1071086v2.pdf.

44. 9/11 Commission Report, at 276. See also id. n.107. http://www.9-11commission.gov/report/911Report.pdf.

45. *United States v. Farinella*, 558 F.3d 695, 700 (7th Cir. 2009).

46. Ryan Lizza, "State of Deception: Why won't the President rein in the intelligence community?," *New Yorker*, December 16, 2013, http://www.newyorker.com/magazine/2013/12/16/state-of-deception.

47. Eric Lichtblau, "In Secret, Court Vastly Broadens Powers of N.S.A.," *New York Times*, July 6, 2013, http://www.nytimes.com/2013/07/07/us/in-secret-court-vastly-broadens-powers-of-nsa.html?pagewanted=all&_r=0.

48. James Staten, "The Cost of PRISM Will Be Larger Than ITIF Projects," *Forrester* (blog), August 14, 2013, http://blogs.forrester.com/james_staten/13-08-14-the_cost_of_prism_will_be_larger_than_itif_projects. Staten wrote, "Earlier this month The Information Technology & Innovation Foundation (ITIF) published a prediction that the U.S. cloud computing industry stands to lose up to $35 billion by 2016 thanks to the National Security Agency (NSA) PRISM project, leaked to the media in June. We think this estimate is too low and could be as high as $180 billion or a 25% hit to overall IT service provider revenues in that same time-frame."

49. *United States v. Robel*, 389 U.S. 258, 264 (1967).

# Bibliography

Allen, Anita L. *Privacy Law and Society*. 2nd ed. St. Paul, MN: West Academic, 2011.
————. *Uneasy Access: Privacy for Women in a Free Society*. Totowa, NJ: Rowman & Littlefield, 1988.
————. *Unpopular Privacy: What Must We Hide?* Oxford: Oxford University Press, 2011.
————. "The Virtuous Spy: Privacy as an Ethical Limit." *Monist* 91, no. 3 (2008): 3–22.
————. "What Must We Hide: The Ethics of Privacy and the Ethos of Disclosure." *St. Thomas Law Review* 25, no. 1 (2012): 1–18.
————. *Why Privacy Isn't Everything: Feminist Reflections on Personal Responsibility*. Lanham, MD: Rowman & Littlefield, 2003.
Bannister, Frank, and Regina Connolly. "The Trouble with Transparency: A Critical Review of Openness in e-Government." *Policy & Internet* 3, no. 1 (2011): 1–30.
Barendt, Eric. *Freedom of Speech*. Oxford: Oxford University Press, 2007.
————. "Privacy and Freedom of Speech." In *New Dimensions in Privacy Law: International and Comparative Perspective*, edited by Andrew T. Kenyon and Megan Richardson, 11–31. Cambridge: Cambridge University Press, 2010.
Bartels, Larry M. "Uninformed Votes: Information Effects in Presidential Elections." *American Journal of Political Science* 40, no. 1 (1996): 194–230.
Benn, Stanley I. "Privacy, Freedom, and Respect for Persons." In *Philosophical Dimensions of Privacy: An Anthology*, edited by Ferdinand D. Schoeman, 223–44. Cambridge: Cambridge University Press, 1984.
Bloustein, Edward J. "Privacy as an Aspect of Human Dignity: An Answer to Dean Prosser." *New York University Law Review* 39 (1964): 962–1007.
*Board of Education v. Earls*, 536 U.S. 822 (2002).
Boling, Patricia. *Privacy and the Politics of Intimate Life*. Ithaca, NY: Cornell University Press, 1996.
Bork, Robert. *The Tempting of America*. New York: Free Press, 1990.
*Bowers v. Hardwick*, 478 U.S. 186 (1986).
Christiano, Thomas. *The Rule of the Many: Fundamental Issues in Democratic Theory*. Boulder, CO: Westview Press, 1996.
————. "The Authority of Democracy." *Journal of Political Philosophy* 12, no. 3 (2004): 266–90.
————. "Democracy." In *The Stanford Encyclopedia of Philosophy*, edited by Edward N. Zalta, Spring 2015 edition. http://plato.stanford.edu/archives/spr2015/entries/democracy/.
Cohen, Joshua. "Deliberation and Democratic Legitimacy." In *Deliberative Democracy: Essays on Reason and Politics*, edited by James Bohman and William Rehg, 67–92. Boston: MIT Press, 1997.

———. *Philosophy, Politics, Democracy: Selected Essays*. Cambridge, MA: Harvard University Press, 2009.

———. "Procedure and Substance in Deliberative Democracy." In *Philosophy and Democracy*, edited by T. Christiano, 1–17. Oxford: Oxford University Press, 2003.

Cohen, Julie E. "Configuring the Networked Citizen." In *Imagining New Legalities: Privacy and Its Possibilities in the 21st Century*, edited by Austin Sarat, Lawrence Douglas, and Martha Merrill Umphrey, 129–53. Stanford, CA: Stanford Law Books, 2012.

Cooley, Thomas C. *A Treatise on the Law of Torts*. Chicago: Callaghan, 1880.

Cunningham, Frank. *Theories of Democracy: A Critical Introduction*. New York: Routledge, 2002.

Davis, Frederick. "What Do We Mean by 'Right to Privacy?'" *South Dakota Law Review* 4 (1959): 1–24.

DeCew, Judith Wagner. *In Pursuit of Privacy: Law, Ethics and the Rise of Technology*. Ithaca, NY: Cornell University Press, 1997.

Downs, Anthony. *An Economic Theory of Democracy*. New York: Harper, 1957.

Dworkin, Ronald. "What Is Equality: Part I: Equality of Welfare." *Philosophy & Public Affairs* 10, no. 3 (1981): 185–246.

Electronic Communications Privacy Act of 1986. 18 U.S.C. §§2510-22. (2006).

Erlenbusch, Verena. "How (Not) to Study Terrorism." *Critical Review of Social and Political Philosophy* 17, no. 4 (2014): 1–22.

Etzioni, Amitai. "Is Transparency the Best Disinfectant?" *Journal of Political Philosophy* 18, no. 4 (2010): 389–404.

Finkin, Matthew W. "Employee Privacy, American Values and the Law." *Chicago-Kent Law Review* 72 (July 1996): 221–69.

Forsdyke, Sara. *Exile, Ostracism and Democracy: The Politics of Expulsion in Ancient Greece*. Princeton, NJ: Princeton University Press, 2005.

Freund, Paul A. "Privacy: One Concept or Many?" In *Privacy: Nomos XIII*, edited by J. Roland Pennock and John W. Chapman, 182–98. New York: Atherton, 1971.

Frické, Martin. "Big Data and Its Epistemology." *Journal of the Association for Information Science and Technology* 66, no. 4 (2015): 651–61.

Fried, Charles. "Privacy." *Yale Law Journal* 77 (1968): 475–93.

———. "Privacy." In *Philosophical Dimensions of Privacy: An Anthology*, edited by Ferdinand D. Schoeman, 203–22. Cambridge: Cambridge University Press, 1984.

Ganascia, Jean-Gabriel. "The Generalized Sousveillance Society." *Social Science Information* 49, no. 3 (2011): 489–507.

Gavison, Ruth. "Information Control: Availability and Control." In *Public and Private in Social Life*, edited by Stanley I. Benn and Gerald F. Gaus, 113–34. New York: St. Martin's Press, 1983.

———. "Privacy and the Limits of Law." *Yale Law Journal* 89 (1980): 421–71.

Gerstein, Robert. "Intimacy and Privacy." *Ethics* 89 (1978): 76–81.

Goodin, Robert E. *What's Wrong with Terrorism?* Cambridge, UK: Polity Press, 2006.

Goold, Benjamin. "The Difference between Lonely Old Ladies and CCTV Cameras: A Response to Ryberg." *Res Publica* 14, no. 1 (2008): 43–47.

*Griswold v. Connecticut*, 381 U.S. 479, 1965.

Gurstein, Michael B. "Open Data: Empowering the Empowered or Effective Data Use for Everyone?" *First Monday* 16, no. 2 (February 2011). doi: 10.5210/fm.v16i2.3316.

Gutmann, Amy, and Dennis Thompson. *Why Deliberative Democracy?* Princeton, NJ: Princeton University Press, 2009.

*Haynes v. Alfred A. Knopf, Inc.* 8 F.3d 1222, 1229 (7th Cir. 1993).

Hobbes, Thomas. *Leviathan*. Edited by Richard Tuck. Cambridge: Cambridge University Press, 1991. Originally published 1660.

Holm, Soren. "The Privacy of Tutankhamen—Utilizing the Genetic Information in Stored Tissue Samples." *Theoretical Medicine and Bioethics* 22, no. 5 (2001): 437–49.

Inness, Julie. *Privacy, Intimacy and Isolation*. Oxford: Oxford University Press, 1992.

Jaeger, Paul T., and John Carlo Bertot. "Transparency and Technological Change: Ensuring Equal and Sustained Public Access to Government Information." *Government Information Quarterly* 27, no. 4 (2010): 371–76.

Janssen, Marijn, Yannis Charalabidis, and Anneke Zuiderwijk. "Benefits, Adoption Barriers and Myths of Open Data and Open Government." *Information Systems Management* 29, no. 4 (2012): 258–68.

*Katz v. U.S.*, 389 U.S. 347, 1967.

Kundera, Milan. *The Unbearable Lightness of Being*. New York: HarperCollins, 1984.

Laborde, Cécile. *Critical Republicanism: The Hijab Controversy and Political Philosophy: The Hijab Controversy and Political Philosophy*. Oxford: Oxford University Press, 2008.

———. *Français, Encore Un Effort Pour Être Républicains!* Paris: Seuil, 2013.

*Lawrence v. Texas*, 539 U.S. 558, 2003.

Lever, Annabelle. *A Democratic Conception of Privacy*. AuthorHouse, 2013.

———. *A Democratic Conception of Privacy*. Authorhouse, 2014.

———. "Mrs. Aremac and the Camera." *Res Publica* 14, no. 1 (March 2008): 35–42.

———. *On Privacy*. New York: Routledge, 2012.

———. "Privacy and Democracy: What the Secret Ballot Reveals." *Law, Culture and Humanities* 11, no. 2 (2012): 164–83.

———. "Privacy, Democracy, and Freedom of Expression." In *Social Dimensions of Privacy*, edited by Beate Roessler and Dorota Mokrosinska, 162–80. Cambridge, UK: Cambridge University Press, 2015.

———. "Privacy Rights and Democracy: A Contradiction in Terms?" *Contemporary Political Theory* 5, no. 2 (2005): 142–62.

———. "What's Wrong with Racial Profiling? Another Look at the Problem." *Criminal Justice Ethics* 26, no. 1 (Winter/Spring 2007): 20–28.

———. "Why Racial Profiling Is Hard to Justify." *Philosophy and Public Affairs* 33, no. 1 (2005): 94–110.

Locke, John. *Second Treatise on Government*. Edited by Thomas P. Reardon. New York: Macmillan, Library of Liberal Arts, 1988. Originally published 1690.

Lovett, Frank, and Philip Pettit. "Neorepublicanism: A Normative and Institutional Research Program." *Annual Review of Political Science* 12 (2009): 11–29.

*Loving v. Virginia*, 388 U.S. 1, 2 (1967).

Luban, David. "The Principle of Publicity." In *The Theory of Institutional Design*, edited by Robert E. Goodin, 154–98. Cambridge: Cambridge University Press, 1996.

Mann, Steve, Jason Nolan, and Barry Wellman. "Sousveillance: Inventing and Using Wearable Computing Devices for Data Collection in Surveillance Environments." *Surveillance & Society* 1, no. 3 (2003): 331–55.

Mathiesen, Kay. "Facets of Access: A Conceptual and Standard Threats Analysis." In *iConference 2014 Proceedings*, 605–11. 2014. doi: 10.9776/14265.

*Melvin v. Reid*, 112 Cal. App. 283, 1931.

Mill, John Stuart. *On Liberty*. Edited by David Bromwich and George Kateb. New Haven, CT: Yale University Press, 2003. Originally published 1859.

Moore, Adam D. "Coercing Privacy and Moderate Paternalism: Allen on Unpopular Privacy." American Philosophical Association *Newsletter in Philosophy and Law* 13 (2013): 9–14.

———. "Employee Monitoring and Computer Technology: Evaluative Surveillance v. Privacy." *Business Ethics Quarterly* 10 (2000): 697–709.

———. "Intangible Property: Privacy, Power, and Information Control." *American Philosophical Quarterly* 35 (1998): 365–78.

———. "Defining Privacy." *Journal of Social Philosophy* 39 (Fall 2008): 411–28.

———. "Privacy: Its Meaning and Value." *American Philosophical Quarterly* 40 (2003): 215–27.

———. *Privacy Rights: Moral and Legal Foundations*, University Park: Pennsylvania State University Press, 2010.

———. "Privacy, Speech, and the Law." *Journal of Information Ethics* 22 (2013): 21–43.

———. "Toward Informational Privacy Rights." *San Diego Law Review* 44 (Fall 2007): 809–39.

Moore, Adam D., with B. Newell and C. Metoyer. "Privacy in the Family," In *The Social Dimensions of Privacy*, edited by Beate Roessler and Dorota Mokrosinska, 104–21. Cambridge: Cambridge University Press, 2015.

Narayanan, Arvind, and Vitaly Shmatikov. "Myths and Fallacies of 'Personally Identifiable Information.'" *Communications of the ACM* 53, no. 6 (2010): 24–26.

Newell, Bryce Clayton. "The Massive Metadata Machine: Liberty, Power, and Secret Mass Surveillance in the U.S. and Europe." *I/S: A Journal of Law and Policy for the Information Society* 10, no. 2 (2014): 481–522.

Newman, Abraham L. *Protectors of Privacy: Regulating Personal Data in the Global Economy.* Ithaca, NY: Cornell University Press, 2008.

Nissenbaum, Helen. "The Meaning of Anonymity in an Information Age." *Information Society* 15 (1999): 141–44.

———. "Privacy as Contextual Integrity." *Washington Law Review* 79 (2004): 119–158.

———. *Privacy in Context: Technology, Policy, and the Integrity of Social Life.* Palo Alto, CA: Stanford University Press, 2010.

———. "Protecting Privacy in an Information Age: The Problem of Privacy in Public." *Law and Philosophy* 17, no. 5 (1998): 559–96.

———. "Toward an Approach to Privacy in Public: Challenges of Information Technology." *Ethics and Behavior* 7 (1997): 207–19.

Nozick, Robert. *Anarchy, State, and Utopia.* New York: Basic Books, 1974.

Nyhan, Brendan, and Jason Reifler. "When Corrections Fail: The Persistence of Political Misperceptions." *Political Behavior* 32, no. 2 (2010): 303–30.

*Olmstead v. U.S.*, 277 U.S. 478, 1928.

Omand, David. *Securing the State.* London: Hurst, 2010.

O'Neill, Onora. "Transparency and the Ethics of Communication." In *Transparency: The Key to Better Governance?*, edited by Christopher Hood and David Heald, 75–90. Oxford: Oxford University Press, 2006.

Parent, William. "A New Definition of Privacy for the Law." *Law and Philosophy* 2, no. 3 (1983): 305–38.

———. "Privacy, Morality and the Law." *Philosophy & Public Affairs* 12, no. 4 (1983): 269–88.

Peled, Alon. "Re-Designing Open Data 2.0." In *CeDEM13: Conference for E-Democracy and Open Government,* edited by Peter Parycek and Noella Edelmann, 243–57. 2nd ed. Krems: Edition Donau-Universität Krems, 2013.

Pettit, Philip. "Freedom as Antipower." *Ethics* 106, no. 3 (1996): 576–604.

Piette, Diane Carraway, and Jesslyn Radack. "Piercing the Historical Mists: The People and Events behind the Passage of FISA and the Creation of the Wall." *Stanford Law & Policy Review* 17, no. 2 (2006): 437–86.

Pitkin, Hanna Fenichel. *The Concept of Representation.* Berkeley: University of California Press, 1967.

*Planned Parenthood of Southeastern Pa. v. Casey*, 505 U.S. 833, 1992.

Pound, Roscoe. "Interests in Personality." *Harvard Law Review* 28 (1915): 343.

Prosser, William. "Privacy." *California Law Review* 48, no. 3 (1960): 383–423.

Rachels, James. "Why Privacy Is Important." *Philosophy & Public Affairs* 4, no. 4 (1975): 323–33.

Regan, Priscilla. *Legislating Privacy.* Chapel Hill: University of North Carolina Press, 1995.

Reiman, Jeffrey. "Driving to the Panopticon: A Philosophical Exploration of the Risks to Privacy Posed by the Information Technology of the Future." In *Privacies: Philosophical Evaluations*, edited by Beate Rössler, 194–214. Palo Alto, CA: Stanford University Press, 2004.

———. "Privacy, Intimacy, and Personhood." *Philosophy & Public Affairs* 6, no. 1 (1976): 26–44.

Robinson, David G., Harlan Yu, William P. Zeller, and Edward W. Felten. "Government Data and the Invisible Hand." *Yale Journal of Law & Technology* 11 (2008): 160–75.

Rössler, Beate. *The Value of Privacy.* Cambridge, MA: Polity Press, 2005.

Rozenberg, Joshua. *Privacy and the Press.* Oxford: Oxford University Press, 2004.

Rubel, Alan. "Privacy and the USA Patriot Act: Rights, the Value of Rights, and Autonomy." *Law and Philosophy* 26, no. 2 (2007): 119–59.

———. "Profiling, Information Collection and the Value of Rights Argument." *Criminal Justice Ethics* 32, no. 3 (2013): 210–30.

Ryberg, J. "Privacy Rights, Crime Prevention, CCTV and the Life of Mrs. Aremac." *Res Publica* 13, no. 2 (June 2007): 127–43.

Scanlon, Thomas. "Thomson on Privacy." *Philosophy & Public Affairs* 4, no. 4 (1975): 315–22.

Schauer, Frederick. "Can Public Figures Have Private Lives?" *Social Philosophy and Policy* 17, no. 2 (2000): 293–309.

Schedler, Andreas, Larry Jay, and Marc F. Plattner. *The Self-Restraining State: Power and Accountability in New Democracies.* Boulder, CO: Lynne Publishers, 1999.

Schoeman, Ferdinand D. *Philosophical Dimensions of Privacy: An Anthology.* Cambridge: Cambridge University Press, 1984.

———. *Privacy and Social Freedom.* Cambridge: Cambridge University Press, 1992.

Shklar, Judith N. "Obligation, Loyalty and Exile." In *Political Thought and Political Thinkers,* edited by Stanley Hoffman, 38–55. Chicago: Chicago University Press, 1998.

Sidgwick, Henry. "Utility and Government." In *Social and Political Philosophy: Contemporary Readings,* edited by George Sher and Baruch A. Brody, 35–55. Fort Worth, TX: Harcourt Brace College Publishers, 1999.

Solove, Daniel. *Understanding Privacy.* Cambridge, MA: Harvard University Press, 2008.

Swire, Peter P. "Privacy and Information Sharing in the War on Terrorism." *Villanova Law Review* 51, no. 4 (2006): 951–80.

Taylor, James Stacey. *Death, Posthumous Harm, and Bioethics.* New York: Routledge, 2012.

———. "In Praise of Big Brother: Why We Should Learn to Stop Worrying and Love Government Surveillance." *Public Affairs Quarterly* 19 (July 2005): 227–46.

———. "Privacy and Autonomy: A Reappraisal." *Southern Journal of Philosophy* 40 (2002): 587–604.

Thomson, Judith J. "The Right to Privacy." *Philosophy & Public Affairs* 4, no. 4 (1975): 295–314.

Waldron, Jeremy. "Homelessness and the Issue of Freedom." In *Liberal Rights: Collected Papers 1981–1991,* 309–38. Cambridge: Cambridge University Press, 1993.

Warren, Samuel, and Louis Brandeis. "The Right to Privacy." *Harvard Law Review* 4, no. 5 (1890): 193–220.

Wasserstrom, Richard A. "Privacy: Some Arguments and Assumptions." In *Philosophical Dimensions of Privacy: An Anthology,* edited by Ferdinand D. Schoeman, 317–32. Cambridge: Cambridge University Press, 1984.

Westin, Alan. "The Origins of Modern Claims to Privacy." In *Philosophical Dimensions of Privacy: An Anthology,* edited by Ferdinand D. Schoeman, 56–74. Cambridge: Cambridge University Press, 1984.

———. *Privacy and Freedom.* New York: Atheneum, 1968.

*United States v. Jones,* 132 S. Ct. 945 (2012).

*United States v. Miller,* 425 U.S. 435 (1976).

*Whalen v. Roe,* 429 U.S. 589 (1977).

Zack, Naomi. *White Privilege and Black Rights: The Injustice of U.S. Police Racial Profiling and Homicide.* Lanham, MD: Rowman & Littlefield, 2015.

# Index

# About the Contributors

**Anita L. Allen** is an expert on privacy law, bioethics and contemporary values, and is recognized for her scholarship about legal philosophy, women's rights and race relations. She is a graduate of Harvard Law School and received her PhD in Philosophy from the University of Michigan. At Penn she is the Vice Provost for Faculty and the Henry R. Silverman Professor of Law and Philosophy. In 2010 she was appointed by President Obama to the Presidential Commission for the Study of Bioethical Issues. Her books include *Unpopular Privacy: What Must We Hide* (2011); *Privacy Law and Society* (2011); *Why Privacy Isn't Everything: Feminist Reflections on Personal Accountability* (2003); and *Uneasy Access: Privacy for Women in a Free Society* (1988). She has written more than one hundred scholarly articles, has contributed to popular magazines and blogs, and has frequently appeared on nationally broadcast television and radio programs.

**Judith Wagner DeCew**'s research focuses on topics in theoretical and applied ethics, philosophy of law, social and political philosophy and privacy. She is a Professor of Philosophy at Clark University and has been a research fellow at Harvard Law School, The Bunting Institute at Radcliffe, Harvard University, and has received fellowships from the National Endowment for Humanities, the American Council for Learned Societies and the American Association of University Women. In 2010 she earned Clark's Senior Faculty Fellowship "presented to an outstanding senior faculty member who personifies the Clark ideal of excellence in teaching and excellence in scholarship." She is the author of three books, including *In Pursuit of Privacy: Law, Ethics and the Rise of Technology* (1997) and *Unionization in the Academy: Visions and Realities* (2003), as well as over forty articles.

**Kenneth Einar Himma**, PhD, JD, is a visiting professor and adjunct at the University of Washington's Law School. His research interests include legal philosophy, applied ethics, information ethics, and computer ethics. He has authored more than one hundred scholarly articles, encyclopedia entries, book reviews, and op-ed newspaper pieces. He is also the author of ten books and ten edited anthologies including, *The Handbook of Information and Computer Ethics* (2008).

**Michael Katell** is a PhD student at the University of Washington's Information School. He worked for many years as a technologist and manager for an antipoverty law firm in Seattle, Washington. Katell has research interests in the use of technology to improve conditions for marginalized people, the ethical implications of data governance, technology and civil rights and the power dynamics of the surveillance economy.

**Annabelle Lever** is Associate Professor of Normative Political Theory at the University of Geneva. Her research centers on problems of privacy, security, sexual and racial equality, democratic theory and intellectual property. Her current project, "A Democratic Conception of Ethics," is supported by the Swiss National Science Foundation and develops the methodological and substantive ideas about ethics advanced in *On Privacy* (2012) and recent articles on freedom of expression, religious exemptions, race and the selection of juries. She has participated in workshops on the ethics of counter-terrorism at the Home Office, in London and at the House of Lords, and works as an ethics expert for the European Commission's DG Research and Innovation. She is the editor of *New Frontiers in the Philosophy of Intellectual Property* (2012) as well as the author of *A Democratic Conception of Privacy* (2014) and over thirty articles.

**Kay Mathiesen** is Assistant Professor at the University of Arizona's School of Information Resources and Library Science with a research focus on information ethics. Her interdisciplinary work brings philosophical ethics to bear on issues such as equitable access to information, privacy, and intellectual property. Her current research project, "Information Rights as Human Rights," focuses on developing an understanding of the Human Rights relevant for a Global Information Society. Professor Mathiesen is the co-director of the Information Ethics Roundtable and author of ten articles.

**Dorota Mokrosinska** is Assistant Professor of Philosophy at Leiden University, the Netherlands. Her research is primarily in political philosophy and ethics with special interest in political authority, state legitimacy and issues related to the place of privacy, secrecy and transparency in democratic politics. She is the author of *Rethinking Political Obligation: Moral Principles,*

*Communal Ties, Citizenship* (2012) and the editor (with B. Roessler) of the volume *Social Dimensions of Privacy: Interdisciplinary Perspectives* (2015). Her current research project on the role of secrecy in democratic governance has been awarded an ERC Starting Grant by the European Research Council.

**Adam D. Moore** examines the ethical, legal and policy issues surrounding intellectual property, privacy and information control. He received his PhD in Philosophy from the Ohio State University and currently teaches at the University of Washington's Information School. He is the author of *Privacy Rights: Moral and Legal Foundations* (2010) and *Intellectual Property and Information Control* (2001). He is the editor *Information Ethics: Privacy, Property, and Power* (2005) and *Intellectual Property: Moral, Legal, and International Dilemmas* (1997). In addition to writing opinion articles and contributing to radio programs he has published over thirty-five articles.

**Bryce Clayton Newell**, PhD, JD, is a post-doctoral researcher at the Tilburg Institute for Law, Technology, and Society, Tilburg University Law School Tilburg University. He conducts research in the area of information law, policy and ethics. More specifically, his research investigates the legal, ethical, and political implications of surveillance and counter-surveillance in modern society—with an emphasis on issues related to information privacy, liberty, free speech and access to information. His articles have appeared in a variety of law reviews, social science journals, and refereed conference proceedings, including *Government Information Quarterly*; *I/S: A Journal of Law and Policy for the Information Society*; *Journal of Law, Technology & Policy*; *Maine Law Review*; *Creighton Law Review*; *Richmond Journal of Law & Technology*; *Intellectual Property Law Bulletin*; and the *International Law & Management Review*.

**Helen Nissenbaum** teaches and conducts research in the areas of information technology, ethics, policy and law. Grants from government agencies and private foundations have supported her research on privacy, trust online and security, as well as the study of values embodied in computer systems and digital media. Nissenbaum has collaborated in the development of privacy enhancing software such as Adnostic, TrackMeNot and Context Aware: Do Not Track, and is also the author of many research articles, reports, and books including the most recent, *Privacy in Context: Technology, Policy, and the Integrity of Social Life* (2010). She is the author of seven books and over fifty articles.

**Alan Rubel**, PhD, JD, is Assistant Professor in the School of Library and Information Studies and in the Legal Studies Program at the University of Wisconsin, Madison. He is also an affiliate of the UW Law School and served as a senior adviser to the Presidential Commission for the Study of Bioethical Issues in 2012. He works in the area of information ethics and policy. His current research concerns the nature and value of privacy, moral issues surrounding public health surveillance, rights to intellectual freedom and theoretical foundations of the criminal law. He is the author of over twenty articles.

**Nadine Strossen**, the John Marshall Harlan II Professor of Law at New York Law School and former president of the American Civil Liberties Union (1991–2008), has written, lectured and practiced extensively in the areas of constitutional law, civil liberties and international human rights. Her writings have been published in many scholarly and general interest publications (more than three hundred published works). Her book, *Defending Pornography: Free Speech, Sex, and the Fight for Women's Rights* (1995), was named a "Notable Book" of 1995 by the *New York Times*. Her coauthored book, *Speaking of Race, Speaking of Sex: Hate Speech, Civil Rights, and Civil Liberties* (1995), was named an "outstanding book" by the Gustavus Myers Center for the Study of Human Rights in North America.

**James Stacey Taylor** is Associate Professor of Philosophy at the College of New Jersey. Branded a heretic by the *London Times* for his arguments in favour of legalizing markets in human organs in his book *Stakes and Kidneys: Why Markets in Human Organs Are Morally Imperative* (2005), he is also the author of *Practical Autonomy and Bioethics* (2009), and *Death, Posthumous Harm, and Bioethics* (2012). He is the editor of *Personal Autonomy: New Essays* (2005) and *Death: Metaphysics and Ethics* (2013). He is currently working on a book defending markets in everything, including votes and children. In addition to his academic writing he has authored numerous op-eds on bioethical issues which have appeared in publications including the *Los Angeles Times*, the *Daily News* (New York) and *USA Today*. He is an occasional contributor to NPR and has been quoted in the *New York Times*.